BILL
CLINTON
and
BLACK
AMERICA

BILL CLINTON

and

BLACK AMERICA

DeWayne Wickham

BALLANTINE BOOKS
NEW YORK

A Ballantine Book
Published by The Ballantine Publishing Group

Copyright © 2002 by DeWayne Wickham

All rights reserved under International and
Pan-American Copyright Conventions. Published in
the United States by The Ballantine Publishing Group, a division
of Random House, Inc., New York, and simultaneously in
Canada by Random House of Canada Limited, Toronto.

www.ballantinebooks.com

Library of Congress Cataloging-in-Publication Data is available upon request.

ISBN 0-345-45032-9

Text design by Holly Johnson

Manufactured in the United States of America

First Edition: February 2002

10 9 8 7 6 5 4 3 2 1

Contents

Acknowledgments

While I didn't move out of the house, this book separated me from my family for much of the time I spent researching and writing it. I could not have taken on or completed this project without the dispensation my wife and daughters gave me to do so. I am grateful to them for this unselfish act of love.

I am also thankful for the friendship and guidance of my literary agent, Denise Stinson, who has stuck with me through thick and thin and for the support and encouragement of Anita Diggs, my editor. The enthusiasm of these dynamic women for unleashing the pent-up voices of African-American writers has stocked the shelves of bookstores with works that otherwise would have gone unwritten—and unread.

A special thanks to the people who allowed me to interview them for this book and etch onto the template of history their views about the special relationship that William Jefferson Clinton, the forty-second president of the United States, had with African Americans. Without them this book—and the understanding of this relationship that it offers—would not have been possible.

Finally, I want to thank Raina Harper, Sheila Lewis, and Kathy Briggs for transcribing the tape recording of the many intervews I did for this book; George Kimbrow for compiling the list of the Clinton administration's black appointees; and my good friend John C. White for his frank and honest assessment of this book while it was a work in progress.

"To be is to be perceived."
—George Berkeley
(philosopher, 1685–1753)

Introduction

The purpose of this book is to give readers an understanding of why Bill Clinton is so wildly popular with the vast majority of African Americans. Throughout his eight years in the White House, this white southerner's approval rating with the descendants of the men and women who were stolen from Africa, shackled to the hulls of ships, and delivered into slavery throughout the Americas was very high. For most of that time it hovered around 90 percent. At its low point, in 1993 when Clinton pulled his nomination of Lani Guinier to be assistant attorney general for civil rights amid the bogus charges of right-wing Republicans that she was a quota queen, his support among African Americans still managed to top the 50 percent level.

By August 1998, a poll done by Lester & Associates, a black-owned survey and research group, found that Clinton's approval rating among African Americans (93%) was higher than that of the Reverend Jesse Jackson (89%). Four months later, when the House of Representatives voted to impeach Clinton, his approval rating with whites was 70 percent, while 91 percent of African Americans said they approved of the job he was doing, according to a Gallup Organization poll. In January 2001, just days before Clinton left office, Gallup found that his approval rating with whites dropped to 62 percent, while it rose back up to 93 percent with African Americans.

Why has Bill Clinton been so popular with African Americans?

1

Do African Americans, as so many of Clinton's critics charge, have a sheeplike allegiance to the Democratic Party? Have black folks been beguiled into their love affair? Those who think so have been blinded by their dislike for the former president and disdainful of the ability of the vast majority of African Americans to take proper measure of the man some say was in his words and deeds the nation's first black president. More than anything else, the use of that moniker to describe Clinton rankles his black critics as well as some of his black supporters.

Derrick Bell, the New York University law professor, complained that while Clinton did a lot in terms of symbolism for African Americans, when it came down to the nitty-gritty, the things we really needed, he wasn't there for us. Armstrong Williams, the acerbic conservative commentator and columnist, blamed Clinton's high standing among African Americas on the treachery of black leaders.

When you have organizations like the Rainbow/PUSH Coalition, the Congressional Black Caucus, the NAACP, and the National Urban League being the most vociferous defenders of Clinton, then obviously that trickles down to their constituents. And when the Pulitzer Prize–winning author Toni Morrison went to the ridiculous length to claim Clinton was a black president, that caused a lot of people to really believe he is one of us, Williams argued.

Clay Carson, the highly regarded Stanford University historian, maintained that Clinton is no more highly regarded among African Americans than any other Democrat who held or sought the White House in recent years. Any Democratic candidate for president in the last forty years is going to get 85 to 90 percent of the black vote. So Bill Clinton, or even someone as culturally klutzy as Michael Dukakis, is naturally going to get 85 to 90 percent of the black vote.

Carson's point is well-taken. Since 1964 no Democratic contender for the presidency has won less than 82 percent of the black vote in the General Election. But with the exception of Clinton, none of those white men were viewed as kindred souls by a vast majority of African Americans. To figure out why so many African Americans view Clinton not just favorably, but warmly, requires more than a clinical analysis of election results. This book does that.

There are some notable histories of the relationship between African Americans and the presidents who have led this country. *Nixon's Piano* (The Free Press, 1995) by Kenneth O'Reilly, and *African-Americans and the Presidency: A History of Broken Promises* (Franklin Watts, 2000) by Christopher B. Booker are excellent historical resources. For those who wish to make a genealogical case for the first black president, Auset BaKhufu's book, *The Six Black Presidents, Black Blood: White Masks* (PIK2 Publications, Washington, D.C., 1993), and J. A. Rogers's pamphlet, "The Five Black Presidents" (J. A. Rogers, St. Petersburg, FL, 1965) are good beginning points.

This book, however, casts a wider net. It places Clinton's popularity in a historical context and it draws on interviews with a broad cross section of African Americans to get both an instinctive and intellectual reading on why so many African Americans have such an emotional attachment for a son of the South who, at the end of his presidency, moved his office from the White House to Harlem's 125th Street, the heart of Black America.

CHAPTER 1

The Past as Prologue

It was a moment that has been replayed in Harlem many times. A favorite son of black America, an icon of the struggle for black empowerment in this country and elsewhere, a kindred soul of the descendants of the diaspora that slavery foisted upon Africa was center stage on 125th Street.

But this time it wasn't Marcus Garvey, Malcolm X, Julius Nyerere, or Adam Clayton Powell Jr. who spellbound a crowd on black America's most famous thoroughfare. The man thousands of people in Harlem turned out to see on the mild summer afternoon of July 30, 2001, was William Jefferson Clinton, the forty-second white man to serve as president of the United States and the only one to delight in being called the nation's first black president.

More than any other person who has occupied the Oval Office, Bill Clinton has a special bond with blacks, a relationship that fueled his decision to move his postpresidential office to Harlem. When his presidency ended in January 2001, Clinton's approval rating among whites was in a free fall, but his standing among blacks was sky-high. Eighty-seven percent of African Americans and just 45 percent of whites viewed Clinton favorably in the weeks before his second term as president ended, a poll conducted by researchers at Harvard University and the University of Chicago revealed.[1]

But to fully understand Clinton's appeal to blacks you must first juxtapose him to the forty-one men—from George Washington to George Bush—who preceded him in the presidency. It is impossible to explain Clinton's popularity with African Americans without first probing the relationship that blacks have had with this nation's long line of chief executives.

Eight of the first fifteen presidents of the United States were slave owners. George Washington, who commanded this nation's fight against British tyranny, owned hundreds of slaves. Thomas Jefferson and Andrew Jackson were also slaveholders. And so too were James Madison, James Monroe, William Henry Harrison, John Tyler, and James Polk. With the possible exceptions of John Adams and his son, John Quincy Adams, all the men who served in the White House before the election of Abraham Lincoln campaigned for the office as proslavery candidates. None of these presidents publicly opposed slavery during their time in the White House.

Lincoln, the nation's sixteenth president, is widely—but mistakenly—credited with ending slavery. The Emancipation Proclamation he issued on January 1, 1863, granted freedom only to those slaves in states and territories under control of the rebel government of the Confederacy. His act was meant to end the Civil War by disrupting the South's labor pool and to use antislavery sentiment in France and Great Britain to keep those nations from intervening on the side of the Confederacy. It was not intended to shut down the "peculiar institution" that had existed in this country since 1619,[2] the year before the *Mayflower* dropped anchor at Plymouth Rock to deliver the Pilgrims from religious persecution in Europe. Lincoln's Emancipation Proclamation did not apply to any slaves held in areas that remained loyal to

---

[1] Lawrence D. Bobo and Michael C. Dawson, *Polls & Polls Apart: Black and Whites Divided on the Clinton Legacy* (A joint project by Harvard University's DuBois Institute and the University of Chicago's Center for the Study of Race, Politics, and Culture, 2001).

[2] Mary Frances Berry and John W. Blassingame, *Long Memory: The Black Experience in America* (New York: Oxford University Press, 1982), 7.

the Union, including those in the nation's capital. Lincoln left no doubt of his true intentions in an August 22, 1863, letter to Horace Greeley, the editor of the *New York Tribune* who used his newspaper to agitate for an end to slavery. An editorial in the paper several days earlier had questioned where the president stood on the issue of emancipation.

"As to the policy I 'seem to be pursuing' as you say, I have not meant to leave any doubt," Lincoln wrote Greeley. "I would save the Union. I would save it the shortest way under the Constitution. The sooner the national authority can be restored; the nearer the Union will be 'the Union as it was.' If there be those who would not save the Union, unless they could at the same time save slavery, I do not agree with them. If there be those who would not save the Union unless they could at the same time destroy slavery, I do not agree with them. My paramount objective in this struggle is to save the Union, and is not either to save or to destroy slavery. If I could save the Union without freeing any slave I would do it, and if I could save it by freeing all the slaves I would do it; and if I could save it by freeing some and leaving others alone I would also do that."

Lincoln's Emancipation Proclamation followed his third option. Slavery throughout the United States actually wasn't ended until the Thirteenth Amendment of the Constitution was ratified on December 6, 1865. Eleven years later, Frederick Douglass—who had met with Lincoln several times to make the case for black emancipation—gave a chilling assessment of the Republican president in a speech to a largely black audience.

"It must be admitted, truth compels me to admit, even here in the presence of the monument we have erected to his memory, Abraham Lincoln was not, in the fullest sense of the word, either our man or our model. In his interests, in his associations, in his habits and thoughts, and in his prejudices, he was a white man," Douglass said at the dedication of a memorial to the former president.

> He was preeminently the white man's president, entirely devoted to the welfare of white men. He was ready and willing at any time during the first years of his administra-

tion to deny, postpone, and sacrifice the rights of humanity in the colored people to promote the welfare of the
white people of this country . . . To protect, defend, and
perpetuate slavery in the states where it existed Abraham
Lincoln was no less ready than any other president to draw
the sword of the nation. He was ready to execute all of the
supposed guarantees of the United States Constitution in
favor of the slave system anywhere inside the slave states.
He was willing to pursue, recapture, and send back the
fugitive slave to his master, and to suppress a slave rising for
liberty, though his guilty master were already in arms
against the government. The race to which we belong were
not the special objects of his consideration.

Douglass said of the man many historians call "the great emancipator."

Of the eight presidents that followed Lincoln into the Oval Office
during the remaining years of the nineteenth century, three, Andrew
Johnson, Grover Cleveland, and William McKinley, were classified as
"white supremacist" by University of Michigan professor Hanes Walton
Jr. and San Francisco State University professor Robert C. Smith in their
book *American Politics and the African-American Quest for Universal
Freedom* (New York: Longman, 2000). One president, Chester Arthur,
was ranked as "racially neutral" and two others, Rutherford B. Hayes
and James Garfield, were labeled "racially ambivalent." Only two presidents, Ulysses S. Grant and Benjamin Harrison, were categorized as "an-
tiracist" in the authors' analysis of the racial attitudes of U.S. presidents.

Grant's good ranking is probably due in part to the fact that in
1869 he became the nation's first chief executive to appoint an African
American to a major diplomatic position when he named Ebenezer
Don Carlos Bassett minister to Haiti. Twenty years later, Harrison be-
came the second president to do so when he appointed Frederick
Douglass chargé d'affaires to Santo Domingo and minister to Haiti.

In the thirty-one years from the start of the twentieth century to
the election of Franklin Delano Roosevelt in 1932, nearly 1,600
African Americans were lynched in the United States. Three years be-

fore the new century began the Supreme Court made "separate but equal" the law of the land with its decision in the *Plessy v. Ferguson* case. The ruling epitomized the nation's retreat from the advances made by the newly freed slaves during Reconstruction. It came at a time when whites in the former Confederate states were moving aggressively to plunge African Americans into a state of neoslavery. Between 1898 and 1910 hundreds of thousands of black southerners were forced off the voting rolls and racial discrimination and segregation were etched into law and social practice throughout the South. Blacks who resisted these oppressive changes often ended up hanging from the end of a lynch mob's rope.

None of the twentieth century's early presidents—not Republican Theodore Roosevelt, whose Rough Riders' charge up San Juan Hill during the Spanish-American War was supported by the more battle-tested black "Buffalo Soldiers," nor Democrat Woodrow Wilson, whose election in 1912 was backed by a group of dissident black Republicans— did anything to stop these attacks on the rights and lives of African Americans. If anything, these early twentieth-century presidents gave aid and comfort to those who carried out these brutal assaults.

Roosevelt surely fueled the passions of those who believed African Americans were unworthy of the benefits of citizenship when he accused the black troops that fought in Cuba of cowardice, despite the fact that five of them were awarded the Medal of Honor, this nation's highest military award for bravery in combat.

Roosevelt showed his contempt for black soldiers—and his willingness to pander to white bigotry—in another way. When some members of the Twenty-fifth Infantry were accused of going on a drunken shooting spree in Brownsville, Texas, that left one white man dead and two others including the police chief injured, Roosevelt ordered an investigation. When the culprits were not discovered, he had all 167 black enlisted men in the unit—including five Medal of Honor winners—given administrative discharges,[3] an action that precluded them from ever holding a civil service job or receiving a mili-

[3] Kenneth O'Reilly. *Nixon's Piano: Presidents and Racial Politics from Washington to Clinton* (New York: The Free Press, 1995), 73.

9

tary pension. (Sixty-six years later the Department of Army reversed that action and awarded all of the men honorable discharges.)

Between 1901 and 1912, neither Roosevelt nor his handpicked successor, William Howard Taft, did much to enforce the Thirteenth, Fourteenth, or Fifteenth Amendments, which were passed in the wake of the Civil War to guarantee the rights of African Americans. Their callous indifference to the widespread oppression African Americans suffered during their time at this nation's helm caused some leading black activists to break with Republicans and back Democrat Woodrow Wilson's presidential bid in 1912. Wilson assured his black supporters that he wanted to see "justice done to the colored people in every matter; and not mere grudging justice, but justice executed with liberality and cordial good feeling." As these black activists quickly learned, Wilson lied.

Once in office Woodrow Wilson purged black Republican appointees in the South and replaced them with white Democrats. He segregated federal agencies in the nation's capital and elsewhere and delighted in telling "darkie stories" to his White House guests. Wilson's mistreatment of African Americans angered W. Monroe Trotter, who along with W. E. B. Du Bois broke ranks with black Republicans to support the Democratic Party's presidential campaign. Trotter, Harvard University's first black Phi Beta Kappa and publisher of the *Boston Guardian*, headed a small delegation of Wilson's black supporters that met with the president on November 6, 1913, to express their disappointment with his administration's bad treatment of African Americans. Wilson assured them "it will be worked out."

But instead of getting better, the Wilson administration's treatment of African Americans got worse. On November 12, 1914, Trotter led another group of African Americans in a White House meeting with the Georgia-born Wilson.

"One year ago we presented a national petition, signed by Afro-Americans in thirty-eight states, protesting against the segregation of employees of the national government whose ancestry could be traced in whole or in part to Africa, as instituted under your administration in the treasury and post-office departments. We then appealed to you to undo this race segregation in accord with your duty as president and with your pre-election pledges. We stated that there could be no freedom, no respect from others, and no equality of citizenship under segregation of races," Trotter told Wilson.

"Only two years ago you were heralded as perhaps the second Lincoln, and now the Afro-American leaders who supported you are hounded as false leaders and traitors to their race. What a change segregation has wrought!" Trotter said.[4]

When Wilson suggested that racial segregation in federal offices was meant to help African Americans by relieving them of their "dependence upon the white element of our population," Trotter struggled to contain his anger. "Now, Mr. President, this is a very serious thing with us. We are sorely disappointed that you take the position that the separation itself is not wrong, is not injurious, is not rightly offensive to you," he said sharply. Wilson responded that if this "organization wishes to approach me again, it must choose another spokesman." The group didn't return—and Wilson never retreated from his efforts to segregate the federal workforce.

In the years leading up to the 1932 presidential election, black frustration with the Oval Office occupants grew. The three Republican presidents who followed Wilson into the White House worked mightily to court the votes of white southerners and to hold black voters—then the Republican Party's most loyal constituency—at bay. The trickle of black support that W. E. B. Du Bois and W. Monroe Trotter produced for Woodrow Wilson in 1912 (about 7 percent) increased dramatically in 1932 when the next Democratic president, Franklin D. Roosevelt, was elected. Roosevelt won nearly 30 percent of the black vote.

Shortly before the 1936 presidential election Roosevelt appointed Mary McLeod Bethune, the founder of the National Council of Negro Women and president of Bethune-Cookman College, director of the Office of Negro Affairs in the National Youth Administration. Bethune, the first black woman to receive a presidential

[4] Christine A. Lunardini, "Standing Firm: William Monroe Trotter's Meeting with Woodrow Wilson." *Journal of Negro History* 64, no. 3 (summer 1979): 244–264.

appointment, was a key member of the "black cabinet." This loose-knit group of midlevel black appointees—whose members included *Pittsburgh Courier* editor Robert L. Vann, Howard Law School dean William H. Hastie, and Robert C. Weaver,[5] who two decades later would become the first black cabinet officer—reversed the political ostracizing African Americans suffered at the hands of Franklin Roosevelt's Democratic predecessors and sparked a mass exodus of black voters from the Republican Party.

Seventy-one percent of African Americans cast their ballots for Roosevelt in 1936; the first time a majority of black voters had not supported the GOP's presidential candidate. In 1940, Roosevelt won 67 percent of the black vote, and in 1944 he got 68 percent of the ballots cast by African Americans.[6] During Roosevelt's presidency the number of black federal workers increased nearly 300 percent. But Roosevelt's record on racial issues was far from spotless. In 1934, he wouldn't back an antilynching law because he feared that outraged southern lawmakers would retaliate by derailing his New Deal legislation. And while he barred discrimination in federal employment, he did little else to end racial segregation during his time in the White House.

In 1948, a year after Jackie Robinson integrated major league baseball, Democrat Harry S. Truman issued two executive orders. One mandated "fair employment practices" in the civil service, and the other ended racial segregation in the U.S. military. Like his successor, Republican Dwight Eisenhower, Truman struggled to balance the pressures coming from a burgeoning civil rights movement with the cold calculations of presidential politics. Unlike Truman, Eisenhower was a closet segregationist. He opposed the Supreme Court's 1954 decision that ended school segregation and did little to enforce the historic ruling. To deflect attention away from his foot-dragging on this and other civil rights issues, Eisenhower named an African American,

---

[5] John Hope Franklin and Alfred A. Moss Jr., *From Slavery to Freedom: A History of Negro Americans* (New York: Alfred A. Knopf, 1988), 349.

[6] David A. Bositis, *Blacks and the 2000 Republican National Convention* (Washington, D.C.: Joint Center for Political and Economic Studies, 2000), 13.

E. Frederic Morrow, to his White House staff. Morrow was the first black person to serve in this position and his selection boosted Eisenhower's popularity with black voters. Later that year Eisenhower won 39 percent of the black vote in the 1956 presidential election, 15 percent more than he received in 1952. Morrow's appointment, which was announced with great fanfare in the black press, was not made official until January 1959.

The following year, John F. Kennedy was elected president. He entered the White House just as the festering Civil Rights movement began to boil over. Whereas Eisenhower had to be prodded into supporting the watered-down Civil Rights Act of 1957, Kennedy—then a Massachusetts senator—played a key role in emasculating the legislation. He joined with Senate Majority Leader Lyndon B. Johnson in supporting an amendment to the federal legislation that required a jury trial in state court for anyone found in contempt of efforts to enforce the voting rights of African Americans. The amendment took the teeth out of this portion of the bill since it was highly unlikely that any southern jury would find a white person guilty of such an offense. But when black voters went to the polls in the 1960 presidential election, they voted heavily for Kennedy and against Richard M. Nixon, who as Eisenhower's vice president had tried to rally enough votes to defeat the damaging amendment.

Kennedy's standing among African Americans skyrocketed in the final weeks of the campaign after he called Coretta Scott King to express his concern following the jailing of her husband, Martin Luther King Jr., on a trumped-up traffic violation charge. News of Kennedy's expression of concern caused King's father, a lifelong Republican and an influential black Baptist minister, to publicly declare his support for the Massachusetts senator.[7] Kennedy, who eked out a slim victory in the 1960 presidential election, won 68 percent of the black vote. Nixon garnered 32 percent, more than double what any Republican presidential candidate would receive in the remaining years of the twentieth century.

[7] David J. Garrow, *Bearing the Cross: Martin Luther King, Jr., and the Southern Christian Leadership Conference* (New York: William Morrow and Company, 1986), 148.

Shortly after taking office Kennedy named Robert Weaver to head the federal Housing and Home Finance Agency, a subcabinet position that made the former member of Franklin Roosevelt's "black cabinet" the highest-ranking African-American presidential appointee in the nation's history. But as much as Kennedy maintained contact with Martin Luther King and other civil rights leaders he did not stray far from the "states' rights" crutch that Eisenhower used to explain his failure to stanch the South's Jim Crow practices.

Kennedy's foot-dragging was tested shortly after he took office when Freedom Riders bent on desegregating the buses and bus stations involved in interstate transportation were brutally set upon by Klansmen. Kennedy ordered his staff to mount a behind-the-scenes effort to stop the Freedom Riders from making any more forays into the South. Only after several violent attacks on the Freedom Riders did the Kennedy administration send a force of six hundred U.S. marshals and FBI agents to Alabama to protect the black activists.

The following year, twenty-four months after entering the White House, Kennedy made good on his campaign promise to desegregate public housing by issuing an executive order that banned racial segregation in new public housing units only. But by early 1963, King was so upset with Kennedy that he accused the president in a magazine article of undermining the civil rights struggle. Prodded by King's criticism, the ambush murder of Mississippi NAACP leader Medgar Evers and a string of televised attacks on peaceful demonstrators, Kennedy sent a civil rights bill to Congress in June 1963. When an assassin's bullets ripped the life from Kennedy's body as he rode in an open convertible in Dallas on November 22, 1963, the civil rights bill he sent to Congress was bogged down by the legislative maneuvering of southern congressmen. Within months of being sworn in as president, Lyndon B. Johnson, the former Texas senator who led the effort to water down the Civil Rights Act of 1957, won passage of the Civil Rights Act of 1964. The bill was the most far-reaching legislation of its kind in the nation's history. It forbade discrimination in public accommodations, provided African Americans with federal protection against school segregation and voter disenfranchisement, and created the

Equal Employment Opportunities Commission. A year later, Johnson won passage of a Voting Rights Act that further strengthened the ability of African Americans to register and vote in areas of the country where many of them had long been denied the franchise.

Johnson elevated Robert Weaver to his cabinet in 1966 when the Department of Housing and Urban Development was created, making him the nation's first black cabinet officer. Two years later Johnson capped his civil rights record by signing into law the landmark Fair Housing Act of 1968. No president before or since has amassed a more impressive civil rights legislative record.

Richard Nixon, who received a third of the black vote in his unsuccessful 1960 presidential race, was backed by just 15 percent of the African Americans who went to the polls when he won the presidency in 1968. Nixon's poor showing among black voters is no doubt due in part to the "southern strategy" he used to defeat Democrat Hubert Humphrey and Governor George Wallace of Alabama, who ran as a third-party candidate. In return for the support of Strom Thurmond, the old Dixiecrat who switched to the GOP, Nixon assured the racist South Carolina senator that he would do as little as possible to desegregate the nation's public schools.

Nixon chose Maryland governor Spiro Agnew as his running mate. Agnew had been propelled into the national spotlight after he publicly derided black leaders in Baltimore for their failure to end the rioting in that city that followed the 1968 assassination of Martin Luther King. Publicly, Agnew was a bigot; privately, he was a common crook who was forced to resign in 1973 after being accused of taking payoffs while a county executive and governor. Agnew was the shrill voice behind Nixon's efforts to lure white voters away from the Democratic Party—which Agnew portrayed as kowtowing to black leaders. Less than a year after Agnew left office under a plea bargain agreement that got him a $10,000 fine and three years probation, Nixon too was forced to resign after being named an unindicted co-conspirator in the cover-up of a break-in into the Democratic Party's headquarters during the 1974 presidential campaign.

But while Nixon was gone, the strategy he and Agnew forged for winning the presidency with thinly veiled appeals to whites turned off by the Democratic Party's close ties to African Americans remained a cornerstone of every Republican White House campaign that followed in the remaining years of the twentieth century. No Democratic presidential candidate—not even Jimmy Carter or Bill Clinton—has won a majority of the white vote during this time.

Neither the presidencies of Republican Gerald Ford, who replaced Nixon, nor Democrat Jimmy Carter, who defeated Ford in the following election, produced many gains for African Americans. Like Lyndon Johnson, both men named a single African American to their cabinet. Carter created another "first" when he named a black woman, Patricia Harris, as secretary of the Department of Health, Education, and Welfare and then later as head of the Department of Housing and Urban Development, and named Andrew Young the U.S. ambassador to the United Nations. But for the most part, nothing happened in either administration to make African Americans more or less likely to vote for Carter or Ford. When the two men faced off in the 1976 presidential election, 85 percent of black voters supported Carter and 15 percent backed Ford—the very same percentages that black voters produced when Richard Nixon defeated Hubert Humphrey in 1968.

That changed in 1980. Ronald Reagan's victory was a traumatizing body blow to African Americans. The former Hollywood "B" actor opened his presidential campaign in Philadelphia, Mississippi, where three civil rights workers—Michael Schwerner, James Chaney, and Andrew Goodman—were brutally murdered in 1964. Reagan perfected the "southern strategy" that Richard Nixon had forged twelve years earlier. His appeal to voters that the media labeled "Reagan Democrats" was actually an outreach to the white opponents of civil rights, an effort that caused the Ku Klux Klan to take to the streets of southern cities to campaign for Reagan in full regalia. The Republican platform, the *New York Times* reported a Louisiana Klan group as saying, "reads as if it were written by a Klansman."

After taking office, Reagan did little to turn on black voters and much to turn them off. He launched an assault on affirmative action, named Clarence Thomas to head the Equal Employment Opportunity Commission, backed away from school integration, and fought to grant a tax exempt status to Bob Jones University, which forbade its students to date or marry across racial lines.

But as bad as Ronald Reagan was, George Bush was worse in his mean-spirited pursuit of the Republican Party's "southern strategy" during his 1988 presidential campaign. Bush's campaign used a foreboding image of Willie Horton, a black convicted murderer who raped a white woman while on furlough from a Massachusetts prison, in a television commercial to attack his Democratic opponent, Michael Dukakis, for being soft on crime. The commercial outraged black leaders who had a vivid memory of the 1951 case in which Matt Ingram, a black sharecropper, was jailed in North Carolina on a charge of "rape by leer" for staring at a white woman from a distance of seventy-five feet. Ingram spent two and a half years in jail for this "reckless eyeballing" offense.[8]

Bush's appointments of Louis Sullivan to head the Department of Health and Human Services and Colin Powell as chairman of the Joint Chiefs of Staff were overshadowed by his cynical assertion that Clarence Thomas was the most qualified person to replace retiring Supreme Court Justice Thurgood Marshall. An icon of the Civil Rights movement, Marshall became the first black to serve on the nation's highest court when Lyndon Johnson nominated him to that body in 1976. Thomas, a darling of right-wing conservatives, was for many African Americans the antithesis of Marshall. Thomas climbed the affirmative action ladder all the way to the Supreme Court and then worked mightily to tear away its rungs.

It is against this backdrop that Bill Clinton was elected president in 1992. While all of his predecessors were personally and, more often than not, politically detached from black America, Clinton forged an unprecedented relationship with African Americans—one that cries out for explanation.

---

[8] Mary Frances Berry, *Long Memory: The Black Experience in America* (New York: Oxford University Press, 1982), 124.

CHAPTER 2

The Man

In Irving Wallace's 1964 book *The Man*, a black senator is thrust into the Oval Office when the president and others ahead of him in the line of succession are killed in a tragic accident. The fate of this black president—and that of the country—hung on his ability to manage the competing pressures of his race, his public office, and a scandal in his personal life. Three decades later, Toni Morrison invoked the same gnarling issues in her assessment of a real-life president for whom race also became an issue. In her controversial 1998 article in the *New Yorker*, the Pulitzer Prize winner bemoaned the hypocrisy of many of the people who attacked Bill Clinton for breaking his marriage vows, ridiculed their efforts to make his personal indiscretion a matter of state, and floated the idea that it all might have had something to do with a question of race.

"Serious as adultery is, it is not a national catastrophe," Morrison wrote. "Women leaving hotels following trysts with their extramarital lovers tell pollsters they abominate Mr. Clinton's behavior. Relaxed men fresh from massage parlors frown earnestly into the camera at the mere thought of such malfeasance. No one 'approves' of adultery, but, unlike fidelity in Plymouth Rock society, late-twentieth-century fidelity, when weighed against the constitutional right to privacy, comes up short."

Then, she offered a reason for the right wing's savage attacks on

Clinton that pierced the soft underbelly of this nation's racial divide and sent shock waves in all directions. The verbal salvos being fired at the president, she suggested, had a familiar ring.

"African-American men seemed to understand it right away. Years ago, in the middle of the Whitewater investigation, one heard the first murmurs: white skin notwithstanding, this is our first black President. Blacker than any actual black person who could ever be elected in our children's lifetime. After all, Clinton displays almost every trope of blackness: single-parent household, born poor, working-class, saxophone-playing, McDonald's-and-junk-food-loving boy from Arkansas."[9]

While whites shrieked at the notion and African Americans debated the merits of the "honorary" blackness Morrison bestowed on the president, Clinton took to the idea like a barnacle to the side of a rusting ship. In a September 1999 speech at the Congressional Black Caucus's annual dinner, the president made his first public acknowledgment of what Morrison said.

"I want you to all listen to this," Clinton said with a seriousness that didn't betray what he was about to say. "The magnificent African American writer, Toni Morrison, agreed with an extreme right-wing journalist that I am the first black president of the United States." The room erupted with laughter.

"Chris Tucker came to see me today," Clinton said, in reference to the black comedic actor. "He's here somewhere tonight ... So Chris Tucker is in there, he looks at me straight face and says he's come in to the Oval Office because he's about to make a movie in which he will star as the first black president. I didn't have the heart to tell him I had already taken the position."

Two months after Clinton's second presidential term ended he raised the subject again during the telecast of the NAACP's 2001 Image Award Program. This time Clinton was seated in the audience and Tucker, the show's master of ceremonies, was onstage. At one point during the program the actor went into the audience to interview the former president.

---

[9] Toni Morrison, "The Talk of the Town." *The New Yorker*, 5 October 1998.

CHRIS TUCKER: Mr. President, how are you enjoying the show?

BILL CLINTON: I'm having a great time. You know, entertainment's wonderful. So many people I like, and then . . . you.

CHRIS TUCKER: I heard you moved to Harlem since the last time I came to the house. You stay right down the street from my cousin Willie. He said he seen you. No, seriously, seriously, I want to thank you. Thank you. Thank you. You've done so many great things for this country and so many great things for our people, my people. I want to thank you so much. We love you.

BILL CLINTON: Now wait a minute.

CHRIS TUCKER: And another thing, I'm mad. I'm mad because I wanted to be the first black president, but you beat me to it.

BILL CLINTON: Hey, wait a minute. That's why I went to Harlem. I thought I was the first black president. So I figured you can make the movie, but if I go to Harlem I'll still be the real thing.

While Clinton was the first White House occupant to claim (if only jokingly) to be black, he's not the only one to be so labeled. During the 1800 presidential campaign, Thomas Jefferson was called "a mean-spirited, low-lived fellow, the son of a half-breed Indian squaw, sired by a Virginia mulatto father."[10] While it's not known whether black blood actually coursed through Jefferson's veins, there is good evidence that the nation's third chief executive fathered children with Sally Hemings, a slave woman who was his concubine.

Andrew Jackson and Abraham Lincoln were both rumored to have had black fathers. But it was Warren Harding, this nation's twenty-ninth president, who came close to having the charge derail his presidency. Harding long had been dogged by accusations that he had black blood. The rumor was so persistent that the father of his wife-

[10] Paul F. Boller Jr., *Presidential Campaigns* (New York: Oxford University Press, 1984), 11.

to-be tried to block the wedding—an action that almost brought him and Harding to blows.[11] A month before the 1920 presidential election, a university professor in Ohio circulated a pamphlet that raised the charge anew. Harding's campaign staff quickly got a historical society to research the Republican presidential candidate's family tree and certify that only "Anglo-Saxon, German, Scotch-Irish, and Dutch"[12] blood flowed through his veins.

While no one argues that a black bloodline runs through Bill Clinton's family tree, more than a few African Americans consider him to be a kindred soul.

[11] Christopher B. Booker, *African-Americans & the Presidency: A History of Broken Promises* (New York: Franklin Watts, Inc., 2000), 97.
[12] Ibid., 97.

Interviews

MICHAEL BROWN
ATTORNEY, WASHINGTON, D.C.

(Son of Commerce Secretary Ronald H. Brown who died in a plane crash in 1996)

Bill Clinton reached out to my family as soon as my father's plane was reported missing. It was a day I'm never going to forget. The president was literally up all night with us. We were getting reports from the secretary of defense and from the secretary of the army and trying to get as much information as we could. He visited with us that night at my mother's house and talked to us often on the phone throughout the night. At some point we were saying, "This guy, doesn't he have other stuff to do? We know he's trying to run a country." I think, like my family, he was just devastated by what occurred.

The next thing that sticks out for me was what the president said about my father at his funeral. During his remarks at the cathedral he gestured to the casket and said if not for my dad he would not be president. I think more than important for us as a family to hear that, I think for my father's people, my father's soldiers, the people that worked for him when he was chairman of the Democratic National Committee, the people that worked so hard at the Department of Commerce, the people that gave their all for him during the 1992 presidential campaign, they really needed to hear that.

That recognition from "the Man"—the president of the United States—that the efforts of a black man, my dad, put him in the White House was important for us as a family to hear, but it was more important for my father's friends—and the nation—to hear.

TOM JOYNER

SYNDICATED RADIO TALK SHOW HOST,
DALLAS, TX

Bill Clinton had, and still has, a way of making people believe they are important—that they matter and that he has genuine concern for their well-being. For a group of people like African Americans who have been treated, at best, like second-class citizens and afterthoughts by most politicians, he was a welcomed change.

After decades of supporting Democratic presidential candidates, finally, here was a man who seemed to be interested in not just black votes, but black voters, too. I watched on CNN as President Clinton spoke to his new neighbors in Harlem on the day thousands of people turned out to welcome him at the opening of his office there. That was something no other president ever contemplated.

I can give several firsthand accounts of how President Clinton reached out to Black America in ways no U.S. president had before. Some have examined his record and claimed that a lot of his "love" for black folks was more talk than action. I'm not sure about that, but I am sure of the connection he had with black people and the connection we had with him.

When he traveled to South Africa with a group of media that included Tavis Smiley and me, he publicly called Africa the cradle of civilization and he apologized for slavery. These are things that white people may have barely noticed, yet for black people in America they were cause for celebration. Here was the most powerful man in the world acknowledging before the world that civilized life began with people who looked like us.

My favorite Bill Clinton story by far is this: A few years ago, Tavis Smiley called to the attention of our radio audience that Rosa Parks, the mother of the Civil Rights movement, had never received the Congressional Medal of Freedom. After many weeks of encouraging our listeners to write, call, fax, and e-mail members of Congress, Rosa Parks was finally given that honor. As I stood in the audience the day she received the medal, Jessye Norman led us all in "Lift Every

Voice and Sing." Not one verse, but three. Every living black dignitary was in the audience that great day and everyone stood and sang the first verse loudly and proudly.

As we got to the second verse, the singing got faint. Most of us left it up to Miss Norman, who had the words in front of her. The only person in the room that sang every word of every verse by heart was Bill Clinton. By the third verse, he and Jessye Norman were doing a duet.

President Clinton may not have been all things to all black people, but he was like no other president we've seen before. And unless by some miracle he's able to run again, I doubt that we'll ever see one like him again.

JOSEPH LOWERY
CIVIL RIGHTS LEADER, ATLANTA, GA

Let me tell you why Bill Clinton is so popular with black folks. Have you ever been swimming and stayed underwater so long that when you did come up that fresh air was like "Glory Hallelujah"? Now I think that's the first thing. We had been under Reagan and Bush for a long time—Reagan eight years and Bush four—that was twelve years during which presidents that made us feel like we were being smothered, if not with direct assault then with neglect and insensitivity. They put issues that we cared about, issues that impacted our lives, way down on the priority scale, somewhere about two notches below the snail darter.

So when Clinton came in and started making appointments and showing interest in issues that related to us, and had some black folks around him who at least enjoyed a reputation for favoring the issues that we were concerned about, it was a breath of fresh air. He made good appointments. Clinton made some very significant appointments. I think his appointment record will probably exceed the level of all the presidents before him, maybe combined. I have to give him credit for that. He promised to have an administration that looked like America and he did. He tried to do that. I think he would have done even better in his judicial appointments but you had people like Jesse Helms blocking a lot of his appointments.

You have to give Clinton credit for the appointments he made— and for his stand on affirmative action where he said "mend it, don't end it." That was a real shot in the arm for the hopes and aspirations of black Americans in the workplace and for educational opportunity. And it was so contrary to what Reagan and Bush had been saying about affirmative action. So that was a great salute to black Americans that he made. On most issues he seemed sympathetic and supportive of positions taken by African Americans, things African Americans felt were important.

And we can get down to the real reason. The real thing is that the boy blew saxophone. He wasn't no Chew Barry or Sonny Hodges, but the fact that he just blew a saxophone made white folks hate him.

See, if he had played the violin or the oboe, white folks would not have been so disturbed. But a saxophone is about as black an instrument as you can get. It even surpasses the piano. You have some white boys who can play it, but really the saxophone is a soul-o-phone—and Clinton played it.

Clinton had another ace up his sleeve. The boy can preach. Jesse Jackson could make a fool out of Walter Mondale and Michael Dukakis, but he couldn't bother Clinton. Clinton could tell a story. That's the first thing I learned about him. I preached in Little Rock when he was governor. He and I became friends because he loved preaching. He can preach, but he also knows how to go to a black church and just melt into the woodwork. He becomes an invisible white man. He becomes a black man in the pews.

There's no question in my mind, he is the greatest politician in my time, and I'll be eighty this year. Prior to Clinton, Lyndon Johnson was the best president we ever had. Prior to Clinton, Johnson was the best friend the Civil Rights movement had in the White House. Lyndon couldn't blow the saxophone. Lyndon couldn't do nothing but hold dogs up by their ears. One thing that helped Lyndon Johnson with us was that he said "we shall overcome" with a southern drawl. Actually, in terms of legislation such as the Civil Rights Act and Voting Act, Johnson did a great job.

But Clinton was the greatest friend the movement had without being an authentic liberal, because he isn't. He is not. He's for the death penalty. He's responsible for the "three strikes and you're out" rule. I have serious questions about the welfare reform legislation Clinton signed, but that was a matter of political strategy. No other Democrat could have beat Bush except Clinton.

Like the White Citizen's Council that took the Ku Klux Klan's garb and philosophy and hid it under their suits and ties, Clinton took many aspects of the Republican program and put a dashiki on them and got them passed. He's a great politician. Who else could have been caught with an intern under his desk performing oral sex and survive? He survived and here he is now getting $10 million for a book, and his wife got elected to the Senate.

GWEN MCKINNEY
PRESIDENT, MCKINNEY AND MCDOWELL,
WASHINGTON, D.C.

I think Toni Morrison said it right when she described Bill Clinton as the first "black president." I know it was a little bit tongue in cheek, but I think the symbolism can't be lost. Bill Clinton has been viewed all his life as an underdog. He came from the other side of the tracks. He was basically the type of person who persisted in whatever it was he set out to do, despite the odds. He was relentless and won the label of "Comeback Kid."

In some circles he was probably called "poor white trash," but from our viewpoint he is an underdog. He was someone who a lot of white people despised because he wasn't part of their group and that in itself was endearing to many black folks. I think the other reason why Bill Clinton is so very popular with African Americans is that he's an astute student of human nature. I think he knows and understands the psyche of oppressed people—black people—people who are on the outside looking in. His experiences in Arkansas in his very early days gave him the opportunity to be exposed to black people in a different way from rednecks. He was probably drawn to us out of a certain level of intellectual curiosity. I think he's very much a promiscuous individual, and I don't mean sexually promiscuous. I mean promiscuous in terms of just his uninhibited desire to engage with people—and that is probably what opened him up to learning about black people. And in so doing he learned some lessons that many of us have not learned about ourselves.

We have an uncanny ability to connect with people based on an emotional appeal. We are very physical as a people so you need to reach out and touch. That's very important to us. We also like the oral cadence that comes from the black church. Clinton has got that down pat. If you heard Bill Clinton talk when he's on the stump, when he talked to a black audience and when he spoke at a reunion of Oxford grads you would think you were listening to two different people. He has the cadence down in terms of the drawl and the rhythm and just even the use of language that works with black folks—language that's visual, that's colorful, that invokes emotion.

I think Bill Clinton was more style than substance. I think that the substance was that he was able to learn what worked and how to use it effectively. So I don't want to in any way diminish the fact that he got that style down because it's not easy, you know.

I think his move to Harlem is indicative of the kind of two-edged sword that Clinton wields in the African-American community. On the one hand it's cause for a celebration—a former president anointing our community and giving us a kiss of acceptance by moving there. And on the other hand I think his move to Harlem will quicken the gentrification that has taken hold there. That's what Bill Clinton gives us. His move to Harlem shows that he feels totally comfortable in an African-American environment.

I think what's important to remember about the relationship between African Americans and Bill Clinton is that we stood by him when he was down. The loyalty and the steadfast support that Bill Clinton garnered from African Americans, I think, will be part of what history records down the road—the fact that Bill Clinton's personal approval rating among whites was, like, in the subbasement, but went through the roof with black people at the height of the Monica Lewinsky controversy.

TIM REID

ACTOR/PRODUCER, PETERSBURG, VA

Bill Clinton was the FDR of this era. You know FDR had the same sort of love and admiration from the black community. When you bring up his name with old-timers you see a trance going over them. They immediately go, ooooooh! Bill Clinton reminds me of a St. Bernard in the sense that he is big and loveable, but he leaves a big mess in the backyard and drools all over your furniture.

I've been in his presence a few times and I have to tell you he is disarming and when he comes in a door you can't take your eyes off of him, male or female. Hopefully you have two different things you admire about him on a gender basis, but you look at him you go, "this guy, he really has that aura." I remember Richard Pryor looking at me one day and saying—this is when I was struggling and wondering if I was going to make it in show business—he said, "You gonna be all right 'cause you got that thing." I said, "What thing?" He said, "I don't know what it is, but I know it when I see it."

Well, Clinton's got that thing. That's why I say he is big and loveable. He's just a big, loveable guy, an intelligent man, who basically represents the underdog in the eyes of a lot of black people. He's the guy who is counter to the system; he goes against the system, he comes from struggle, and his family background mimics much of our own.

I say he's incredibly intelligent because it takes a lot of intelligence to shape that sort of image for himself. But I think he was sixty percent style and forty percent substance. I think the substance deficiency comes from the fact that people with his kind of drive sometimes outrun their mission. Clinton was cut out of a mold that a lot of black folks' heroes come from.

It's that underdog mold. We champion underdogs, whether they come from wealth like Kennedy, or not. Kennedy really came in as an underdog. His hurdle was religion. The question he had to overcome was can a Catholic be president of the United States? FDR triumphed over illness. This man was president of the United States in a wheelchair at a time when people had to hide their disabilities to get ahead.

Because we see ourselves as the underdog, we see ourselves as the out-cast, we align ourselves with people we view in the same way.

But as anyone who owns a St. Bernard will tell you, you can't have the big and loveable piece without getting the big mess in the backyard. You can't have one without the other.

When Clinton was catching all that impeachment hell from Congress, I read an article in the *New York Times* in which a guy called Clinton a "trickster." He didn't mean it in a derogatory way. It's a term that comes out of medieval times. The "trickster" was part of the mythology of that time. The trickster's job is to test your spirit, to test your resolve, and if you don't give the trickster respect, the trickster will win because you are not pure of heart. That's what happened to Clinton's enemies in Congress. Everyone who came before him was defeated. The closet doors started opening and bones were falling out faster than the reporters could report them.

Much of what I know about my relationship with women was not learned in church, it was learned in discussions with my uncle, who was a player, and another guy in my neighborhood who was a ladies' man. They taught me how to deal with women, how to be nice to them, and how to be open with them. Well, if you use that sort of simple philosophy at the ghetto level and take it into politics, that's what Clinton has done. He's given black people something that no one has given: hope. He put a lot of black people in office, some incredibly qualified people. But he created that big mess in the backyard with Monica Lewinsky. That's the St. Bernard thing I'm talking about—as loveable as they are, they drool all over your furniture and leave a big mess in the yard.

I'm not surprised that Clinton moved his office to Harlem. He had nowhere else to go. We are his constituency. Harlem is his safe haven. He can go anywhere around the world and they love him. But in this country I think he has infuriated white America to the point that he feels most comfortable among black people. For them it's really about race. The fact that he has loved or embraced black America has pissed them off. I think white Americans feel he has betrayed them. Not because he slept with someone and got caught. It's that he has embraced black America that angers them. It's like in the *Wizard of Oz*. The power of Oz, that voice that made everybody quake, was a frightened white man behind a curtain yelling into a megaphone. For us it's white America behind that curtain and those people are frightened that they are about to lose their grip on power in this country. They are about to become a minority. They look at Clinton as someone who betrayed them.

To them, he was a little too liberal with his appointments. I was on a plane yesterday coming back from Detroit and behind me were two white gentlemen. We were stuck on the runway for a long time and I was just listening to their political talk. They were just two strangers who struck up a conversation. I assume they were Republicans, but I wouldn't bet on it. Well, the hatred they had for the Clintons was unbelievable. What I heard was the fear of that white man behind the curtain.

They attacked Hillary. They said she's an evil woman, that she's a mean woman. It sounded so chauvinistic. Then they went after Clinton. It was clear they thought Clinton and his wife had not behaved in the way that the little white man behind the curtain thought they should have acted.

There have been only a few presidential idols in the black community. FDR, Kennedy, and Johnson never really quite made it to that level. Truman, probably more than Johnson, was respected by blacks. When I hear old-timers talk about presidents they respect, they mention Truman. Eisenhower, Nixon, Ford—none of them really cut it with black folks. A lot of black church people liked Jimmy Carter because of his spiritualism. But black people certainly do love Bill Clinton.

DWIGHT ROBINSON
SENIOR VICE PRESIDENT, FREDDIE MAC,
VIENNA, VA

Bill Clinton is multilingual. What I mean is that he has the understanding that most African Americans have—that to be successful we
have to be able to operate and verbalize in two worlds. Clinton is able
to do that. He's actually able to operate in more than two worlds. This
is what makes us comfortable with him. He was the president of the
United States and the guy next door playing the saxophone. He was
the dutiful husband and proud father and he was the cat hanging out
in the bar up the street talking with the fellas. He was the expert on
bilateral issues and could sit down and rag people with the best of 'em.
All of those traits, I think, resonate very well with black folks because
that's an element of our character that we cultivated during our time
in this country. It's an element of our character that allows us to be
successful in this environment.

Clinton exuded those characteristics. People picked that up not
only in what he said, but in what people said about him; not only in
what he did, but in the things that he didn't do. All of those things resonated with black folks and that is what made him so popular. I think
the other thing that made him so popular in the African-American
community is his tendency to talk about teaching people to fish, giving them the wherewithal to do for themselves, as opposed to someone doing it for them. Too many white liberals always want to do for
us. Clinton gave off a signal that said, "Wait a minute, with a little
help, you can do for yourself."

On the other hand, Clinton has his share of warts. But he always
seems to find a way around them, from the Sister Souljah episode to
his real desire to have a discussion, but not a real discussion, about
race.

When Bill Clinton got into trouble black folks didn't take to the
lifeboats like so many white folks, because we understand the difference between "shit and shineola." We know the rhetoric and we know
the rhetoric always exceeds the reality. So when the reality catches up

with the rhetoric and we see the gaps that exist, we're never surprised. We've seen those kinds of things happen in our families and we understand the difference between a person's public duties and their private business.

NORMA JOHNSON
RETIREE, FISHERS, IN

I think Bill Clinton is very comfortable with African Americans. I think it's apparent that he's a lot more comfortable with us than he is with his own people. I think also the kind of ire that he draws from the right-wing conservatives, even the ire that he draws from the right-wing black conservatives, just makes us like him even more.

Just the other day I was looking at C-SPAN and they were talking about the payment of pension and retirement money for these ex-presidents, and the black folks who were calling in were saying stuff like "you know the Republicans never said nothing as long as Reagan and the others were getting money." Let them mess with Clinton and they're gonna have war. One woman said if they want a fight, they gonna get a fight.

It was funny because that is exactly how we feel. A lot of what his enemies don't like about him is exactly what makes us like him—his comfortableness with us, and I don't think it's a condescending kind of comfortableness. You know, you have some white folks, like the present president, who are very condescending toward us. And I don't have a whole lot of respect for the black folks around him, not even Colin Powell. I mean, I think he's probably a nice person, but white people like him too much, and if white people like him that much there's got to be something wrong. We feel the same way about Clinton. If they hate him so much that they would try to destroy his career, that they will send a woman in like they did with Monica Lewinsky—a lot of my friends feel like that was a setup—then that's a good reason for us to like him. And so that's why I think black folks like him.

Black folks knew he wasn't perfect, that he made mistakes. He's human. Sure we got angry with him when he did those things, but he's part of the family. So just like Jesse Jackson made mistakes, Jesse's part of the family. You don't mess with the family. I hate the way the Congress jumped on Clinton and the press went after him 'til they almost sucked the life out of the man. That's what I resented. But I was upset with him, too. I was upset with him just like I would be with my brother if he went out and played around on his wife and got caught. But what he did is not an unforgivable sin. That's all I'm saying. It's not an unforgivable sin. They had no right to try to destroy him the way they did—and are still trying to do. They just need to get a life and leave him alone. That's how I feel. They need to go get a life.

The thing about Clinton and his shortcomings is that his shortcomings are public while those of a lot of other people aren't. I mean these hypocrites, they're doing the exact same thing that they accused Clinton of and we're now seeing that come out. Like Gary Condit, who was calling for Clinton to step down. Now he's got all these women coming out of the woodwork. So I think we should beware of those who were out there throwing stones at Clinton, because they often are the very ones who have the most to cover up.

I know that on paper it looks like Clinton didn't do a lot for black people, but I think he did a lot in terms of the image of black people in this country and worldwide. You know he was the first president to make a trip to Africa and really try to do something about things over there. He was the first president that even gave Africa some respect. He went. His wife went. His daughter went. You could go all the way back to when I was born and you won't find another president who did that.

Now there were things he did that I disagreed with. I totally disagreed with his position on welfare reform. I think it's done more to push those who were on the edge of poverty into poverty, but you can't be all things to all people. The part of him I do like is the respect that I think he gives black people. I don't know how to phrase it, if it is style or substance. I think it's substantial considering that we're not getting any respect right now. Bush ain't giving us no respect. It's like he's going to fry all of us, give us all the death penalty, and the ones who don't die on death row, well then he'll find another way to do them in.

I think Bush and his cronies would love for Bill Clinton to go away. He ain't going anywhere. The man is the same age as me. He's got another good thirty to forty years that those right-wingers will have to put up with him. I don't believe that we've seen the last of him. Who knows? We might have an ex-president in the Senate. I mean, I don't see why he would. I think he's got a lot more clout not being elected, but you know he likes the spotlight. If he feels like he and Hillary can hog the spotlight being in the Senate, being Clinton and Clinton, he might do it.

I think anything that would upset those right-wing conservatives is a good idea. They hate his guts—and that's exactly why black folks love Bill Clinton. And I think a lot of black folks think it was cool that he put his office in Harlem. That was a real slap in the face to those conservatives who tried to bring him down. It was a good decision on his part and I think it will be good for Harlem. I don't really know that much about Harlem, but I think it will be good for the people there. They'll get whatever economic development he can bring to that area.

Bill Clinton will be safe in Harlem.

REVEREND FRANK REID

PASTOR, BETHEL AME CHURCH, BALTIMORE, MD

Black folk relate to Bill Clinton is many ways. He has charisma. He's a tremendous speaker. He came from a dysfunctional family where the father for all intents and purposes was absent. The mother was the matriarch of the family. And so in many ways, I believe African Americans identify with him because he identifies with us.

And it was because of the way we identify with him—that connection a lot of black folk feel with him—that we didn't desert Clinton during the impeachment. We don't throw away our leaders. We didn't throw away Jesse Jackson, Adam Clayton Powell, Martin Luther King Jr., and Elijah Muhammad. We look at the public work of a person and if they are truly sorry for their personal failings, if they really try to change, then we're willing to give them a second chance. That's why I think you saw people like Reverend Jackson and Bishop T. D. Jakes and many other pastors really support Bill Clinton at that low point in his White House career.

Now, as for his relationship with black folk, I think he is sincere. I'm not blind to the fact that he's a politician. When I look at his life history and see what he's been through I can see why there may be some dysfunctional sides to his character, as there are dysfunctional sides to everybody's character. When you look at what he has achieved, and what he stands for, then it becomes easy not only to support him—but also to like him.

MICHAEL COLYAR
ACTOR/COMEDIAN, LOS ANGELES, CA

I have nine reasons why Bill Clinton is popular with black people or, in other words, why they like him. First, he's a regular guy. I mean he appears to everybody like regular folks. He doesn't seem like he's haughty and above other people, or that he's elitist, or different. He seems like a regular cat that you'd hang out with and that's appealing to our people.

Second, some politicians go to black churches and other places in the black community and you know they were just there because they needed our votes. But with Clinton, I always felt like he sort of belonged at the black picnics and the black fund-raisers and all the events that he would go to, because he always came across as just one of the guys. There was a comfort zone, I guess, with him.

Number three—he's got natural rhythm. You've got to respect that. This guy played the saxophone and he could actually play that thing. You know, he got up there with the brothers and played. He's got rhythm, natural rhythm, and of course we love that about him.

Fourth, he appointed a lot of minorities to his cabinet, probably more than anybody. Every time we saw him speaking somewhere he would be surrounded by people of all nationalities.

Five, everybody can respect a brother who likes the ladies. That's an important thing for him. You know he's going to get it. I mean he went about it wrong, but he likes the ladies.

Six, Bill Clinton always came across as fair. Now that may be because of his great ability to communicate with people, to speak in a really nice and positive and convincing way, but he always came across as fair, always seemed like he was trying to do the right thing. In fact, I think he tried to do the right thing for black people a lot and that may be why he had so many people trying to bring him down.

Number seven, he wasn't about tokenism. It seems like a lot of times presidents have a couple of black tokens, you know, one here and one there just 'cause they know they have to have a brother on their staff. Clinton didn't have any tokens around him, or at least there didn't appear to be any.

Eight, his brother—he had one of those brothers that everybody's got. You know what I'm saying. He ain't no presidential brother. He's a regular brother. He's always in trouble. He's always getting plenty of negative press.

And nine, when Bill Clinton got in trouble with Monica Lewinsky, who did he go to: black people. He went to Vernon Jordan and Jesse Jackson. Those were the first people he turned to. Black people saw that and realized that when it came down to the real deal, the president of the United States came to us when he was in trouble and needed somebody to protect his back.

Plain and simple, this is why black people love this guy.

JOHNNIE COCHRAN
ATTORNEY, NEW YORK, NY

Bill Clinton is probably the most comfortable caucasian around black people that most of us have ever seen. He feels totally comfortable around black people. There's not a difference, there's nothing awkward about his relationship with us; there's nothing uncomfortable about it. You know he just seems very much at home when he's with us and hence all those jokes from Chris Rock about him being the first black president.

Let me tell you a story about the night Clinton won the presidency in 1992. I was very close with Ron Brown and Mickey Kanter. They invited me to Little Rock. I spent three or four days there around the time of the election. Well, I remember going into a black-owned barbecue place that Clinton went to often. The people there told me how he was so comfortable around them, and how he seemed to genuinely care about them. They said he wasn't one of those white politicians that wouldn't look you in the eyes and couldn't remember your name. They said that wasn't the situation with Clinton. This guy really seems to really care, they said.

And then later when I saw him at the White House I saw what those people at the barbecue place were talking about. My wife and I were in a White House reception line one evening. I had been on the *Today Show* that morning. The first thing Clinton said to me was, "I saw you on TV this morning," and then we talked about our families and joked about a couple of things. That's the kind of president he was—easy to talk to. Clinton not only knows black people, he knows things that are important to us. So if it's civil rights, or judicial appointments, or just diversifying the staff in the White House, I think he felt that was an important thing to do and I think he worked very hard to make black folks a part of all of those things.

I didn't always agree with him. I thought Clinton went too far on the crime bill. But I think he was a smart politician, too. And he worked very hard to position himself at the political center. He didn't do everything right. He had some ethical lapses, which I think gave his enemies a stick with which to beat him. But in the crunch he was still the person in the White House with whom we felt the safest.

When things didn't go right, when we disagreed with something he did, he would listen to what we had to say. We didn't close the door on him because he was like a family member. Things don't always go right even among your siblings; sometimes you have disagreements. And we would disagree with Clinton. We disagreed with him on welfare reform. We thought that was a real attack on the poor. We differed with him on Lani Guinier. I thought he ran away from her much too soon. He should have stood up for her.

Now on the other hand, I think he and Vernon Jordan are friends to the absolute end. I admire that. It's good to have someone who will protect your back. When Clinton got in trouble, it was African Americans who, by and large, stood by him during his politically driven impeachment. We stood up for him because we came to believe that it was a politically inspired attack. His sexual indiscretion was a private matter that his enemies really blew out of perspective. Black people knew that what these people were doing had nothing to do with whether Clinton could run the country.

We know Clinton didn't always tell the truth about his sexual behavior, but we didn't think he should have been impeached for that. It was political. Other presidents have lied about far more serious stuff—about matters of state—and they didn't get impeached. Black folks stood beside Clinton because we could see through the phoniness of the people who attacked him.

I think Clinton did a lot to earn that support. He went to Robbins Islands to retrace the steps of the great Nelson Mandela. He went to the great continent of Africa—and unlike George W. Bush, he knows that Africa is a continent, and not a country. If you compare Bill Clinton's trip to Africa with the message that was sent when President Bush said something to the effect that Africa "is a country" with a great amount of disease, it's easy to understand the different feelings black folks have for both men. Clinton is seen as somebody who really cares about us. Bush is seen as someone who, when it comes to black people, can't get his geography right.

I think there was both symbolism and substance in the fact that during his Africa trip Clinton acknowledged that slavery was wrong. When other people wouldn't even raise the issue, this man in essence apologized for the injustices of slavery. I think that was important, certainly for us, and important for the country.

I think Clinton will be judged ultimately as the president who had the greatest relationship with African Americans, who bonded with us more than any president, and who was really sensitive to the issues of African Americans. I believe that. I also think that history will treat him kindly overall when you look at what happened with the economy and peace in the world during his time in the White House.

TERRIE WILLIAMS

PRESIDENT, THE TERRIE WILLIAMS AGENCY,
NEW YORK, NY

I think it is Bill Clinton's humanness that appeals to black people. He connects with the humanness in everyone; he connects with the God in everyone. We have a greater affinity for people who treat us like we're special, or we're someone. But it's the God presence in him, that's all that is; it's very simple.

Historians will probably say that he connected with black folks in a way that no other president ever did. If another one comes along it will be a very, very long time. People see themselves in Bill Clinton. I see him on a lot of levels in the same way that people reacted to Marion Barry. It was the God presence in him. It was the human quality in him; it was the everyman quality about him. There is no difference between the street sweeper and Marion Barry. There is no difference between the street sweeper and Bill Clinton. We are all the same. I don't care what your title is because underneath the face we're all identical, fragile, scared human beings—every last one of us.

Bill Clinton has that human quality. It's his heart that you feel first and foremost. When I say he walks in God's presence, he has a human quality. And so, on a lot of levels that's why black people reacted to him in the way that they did. Maybe on some levels, once you are aware how you affect people, you turn it on. There are times when you are aware that when you do things it makes people melt. But I don't think that you can fool many people for long. I think most black people spot insincerity a mile away.

I have a friend who saw Clinton recently on the street in midtown New York. It was kind of like, "what's up bro?" Either Clinton said it first or this guy said it first, but it was responded to in kind. On one level you think, who does he think he is to address a former president as brother? But on another level you feel it's all right with him because he knows we are all the same.

43

MARGARET JONES
PUBLIC SCHOOL ADMINISTRATOR,
LOS ANGELES, CA

Well, I suppose that by and large many African Americans empathized with Bill Clinton. We could relate to him and relate to his life struggles—to the events that occurred during his presidency that somehow seemed to have been blown completely out of proportion. I know that's basically the way I feel. I felt that he was a person who was compassionate, who really understood the plight of the working poor. He certainly was able to relate to black Americans and did so through the appointments he made and through his associations. So I think at least from my own perspective, he identified with those issues that were critical to us: education, health care, looking at how to help folks who had no bootstraps. And perhaps much of that had to do with his experience growing up in the South.

I think that black folks tend to have a greater sense of humanity and willingness to have hope, to help others perhaps in greater preponderance than other groups—and that's why so many of us supported him. I think he was special in that he didn't appear to have a problem expressing his concern about African Americans, about the plight of African Americans, and what had happened to African Americans historically. I also think that there was a sense that he had a vision for helping folks that were poor. I know that there are African Americans who may not feel quite that way, but I think that the vast majority do. I certainly think that Clinton was a president that many black Americans felt they could identify with more than anyone else. I didn't view him as a black president. I think he tried to be fair and he tried to be sensitive to various groups that were different, groups that have been discriminated against in our society. Black folks tend to rally around those kinds of people more readily than other groups.

I met Clinton once. It was a very brief encounter through my daughter. She had a friend who was a secret service agent. Clinton was in Los Angeles. It was right after the Monica Lewinsky stuff broke. He had been here for a fund-raiser and was leaving to go back to Washington. My daughter's friend called us and said that if we could come out to the airport early the next morning she could arrange for us to meet Clinton as he embarked on Air Force One. And so we did.

They checked us out, identification had already been given, and we proceeded with some other people who were able to go to the area, and we waited for him to drive up. He came in with the flags flying on his cars. He was running a little late so I was standing there thinking, oh he won't have a chance to shake our hands or anything. But he got out of his car and most graciously took time to shake the hand of everyone who stood in line to see him. I'm an oxygen patient. I had my portable tank with me and as I was talking with the president—we were talking about some educational things—my tank knocked over and he reached over and straightened it up. He picked it up. He was just a very charming man. And in light of all of the attacks that he was undergoing, I was most impressed that he took the time to be that sensitive to those of us who were there.

We didn't reject him when he got into that Lewinsky mess because basically we're not hypocritical. We knew that he was a victim of the circumstances that he had grown up in. He was a child of the '60s and there was free love all about and so many people had a cavalier attitude about sex. I think that we also are very loyal and have a tendency not to destroy you when you are down. I think we have a tendency to support the downtrodden. For me it wasn't something that I cared about. I mean, we know what powerful men have done throughout the years, throughout the centuries. We start with George Washington. You know why they say "George Washington slept here?" You know Thomas Jefferson and the other big men in our country who were never caught because they grew up in a time when we did not have media lynchings? I think that's what happened. Black folks recognized that whole thing for what it was and decided they were not going to take that opportunity to destroy somebody who had basically supported the causes that we believed in. I would have loved to have seen the media jump up and down on the abuse of power in this last election more so than who slept with whom.

I hope history will judge Bill Clinton well in terms of his relationship with African Americans. He was the president who had vision and who brought forward some of the key issues that needed to be dealt with in our time. I think he was a very brilliant man who did a stupid thing and I hope that that stupid thing does not destroy his place in history.

CHAPTER 3

A Kindred Soul

Ten days before Bill Clinton stepped up to the pulpit of Jesse Jackson's Rainbow Coalition Leadership Summit in June 1992 and quickly angered his host by attacking the lyrics of black rapper Sister Souljah, he hauled a saxophone onto the stage of the *Arsenio Hall Show* and played a set with the show's "posse."

After blowing a spirited rendition of "Heartbreak Hotel" and "God Bless the Child," Clinton spent a half hour talking to Hall, the popular, black late-night television host, about the rioting that had occurred in Los Angeles that year, his views on race relations, and his use of marijuana many years earlier. Looking on through their televisions were the millions of African Americans who regularly tuned in to watch Hall's show, whose guests included some of the most popular black and white entertainers. Clinton's performance that night helped cushion him against the criticism that Jackson and others lobbed his way after he bashed Sister Souljah. In his appearance on Hall's show and the many others Clinton made before black audiences during the 1992 presidential campaign, he "banked" a lot of goodwill—credits that held him in good stead with many African Americans at critical times during his presidency.

This was especially true when Clinton, who won 82 percent of the black vote in November 1992, saw his approval rating among African Americans drop sharply seven months later after he withdrew his nomination of Lani Guinier to be his assistant attorney general for civil rights. Guinier and Clinton were friends. In 1986, he and his wife, Hillary, attended her wedding. The weekend after Clinton's 1992 inauguration Guinier helped put on a small dinner party for the First Couple. A year later she recalled that evening in an article in the *New York Times Magazine* by saying: "The significance of the occasion did not escape those of us in attendance. The party was a poignant reminder that this President had black friends who were his peers. Indeed, for a brief moment, I could even imagine the President as he was at Yale Law School, when he would sit down with us—his classmates—in the law school dining room. Back then, he stood out as a white student who was obviously comfortable eating at a table in the company of more than one black person."[13]

Five weeks after Clinton nominated his law school classmate to be his administration's top civil rights officer, he withdrew the job offer amid blistering criticism from a cabal of right-wing critics that distorted her views. The most damaging charge was that Guinier was a "quota queen." Ironically, while most African Americans supported the use of racial quotas in affirmative action programs, Guinier did not. Still, the charge stuck and Clinton—whose promise to end the ban on gays in the military had already put his approval rating in a free fall—pulled the plug on Guinier's nomination.

Within days, Clinton's approval rating among African Americans fell to 53 percent, a drop of 34 percentage points from February of that year. But in the remaining six years of his presidency, Clinton's approval ratings and his personal standing with African Americans soared—driven largely by the great economic gains African Americans experienced during that time and the force of his personality.

---

[13] Lani Guinier, "Who's Afraid of Lani Guinier?," *New York Magazine*, 27 February 1994, 40.

Interviews

DONNA BRAZILE
DEMOCRATIC PARTY STRATEGIST,
WASHINGTON, D.C.

Bill Clinton got off to a rough start with black folks, but as the years wore on he became more and more popular with us. Prior to the 1996 election, there was a lot of dissatisfaction with him over some of his policies and yet while black leaders and members of the Congressional Black Caucus privately, and in some cases publicly, grumbled about his backing of some conservative initiatives, his support in the black community didn't waver. By this time black folks were with him. They were with him on the death penalty. They were with him on welfare reform. They were with him on taking a tough line on crime. It was almost as if he spoke in unison with the black community. So I think Bill Clinton had a rare gift. I haven't seen any other white politicians in the twentieth century master the black vote and the black community as well as Bill Clinton.

We did polling in each of the last three years of his presidency and in every poll Bill Clinton was the number one African-American leader. He remains number one. Black pollster Ron Lester just did another poll in Virginia and Clinton came out on top. He's number one. When you ask "what leader would you most like to hear from," he's the number one person. He comes out higher than Jesse Jackson and Colin Powell. He beats all the black people. I'll never forget I had to break it down to Reverend Jackson—he said "No, not Bill Clinton." I said, "Yes, Bill Clinton is the number one African-American leader." Now that's amazing.

He not only connected symbolically with African Americans but, after twelve years of Reagan and Bush, he appeared to be somebody that was on the side of African Americans. He not only understood our language and our songs, he understood our dreams and aspirations. I'll tell you a story. It was in June of 2000. We had an event at the home of the songwriter Babyface, I believe his real name is Kenneth Edmonds. He was hosting a fund-raiser for the Democratic Party and the president was the featured guest. The party was at Babyface's Los Angeles estate and he got a lot of other celebrities, like Lionel Ritchie, Chaka Khan, and Quincy Jones, to show up. There were a lot of Hollywood's "Who's Who," as well as a number of regular people, but mostly black folks.

The food was served buffet style. When the time came to eat, the president, rather than have someone serve him, stood in line with everyone else. I'll never forget it. He was standing right behind Chaka Khan, talking to her and the other people around him. When he got to the front of the line, the first food he went to was the black-eyed peas and smothered pork chops. I don't know, maybe it's his southern roots, his southern heritage. I've met other southern politicians who were timid around African Americans, especially powerful African Americans.

Later, when they started partying Bill Clinton just hunkered down. He understood every song that was being played—music that ranged from the '60s to the '70s. It's like he grew up with us. When I was in his presence I never felt as if I was with a politician who didn't understand me. I never had to break it down to Bill Clinton. When I told him what was going on in the black community, he understood it right away, like he was part of our culture, part of what we experienced. Clinton understands the history of our country, the history of race in America, and I think he sees himself as someone who can help bridge the racial divide and to help bring about healing. There was not a pollster telling him that he had to hang out with us to get the black vote. He really liked being around black people.

In White House meetings the president would always remind people, his top advisers, that he wanted African Americans around his table. He didn't want to go to all-white meetings. He didn't want to be involved in all-white events. You know the one mistake that white politicians make, especially liberal white politicians, is that they believe they know more about the black experience than do black people. Bill Clinton never treated African-American leaders or African-American voters as if he knew more about our experience. He understood it. He shared our pain. He just understood what we were going through, more than any other white politician, and I think that's why he will always remain the most popular figure in black politics for African Americans.

HUGH PRICE

PRESIDENT, NATIONAL URBAN LEAGUE,
NEW YORK, NY

There are several reasons why Bill Clinton is so well liked by African Americans. One huge reason is because he made a highly emotional and emotive connection to the African-American community. There was a comfort level in his dealings with African Americans, in his interfacing with African Americans, going to the churches, connecting, preaching, and baring his soul with us.

So, I think there was a strong—let's say—an effective, emotional connection between our community and the president. Secondly, I believe that the black appointments that he made, the sheer volume and quality of the appointments were quite striking. They were unusual. They broke new ground. The appointment of Franklin Raines to be head of the Office of Management and Budget broke new ground; Rodney Slater at Transportation; Alexis Herman at Labor, and on and on. And these were appointments that were not traditional. They were appointments that put African Americans in very important domestic policy roles. In the case of Raines, as the chief of budget, Clinton gave a black man unprecedented power. So I think that's the second reason.

For me, by far the most compelling reason is that during Clinton's tenure the economy really lifted off, and the economic circumstances of African Americans were the best in our history. The unemployment rate of African Americans went down to record lows, our labor force participation rates rose to a record high; he had a record low reduction in out-of-wedlock births among teenagers, a substantial reduction in teenage unemployment, and a substantial reduction in poverty.

There's a new study that shows that child poverty dropped in the late '90s and that was during Clinton's period. There was also a quite substantial recovery in the economic conditions of a lot of cities, a revitalization of neighborhoods that occurred on his watch. But I think what the public paid the most attention to was the emotional connection Clinton made with African Americans—and the economic benefits we received while he was in the White House. This is not idle speculation on my part. When you read the surveys that the Joint Center on Economic and Political Studies has done on the level of optimism of African Americans, you'll see that it exceeded the optimism of whites. Many of us attribute these gains to Clinton's presidency. I think he found the way to our hearts was through our wallets.

I don't think Clinton would have gotten very far with us on style alone. The economic progress African Americans made was not gradual; it was really quite substantial and swift. The improvements in our economic circumstances were very robust. The black unemployment rate dropped from double digits down to 7 percent—a huge drop.

Under Clinton the labor market got so tight that the demand for workers reached deep into our community. The economic conditions he created caused employers to go looking for workers in places they had long ignored.

ALICE RANDALL
AUTHOR, NASHVILLE, TN

It's certainly been my observation that President Clinton made a unique alliance with African Americans. I think white southerners have an intrinsic blackness. Down in the South there is a common culture, particularly among people in the underclass. The language of Toni Morrison and the language of William Faulkner is essentially the same language, and each of them has been deeply influenced by black and white southern voices. And so, I think white southerners owe a great debt to black culture. Some of them cannot tolerate this truth and reject it. And this is why I think some southerners have so much hatred for black people. But you cannot live in the South and not be influenced by black speech, black language, black culture.

If you are in one of those plantation towns, you are in a place that has been built and designed by black people whether or not they've been given credit. If you have someone cooking for you in the kitchen, the flavor of Africa is coming in to you, right there. And so to be a southerner is to understand, whether you like it or not, the power of black culture.

Bill Clinton acknowledges this very openly, in terms of his body language and the way he presents himself. That's one of the things I love about him. I hate it when people call him a liar. The biggest liar is sitting in the White House right now saying that every child has an equal chance in America. The biggest liar is saying, "I am the education president" when he is taking money away from education. Those are fundamental lies and black people who are deep in their culture understand that. I hate those literal, weird things that we call a truth, but that is everything but the truth. And black culture hates those things too.

Black culture has a great impulse toward reality truth, not something that is legalistic truth. And I think the saddest point of Bill Clinton's presidency for me was when he was hiding behind legalistic words, like, "it depends on what your definition of what the word *is*, is." Fortunately, he found a way to tell America the truth. At least that's what he conveyed and I think that was so important.

You know, black leaders in this country have often been attacked on personal grounds. Martin Luther King is certainly a case in point. Another example is the surveillance that J. Edgar Hoover ordered on the personal lives of black leaders. Because so many African-American leaders are subjected to exhaustive personal investigations, on the basis of which their public legitimacy is questioned, we relate to what Clinton went through. I think many black people feel that the economy and certain social justice issues were more important to the nation than Clinton's personal life. We understood that he could be an excellent president and a bad husband, that he could be a great public leader and have a troubled private life.

I'm not saying that this is a casual relation, but I'm saying that it is something that African Americans can identify with. And we did not assume just because Clinton was being investigated—that just because there was smoke there was fire.

The reason I like Bill Clinton, admire him, and feel extremely attracted to him is because he has probably the highest IQ of any president that we've had during my voting life. The other president that is also extremely intelligent is Jimmy Carter. As president he was very intelligent but didn't have leadership skills. I think this intelligence, this raw intelligence, is very attractive to African Americans. I actually think that there is a tremendous prejudice in the African-American community toward very bright people, which I would distinguish from very well educated people. I'm talking about innately bright people. George W. Bush, I think is the exact opposite of this. He is clearly not very bright. I mean, on an objective level he's a man who had every privilege and managed to be a C student at Yale—and is proud of it. If my daughter, an African-American girl, went to Yale and was a C student, she wouldn't have much of a future in front of her. This is one of those truths about black life that Clinton understands so well. Black people can identify with the very hardworking, very bright person, who makes something of himself from nothing. And that's Bill Clinton.

He's a very much self-made president. You know why I think people forgive him for his affair with Monica Lewinsky, and why it ultimately is not that important to me? And I'm speaking as an African-American woman. The story that I remember much more in my heart about him and women is that he defended his mother from an abusive stepfather. The fact that he intervened when she was being beaten, that he put his body between her and the man who was attacking her, even now that makes me want to tear up. There are millions of men who have cheated on their wives and there will be millions more. And there are millions of men who grew up in houses with abusive fathers and all too few of them, when they got big enough, stood up and said to a man who was abusing their mother "I won't let you do it again."

And so from my point of view as a woman, a black woman, I think what Clinton did to defend his mother was heroic. I want a son like that. He could be in my family, because in the black community we appreciate that kind of unsung heroism. I think this is why so many black women stood behind him. You know that lovers will betray you, and husbands, too, but you pray for a son that will stand by you in your real time of trouble.

There's another thing that I like about Clinton. He had black friends. For all of Jimmy Carter's good qualities, I certainly am not aware of any black person that I perceived as his best friend. Clinton on the other hand clearly has some black friends.

And so I think it is very important for the real legacy of the Clinton administration to be discerned. I think this nation enjoyed unparalleled prosperity during his presidency—a period that was also very social justice oriented. I think Bill Clinton's presidency proved that this nation can do good while it does well.

People ask the question, why do African Americans love Bill Clinton? The other side of that question is, why does Bill Clinton love African Americans? I think it is that he recognizes the intelligence and the resilience of our spirit. Take people from six different countries in Africa and shuffle them around on a ship, and then shuffle them around in a country and then put these people—who all speak different languages—to work in a cotton field. You've not just assaulted their written language skills, you assaulted their oral language skills, as well. Very few people have ever been subjected to this kind of assault. But then, from poetry to rap music, to the language of Faulkner and Toni Morrison, you see the emergence of this extraordinary thing we call the African-American poetic voice. Bill Clinton, who was in touch with the black roots, often spoke to America in this voice.

That's something that I think is highly affirming.

BILL CAMPBELL
MAYOR, ATLANTA, GA

More African Americans served in Bill's Clinton's cabinet, more African Americans served as department heads, more African-American judges were appointed by him than in the previous history of the United States. That alone goes a long way in explaining why this guy was so popular with black folks.

He put black people in real power positions that allowed his African-American appointees to make public policy decisions that were sensitive to the needs of African Americans. Clinton had a true commitment to diversity that was not seen in the presidency of the United States before his election—and black folks understand that. Many people fail to understand that we are as smart as everybody else. When we saw a lot of people that looked like us in positions of enormous influence in the Clinton administration, it gave us a sense of pride. And it made us feel a kind of kinship to Bill Clinton.

And we knew this just wasn't about politics. We know when white folks are comfortable around us and when they're not. They don't have to sing our songs, or play our records, or even cheer our leaders for us to know them. Black folks have a way of figuring out what's in a white person's head and sensing what's in their heart. I think African Americans got the chance to really look into Clinton's soul and they determined that he understands us. He appreciates what we've been through, and in many ways he really does feel our pain. I think that empathy was one of the reasons why we came to feel so comfortable with him.

Another reason why he has such closeness to us is his young age. He came of age during the civil rights era. So he didn't have a lot of preconceived notions that I think have hurt other leaders in their ability to understand what African Americans have endured. So the combination of how he grew up, where he grew up, the people he grew up around, but also the fact that he was young enough to really appreciate the African-American quest for equality, helped him to connect with us in a way that is rare. I don't think we've seen this before, certainly not in my lifetime.

When the history of his time is written, I think Bill Clinton's real legacy will be what he did for urban America. The changes have really been phenomenal—and they have benefited everyone, because most people in this country live in cities. I'm talking about the remarkable drop in the crime rate that came about because of his program to put more cops on the streets. He put money into programs that allowed us to employ more people and redevelop abandoned run-down areas. This helped us tackle the areas, the pockets of poverty, where most of the crime occurs. Clinton's holistic approach to the nation's cities was invaluable in causing this era—the Clinton era—to experience the largest ever drop in the nation's crime rate, the largest drop in African-American unemployment, the greatest increase in African-American homeownership, and the greatest increase in African-American entrepreneurship. If you look at cause and effect, its impossible not to give him credit, because when you see all these things happening during his eight years in office, and then look back over the last fifty years, it's impossible not to give him and his African-American appointees enormous credit for having done things that changed the face of urban America.

There's no surprise that for the first time in thirty years people are moving back into cities. Virtually every major city in America is now experiencing a population growth after thirty years of decline, due to a combination of factors. One of those factors is that the Clinton administration gave us the tools we needed to turn things around. Now we're seeing a lot of people, not just minorities but whites as well, moving back into the city. I don't think too many black folks doubt that Bill Clinton deserves enormous credit for making these changes possible.

On the other hand, there was a great deal of consternation among conservatives because those resources were being directed at inner-city communities. That's one of the reasons why they went at Clinton with such a vengeance. They waged an unprecedented, brutal frontal assault on Clinton, and that's why black folks rallied to his defense.

BLAIR WALKER
JOURNALIST AND AUTHOR

The really funny thing about Bill Clinton is that he got off to such a bad start with African Americans. He dropped Lani Guinier like a hot potato the minute he got a whiff of the Senate's opposition to her nomination as assistant attorney general for civil rights. That led a lot of black folks to say, "Oh here we go again, another white boy in office who is talking the talk, but definitely not walking the walk."

But Clinton has a capacity for rebounding. That's one reason why we embraced him. Another was that he, like a lot of brothers, has a life force. Brothers just have this special thing going on. They approach life differently from white males and white women. I see this in Bill Clinton. It was the swagger in his walk as he went about his business of leading this country. It was the defiant way he stood up for himself when the Senate and the House of Representatives tried to impeach him. He just seems to have a huge appetite for life; the same as most brothers and sisters. He pretty much approaches life the same way that we do. We work hard, but we realize that what we happen to be doing at the moment isn't the sum total of what life is all about. Clinton has a way of communicating that to people.

It also didn't hurt that he had charisma by the megawatts. I've watched him give a speech. I've seen him stick to a script, and I've seen him talk extemporaneously. The man has a very quick wit. Brothers can appreciate that. Brothers grow up playing the dozens, cracking on each other—talking about each other's mamas and what not. Bill Clinton has a lot of those same qualities, you know, the way that he thinks very quickly on his feet. What so many black folks feel for him is the sum total of a lot of things. It was the symbolism of his administration; his selection of Ron Brown to be secretary of commerce. It was his choice of Mike Espy to head the Department of Agriculture, and the other blacks he put in his cabinet. His chief speechwriter, Terry Edmonds, is a black man. There was a sense that he was a lot more inclusive, certainly more than George Bush and Ronald Reagan had been. And you know I think that's a very important piece. I mean, black folks were starving when Clinton came into office. We'd been put on a starvation diet for any sort of gesture of kindness for twelve years by Reagan and Bush. So that had something to do with why Clinton was so popular among us. And then it was the other things he did, like his trip to Africa. Man, that just speaks volumes. That just says so much because he really did not have to go there. There was no compelling reason, no strategic interest, that called for Bill Clinton to jump on Air Force One and fly over to Africa.

But to a large degree if you look at his policies I think there wasn't as much substance as one might have hoped. You know, I don't think the substance matched the symbolism. No. I think that if you look at a lot of Democratic administrations you will find that the same types of policies were pursued. But then I don't think we should ever look to the occupants of 1600 Pennsylvania Avenue to dramatically change our state of affairs in this country. That's not going to happen. It wasn't going to happen in Clinton's administration, nor will it happen with any other president until we have a brother or a sister sitting up in the Oval Office. That's the only time we can really expect those kinds of changes.

So why has Clinton been so wildly popular with African Americans? I don't think you can really point at any one thing. It was more than his symbolism, more than the record of his administration, or even his life force. It's really the total package of who he is—it's a confluence of all those things. Jimmy Carter did a lot for African Americans, but he doesn't have Clinton's charisma. He certainly didn't have that life force. He didn't have Clinton's defiance.

And there's something else. A lot of black folks in this country just feel that the system isn't for them, it's against them, and they sort of rebel against that. And I think a lot of us saw the same thing in Clinton and admired him for that reason, too. I think that is another piece to the puzzle—maybe the most important piece.

APRIL WOODARD
TV REPORTER, NEW YORK, NY

Bill Clinton has an "it" quality that any celebrity who is loved by the audience has. It's a quality that he would have whether or not he was president; a quality he will always have with him and to which people are naturally drawn. A part of that "it" quality is his charisma. We see him in the pulpit of black churches speaking with the intonation of a black preacher. We see him as a spiritual man, having grown up as a southern Baptist. We also see him as a person who is not afraid to mingle with African Americans.

He didn't grow up rich. He had a poor upbringing. His father died before he was even born. His mother had to struggle to get him an education. She ended up marrying a man who was an alcoholic and abusive. This is the environment that he grew up in and this is an environment that many African Americans know. We have dealt with struggle. We know about families that have grandmothers raising us, have extended family types of relationships, and we can identify with how Clinton was raised.

There's another reason why we like him. He acknowledged us. For many years African Americans had been ignored, had been alienated, had not been treated right, and what President Clinton did was to acknowledge us. He may not have done a lot of things for us in office, but many African Americans are just happy that he acknowledged that we are talented people, that we are brilliant people, that we are creative. He came up to us on the streets and shook our hands. He hugged us. He answered the call. If I can use the analogy of a telephone, for years politicians did not answer our call and even ignored that the phone was ringing. President Clinton answered our calls.

He reached out to us, and we reached back to him. We didn't join in on the attacks on his personal behavior because we looked at it from the spiritual standpoint. We understand that a man can fail, but also that he can be forgiven for his sins. African Americans are a very accepting people. We are very forgiving people. Once he embraced us, once he let us know that we were important to him, we were not going to turn our backs on him because we saw all of the good things that he did for this country, the way he turned around the economy, the way he vocalized his concern for minorities and people who struggle. That's why we stood with him.

Look at where he is right now. He's in Harlem. He set his digs in Harlem, in black America. While a lot of white people may not feel comfortable with black people moving into their neighborhood, here he is moving into our neighborhood. He is moving into our digs, eating at Sylvia's, eating up some grits with gravy, and we are able to say hello to him and he is very accessible to us.

I met Clinton when I first began working in TV. I was in Norfolk, Virginia, my first job, and was anxious to prove myself, but also wanted to do it the correct way. President Clinton came to Williamsburg, and I was sent to the airport to cover his departure back to Washington. We were told that he was only going to talk to the White House correspondents, the national press that was traveling with him. During the eight hours I was sitting there waiting for him I got to know some of the White House people and I let them know it was my birthday.

"If you yell out 'President Clinton it's my birthday,' he will come over and do an interview," one of his aides told me. I said I couldn't do that. You know all of these national reporters are here and I'm a reporter in Virginia. I don't want to do anything to embarrass myself. I didn't think it would be right, but his aide kept pushing me to do it. Finally, when Clinton was about to walk up the steps of Air Force One, I yelled out, "President Clinton. It's my birthday." At first he just waved me off saying, "Oh, yeah, sure it's your birthday." And I said, "No, really, it is my birthday," and he came over, shook my hand and said, "Well, happy birthday to you." And then I did an interview with him right there on the spot. When I went back to the station with that interview they treated me like a hero. That showed me that Bill Clinton was not your typical president, he was not unapproachable.

I think he will be remembered as a president that some people believe is the closest that we were able to get to having "a black president." I've interviewed people who have said that. Some people will look at his track record and say he really didn't do much for us. He did uphold affirmative action while he was in office. He appointed blacks to his staff. He attended functions. He showed up places where other presidents never went. He answered the phone. He took our calls.

Will black Americans place so much emphasis on his indiscretions? Probably not. I think that we are more concerned about what he did for us. I think he will be remembered as a president who, for us, was very approachable. He is the uncommon man. He's the man that broke the mold in the White House and made himself accessible to us. Someone told me he must have been breast-fed by a black woman because he's so comfortable around us.

DANNY BAKEWELL

PRESIDENT, THE BROTHERHOOD CRUSADE, LOS ANGELES, CA

Bill Clinton demonstrated early on that he embraced black America and was very comfortable with black America. He understood and believed that black people were essential to his being elected president. I mean, we were an interest group that he courted and he saw us not as just an adjunct piece, but a principal part of his campaign to be elected. Of course, our numbers make us relevant to anybody who's running for the presidency, but most candidates either take us for granted or write us off. Bill Clinton embraced us.

Some candidates see conservatives as their core base. Some people see the middle of the road folks or the liberals as their core voters. But Clinton saw black folks as the group that he needed most to win the White House. In part, I think that's because he felt very comfortable being around us. Bill Clinton has a special relationship with black America. When he came out of Arkansas black America didn't know him the way Vernon Jordan knows him, or the way black folks in Arkansas knew him. So for us we were interested in what he did, not what he said.

We had to measure whether or not he was really prepared to do what he said and, of course, without going through all of the little nuances of the campaign, once he was elected president we saw that his coming down to our community during the campaign, embracing us, saying the right things, and making sure that black people were in the right positions in his campaign was really just the predicate for doing the right things as it related to us once he got into the White House.

All you have to do is look at his cabinet to see my point. I mean, it was unprecedented in terms of where he put black folk. Before he got into the White House there was just one job in a president's cabinet for one of us, either at HUD or the Department of Health and Human Services. Those were our spots. Clinton put us at the head of the departments of agriculture, energy, labor, commerce, and veterans affairs. He named one of us surgeon general. I think he actually nominated three black surgeon generals during his time in office. One didn't make it. He nominated another one. That one got knocked out of the box. And she was replaced by another black person.

All of the black appointments Clinton made at the top levels of government made black folks stand up and take notice of his relationship with the Congressional Black Caucus. His friendship with Vernon Jordan caused a lot of black folks to take him seriously. When he got into the White House, Clinton did what he told us during the campaign he would do. He had a real sense of fairness, a genuine sense of equity. So we began to see early on that he is a guy who was worthy of our support—and for that we really needed to protect him. I mean we knew early on that this cat better look out because they—I'm talking about some of the same people who have it in for us—were going to go after him.

By doing all those things for us, Clinton defied the system. He defied white America in a way it had never been defied before. History has taught us that people who did that, even in some nominal way, all ended up dead before their time. I mean Bobby Kennedy, John Kennedy, and Martin Luther King; people who embraced black folk usually never made it to the end of the line, to the end of the game. Bill Clinton is a hand-slapping, almost a "hey brother, what's happening" kind of guy. When this guy would get in a small cluster, I mean he'd be talking to you like he was just one of the guys. He had an aura about him—an ability to pick up on the nuances of the pain that black America has felt for generations.

It will be a long time before we see another Bill Clinton. I think the guy has established a precedent that allows us to hold people accountable in some serious ways because no longer can people say, "Well, you know, I'm not sure black folks can rise to the occasion. I'm not sure that black folks can perform." Clinton showed this country that black folks are up to the job of running this nation. He had us operating at all levels, not only in the cabinet but on his White House staff. Now don't get me wrong. Clinton had rough spots. I think he jumped ship on Lani Guinier, and for a time that made a lot of black folks pull back from him. But Clinton built up enough goodwill with the masses of black people that he was able to ride out those bad times. People would say, "Yeah he messed up, but look at all these other things he did for us."

When you step back and analyze it, you might think he thought to himself at the time, "I ought to stick with Lani. That's really the right thing to do, but I'll get blown to pieces by my enemies in Congress if I do that. And if that happens I won't be able to fulfill my agenda." Now it's true I think he ran hot and cold on us. But overall, Bill Clinton did the best he could for black folks, given the political cards he was dealt. Was he perfect? Absolutely not. Was he consistent in terms of dealing with our interests? Absolutely not. But when it came to how he treated us, was he head and shoulders above every other president this nation has had? Absolutely!

CHAPTER 4

Guess Who's Coming to Dinner

While it's possible that Thomas Jefferson shared a few late-night repasts with Sally Hemings, the slave with whom he fathered at least one child, instances of presidents breaking bread with African Americans have been rare occurrences throughout much of this nation's history. It is widely believed that the first formal White House dinner invitation was given to Booker T. Washington by President Theodore Roosevelt, 112 years after this nation's first president took office. Roosevelt invited Washington to the White House for dinner to get advice on which blacks he might appoint to patronage jobs in his administration. Their dinner meeting took place on the evening of October 16, 1901—the last time that Roosevelt would invite an African American to eat at the White House.

Southern congressmen and newspapermen reacted bitterly. By allowing Washington to dine with him in the White House, Roosevelt had given a presidential stamp of approval to the "social intercourse between blacks and whites," an act that so badly saturated the building "with the odor of the nigger that the rats have taken refuge in the stable," complained Mississippi senator James K. Vardaman.[14] In an effort to staunch the harsh criticism he was getting for his dinner with Washington, Roosevelt quickly explained that neither his wife nor

[14] O'Reilly, *Nixon's Piano*, 68.

daughter shared the table with the Tuskegee University president. And when that didn't satisfy his critics, Roosevelt arranged for Washington to make an appearance at the Gridiron Club dinner, where presidents have subjected themselves to crass ribbing from journalists and politicians since 1885.

That evening Washington was actually the brunt of the joke. On cue he entered the room after someone announced loudly that "Booker Washington" was trying to crash the whites-only affair. After a southern senator who was in on the joke objected, Washington was admitted and then proceeded to sing "one of his inimitable coon songs."[15] Roosevelt didn't have another black dinner guest during his remaining seven years in the White House. Ninety-nine years later scores of African Americans were invited to attend the State dinner that Bill Clinton gave in the final year of his presidency for President Thabo Mbeki of South Africa on May 22, 2000.

The list of black attendees, a "who's who" of the nation's most influential African Americans, included Detroit mayor Dennis Archer and Atlanta mayor Bill Campbell; *Black Enterprise* publisher Earl G. Graves Sr.; singers Stevie Wonder and BeBe Winans; Reverend Jesse Jackson Sr.; New York City's Manhattan Borough president C. Virginia Fields; actor Morgan Freeman and Robert L. Johnson, CEO of Black Entertainment Television; Howard University president H. Patrick Swygert; Labor secretary Alexis Herman; NAACP president Kweisi Mfume; filmmaker Spike Lee; and Representative Eddie Bernice Johnson of Texas, the chairman of the Congressional Black Caucus.

But as impressive as Clinton's efforts were to have large numbers of African Americans attend White House social functions as guests, and not just as waiters, his most revealing instance of "social intercourse" at a dinner table with African Americans came on July 22, 1999. That evening he slipped into a yellow Oxford shirt and a pair of dark khaki slacks and climbed into the back of the presidential limousine for the short ride from the White House to the home of a black

[15]Ibid.

reporter in a middle-class neighborhood in the northwest section of the nation's capital. For more than three hours, Clinton ate soul food, listened to jazz, and talked freely with seven black journalists about matters of state—and the adulterous affair that nearly toppled his presidency. Among the black journalists who attended that historic gathering were Michael Frisby of the *Wall Street Journal*, April Ryan of the American Urban Radio Network, and Bill Douglass of *Newsday*.

Interviews

MICHAEL FRISBY
SENIOR VICE PRESIDENT, PORTER NOVELLI,
WASHINGTON, D.C.

Let me begin by telling you about my first real one-on-one interview with Bill Clinton. It was during the '92 campaign. Early in the campaign we were in New Haven, Connecticut, and I was working for the *Boston Globe* at the time. I rode in a car with him from a campaign event to the airport. We were crunched into the backseat. I covered politics most of my journalism career, which was twenty-two years. Usually when I interviewed a white politician there was a sense of uneasiness. I think they are often uncomfortable talking to black journalists. It doesn't necessarily mean anything, but it's just that you know a lot of these white guys aren't used to talking to a black political reporter.

The thing I will never forget is that Clinton was *so* comfortable talking to me. There was no uneasiness at all. That's what struck me about him and I think that really goes back to his roots. I did a lot of stories on Clinton and what separates him from every other president—and basically from most white politicians—is that he grew up with a lot of black kids. He had black friends at a very young age. Ernie Green, who's a good friend of Clinton's, once told me a story that helps explain why Clinton is such a believer in equal opportunity.

Ernie said Clinton told him about some black kids he knew when he was a young boy in Hope, Arkansas. They all used to hang out at his grandparents' store. Those guys were his friends. Clinton said he knew some of those kids were smarter than him. When it came time to go to college, Clinton went to Georgetown. On his trips home he would see these guys and he was stunned at how nothing was happening in their lives, how they were just hanging out on the street corners. He knew many of them were just as bright as he was—they were

71

just as smart, yet because he was white he got opportunities that they didn't get. He got to go to Georgetown and they didn't. That really bothered him. And that's why whenever you hear Bill Clinton talk about race, he always talks about it in terms of giving people equal opportunity. Clinton didn't grow up privileged. He grew up like so many black kids grow up around the country.

Clinton is a master politician, but when it came to race his heart was always in the right place. Now politically he sometimes had to do things that were quite frankly against the interests of people of color. When he had to do those things it was always a struggle within him because his heart was always in the right place, even if his politics had to be somewhere else. The welfare reform bill was one of those times. He struggled dearly with that. He knew he was going to have to sign some kind of welfare reform bill—and he knew the compromise he eventually signed was going to hurt some poor people, and hurting some poor people means you're going to hurt some African Americans. Ultimately he felt that he had to sign the bill for his own political survival.

Now let me tell you something else that always struck me about Clinton. He was deeply, deeply hurt by the death of Ron Brown. When he spoke at Ron's funeral at the National Cathedral he pointed to the casket and he said, "If not for you my friend, I would not be here today." When has a president of the United States ever come out and said that if not for this black man, I wouldn't be president? Things like that, I thought, were really important. When I covered the White House, by then I was working for the *Wall Street Journal*, Clinton was great to me. He called on me at every single news conference. When I left I wrote him a note. That was at the worst point of the Monica Lewinsky scandal. It was right after he acknowledged that he had had the affair with her. I wrote him a note that basically said "thank you, for being so kind to me over the years" and I said that what African Americans will always appreciate about him is that he didn't just talk about racial equality; he actually did things to try to bring it about. I also told him that I looked forward to someday telling my grandchildren that a black kid who grew up poor in Springfield, Massachusetts, traveled around the world with a president who grew up poor from

Hope, Arkansas. About a month later I received a very nice handwritten thank-you note.

The next time I saw him was almost a year later at the home of Bill Douglas. Bill covered the White House for *Newsday*. While I was still at the White House a small group of black journalists had Clinton's press secretary, Mike McCurry, out to Douglas's house for dinner. We had a really good time. We ate some good soul food, drank some wine. We were dancing. We just had a great time. McCurry said I'm going to get Clinton to do this. That must have been in '97. Our dinner with Clinton was scheduled a couple of times; it was always canceled because something came up. But finally after I left the White House I get this phone call telling me that the dinner had finally been set up and that Clinton wanted me to be there. I was asked to bring the music. Vanessa Rubin's new disc was out and I put it on after dinner. Clinton's listening to her CD and he says, "Who's that?" I tell him it's Vanessa Rubin and he's says, "Aw man, that's really good." I said I'll send it to you at the White House. So I picked it up and sent it to him and he wrote me back this great note thanking me and everything. And then what happened is that Bill Douglas wrote a story about the dinner and mentioned in it that Clinton liked her CD. Rubin saw this and called Douglas, and he told her I had hooked up the music, so she called me. She autographed a couple copies of her disc and sent them to me so I could pass them on to Clinton.

As it turns out I was also a go-between for Walter Mosley. Back in '92 I was on the campaign plane with Clinton and he was talking about the books that he'd read. He started talking about Walter Mosley, who writes these books about this black detective. I wrote a story saying that this black author was one of the candidate's favorite authors and that he had been reading his book on the campaign trail. And then ultimately what happened, after Clinton was elected, is that Walter was invited to the White House.

I did a front-page story in the *Wall Street Journal* about Clinton and Walter Mosley's books. The president actually called me at my home on New Year's Day to talk about it. Well, one of Mosley's characters in these books is a guy named Mouse. So here I was on the phone on New Year's Day with the president talking about a character in a black mystery writer's book. How many presidents have ever read fiction by black authors? We know he's the only president to go to dinner with black reporters who covered the White House.

You know, at that dinner, while we were waiting for Clinton's motorcade to show up, there was a lot of security throughout the neighborhood and one of Bill Douglas's white neighbors came up and said, "What's going on?" I just smiled and said, "Guess who's coming to dinner."

APRIL RYAN

WHITE HOUSE CORRESPONDENT,
AMERICAN URBAN RADIO NETWORK,
WASHINGTON, D.C.

The first time I realized that Bill Clinton was serious about having a relationship with African Americans was when I heard him sing "Lift Every Voice and Sing." A lot of black people don't know the first verse of the Negro National Anthem, but he sang all three verses. I saw him do this on Capitol Hill when Rosa Parks was being honored with the Congressional Medal of Freedom. He stood behind Jessye Norman and sang that song word for word. It was amazing.

I remember talking to him about that moment during the soul food dinner the black White House reporters put on for him in the summer of 1999. When we walked over to the table to eat I said, "Mr. President, sometimes you have to find the right time to say things." Then I told him, "You really impressed me at the Rosa Parks event. I could not believe you knew all the words to the Negro National Anthem." He said it's a song with some of the most beautiful words he'd ever heard.

But I'm getting ahead of myself. Let me tell you how the dinner came about. I don't know what you've heard but this is how it went down. Mike McCurry, the White House press secretary, and I got into this huge debate in front of the West Wing of the White House. I asked him if President Clinton was going to apologize for slavery. I said, "Let me tell you something, black people want to hear the words 'I'm sorry'." McCurry said, "You're not going to get what you want." As we were talking some black White House employees came by and one of them said she didn't want an apology, she wanted economic empowerment.

I told her she was crazy. I said an apology would lead to reparations, forty acres and a mule, which in today's dollars translates into a house on the Potomac River and a seven-series BMW. So Mike said, "Look, here's what we need to do. If you really feel this strongly, we need to all sit down and talk about this." I mean it was just like a tongue-in-cheek conversation that turned into something really big. I said, well, let's discuss this over some chitlins. Bill Douglas offered to have the dinner at his house and we invited the black journalists who work at the White House.

There was Sonya Ross from the Associated Press, Ann Scales of the *Boston Globe*, Bill Douglas of *Newsday*, and a couple other folks. It started at about 7 P.M. and lasted until around midnight. McCurry had such a great time and he said he wanted to get the president in on this. So Mike mentions our dinner to Clinton and he said he'd like to come to one with us. But the date kept getting put off. But I wouldn't let it rest. Sometime later we were in Cape Town and I was doing an interview with the president on his historic trip to Africa. Before the interview got under way, I asked Clinton what he thought about chitlins, fried chicken, and a lot of other soul food. He said, "Where and when?" When we finally got a date it was around the time that John Kennedy Jr. died and we thought we were going to lose it. But everything worked out. The dinner was the night before Kennedy's memorial service. We were so excited.

The dinner with Clinton was at Bill Douglas's house, too. My aunt Pearl came over from Baltimore and cooked most of the meal. She bought twenty-five pounds of chitlins, cleaned them so much she only had five pounds left to cook. You ain't ever had chitlins cleaner than my aunt's. Before the president arrived we were sitting outside waiting for the Secret Service to finish their security sweep of the house when one of Bill's white neighbors came by. He saw all the security and wanted to know what was going on. Mike Frisby just looked at him with a big grin and said, "Guess who's coming to dinner." That was *so* funny. We fell out laughing.

The president arrived about 7:30 P.M. It was amazing. We tried to play it cool, but we were so excited. For an American president to come to the home of a black family and have dinner with black reporters so we could talk about race and about what matters to African-American people, that was a big deal for us.

This was a real soul food dinner. We had garlic fried chicken, catfish, chitlins, pinto beans, black-eyed peas, collard greens, potato salad, and corn bread. When I saw Bill Clinton eating chitlins, that was a rite of passage for me. He went to town on the fried chicken. He ate it with his hands and he used a lot of hot sauce. He didn't mess over his plate. He was a hungry man. He enjoyed the meal so much that weeks later when I saw him in the White House he said, "I'm still full. Tell Aunt Pearl I said hi." Can you imagine that? After all that time he remembered her name and she spent most of the night in the kitchen. This is why black people like him so much.

Some time later Clinton was about to go to North Carolina for an event and I was going along to cover his trip. The place was about fourteen miles from my mother's home. I went down on Air Force One. My family met the president and we have a picture of that. I told Betty Currie, Clinton's personal secretary, that the president was going to my mother's hometown and she said, "Well, let's get your family a meeting with him." And she did. So they arranged for the president to have a brief meeting with my family. This is over a year after our soul food dinner and when he meets my North Carolina relatives, he starts telling them about the meal Aunt Pearl cooked. Now can you image with all that he had on his mind that the president still remembered my aunt Pearl?

I didn't always agree with what the president put out policy-wise. I was angry with him about the fact that he never really apologized for slavery, but at the same time he changed the dynamic of how a president has to deal with black America and I am very appreciative of that, as I was of his decision to visit Africa.

Now we have a Republican president, who is farther to the right than Ronald Reagan, talking about going to South Africa. Bill Clinton did that. Bill Clinton put Sub-Saharan Africa on the map.

BILL DOUGLAS

WHITE HOUSE CORRESPONDENT, *NEWSDAY*,
WASHINGTON, D.C.

I think the reason why black folk like Clinton is because he came into office when black people had been in the political wilderness for twelve years, four years of George Bush and eight years of Ronald Reagan. Blacks had no affection for those two presidents and those two presidents definitely had no affection for black people. They didn't deal with black people. They didn't deal with black issues.

So by the time Clinton came along, people were impressed with how comfortable he was around blacks. I mean, politicians—when they're campaigning—they'll do the black church thing. They'll stiffly dance. They'll mouth the words to the music. They'll say some nice pat phrases and then they'll get the hell out of Dodge. Clinton would go to the churches, sway to the music, *loudly* speak the words, and not leave. And I think that's a big difference. So I think that sort of endeared him rather quickly to black people. I mean here was a guy that basically came from nothing in Arkansas, got educated and succeeded against the odds. He wouldn't go away. He was a guy like a lot of black people who was from little-to-humble means. I mean this is a guy who was a public official who had no home. Once Clinton left the governor's mansion, he had to go out and find a home. He wasn't like Bush who had Kennebunkport or Reagan who had the ranch in California. So I think that's part of Bill Clinton's attraction for black folks.

On its face, if you look at his eight years you would wonder why we have such affection for Bill Clinton. I mean, in essence he caved on welfare reform. He vetoed three versions of the bill and then signed the last version Congress sent to him. The White House's sense was that a bill was going to eventually pass with enough votes to override a veto. I think Clinton believed he had to make the most of a bad situation. So while there were things he did that weren't in our best interest, black folks seemed to either understand, forgive and forget, or just sort of shrug and say that's the way the game is played.

I think we felt vested in him because he got so much of the African-

American vote, because he was so personable with us, and because we remembered how bad it was for us during the twelve years we spent in the political wilderness of Reagan's and Bush's presidencies. In those days if we had a problem with the White House it didn't matter because they didn't care. But with Clinton we could go to the White House and express ourselves. We might not like what we got, but he would listen. So we felt that we had an ally or at least an advocate or at worst an ombudsman, someone who would at least give us the time of day.

Even the handful of black reporters who covered the White House thought we had special access to Clinton. We had a dinner for him at my house in the Friendship Heights section of Washington in the summer of 1999. Can you imagine that? I can't think of a president in my lifetime, which spans from Kennedy to Clinton, that would have done that. The thing that was very surprising about this event was that he was very much at ease. He was not some guy that stiffly walked in, posed for pictures, sat down, and got the hell out. He was supposed to stay for an hour, an hour and a half. He stayed for three, three and a half. He had to be pulled out the door by his aides. He stayed for a long time and what was surprising about that was that the dinner happened the evening before he had to go to New York for John Kennedy's memorial service.

He had a speech to write but he hung out with us for several hours. He ate. He presided over the table. When the White House social office told us all the rules of what he does and does not like they stressed he does not want to sit at the head of the table. He is not the king, but you sit him down and he's the king of the table because he controls the conversation. He was just very breezy. We didn't talk about just black issues; we went from foreign policy to economics and to impeachment. He shifted the conversation to Monica Lewinsky and to impeachment. He went there. He just went over what happened and said he made some mistakes. He just laid it out. He expressed remorse, but he definitely felt his impeachment "was a Republican coup attempt."

When Clinton arrived for the dinner he walked into the living room, which was filled with a lot of black artwork, and he headed for a poster I got from France of the Paris Opera's version of *Porgy and Bess*. It was of a black man holding up a white woman with an ample butt. He said, "I like this." We had some Josephine Baker prints that also caught his eye. Finally my wife ushered him into the dining room. This was a soul food dinner. We had fried chicken, catfish. We had chitlins. April Ryan's aunt cooked the chitlins and he piled them high on his plate, slapped on about half a bottle of hot sauce and just sucked them up. He knew how to eat them. He had corn bread on the side. He dipped a little corn bread in the hot sauce and he was just gnawing on those chitlins. He served himself. I just looked at him in amazement because I don't eat that stuff.

It was just an amazing evening—seven black folks sitting around a table eating soul food with the president of the United States. There was me; April Ryan of the American Urban Radio Network; Sonya Ross of Associated Press; Ann Scales of the *Boston Globe*; Wendell Goler of Fox News; Kenneth Strickland of NBC News; and Michael Frisby, who had covered the White House for the *Wall Street Journal*, but by then had gone to work for a public relations firm.

I think everybody left sort of awed by what happened that evening. This was also the time when Hillary was still trying to decide what the hell she wanted to do, and we asked how he felt about her running for the Senate and he had this sort of—his eyes sometimes look alive but at that point his eyes looked a little uncertain and what he said was like a mantra. It was sort of like, well, she supported me for twenty-five years and now it's my turn. I think at that time he had no idea what his postpresidential life was going to be all about. Then a couple of years later, I watched on TV that "Welcome to Harlem" ceremony they put on for him when he moved his office to Harlem and I thought, damn, this is one white guy who must really love soul food.

CHAPTER 5

In Trotter's
Footsteps

Frederick Douglass was the first black journalist to get inside the White House, although it's not clear that he went there in that role. He often met with Abraham Lincoln to advocate for the end to slavery. During the Civil War, Douglass successfully pressed Lincoln to allow blacks to serve in the Union army. The fabled Fifty-fourth Massachusetts Regiment, in which two of Douglass's sons served, came into existence as a result of that effort. But more often than not Douglass used the time he had with Lincoln to try to lobby the president, not interview him for his publication.

It wasn't until after the turn of the century that another prominent black journalist found his way into the White House. W. Monroe Trotter, the publisher of the *Boston Guardian,* had two documented meetings with President Woodrow Wilson. Trotter was one of the leaders of a small band of black Republicans who campaigned for Wilson's election in 1912. At the time African Americans voted for GOP presidential candidates in about the same high percentages as we do now for Democratic seekers of the Oval Office.

During both of his White House visits, Trotter pleaded with Wilson to undo the segregation of federal offices that his administration had put in place. Each time Trotter was rebuffed, but the black newspaperman had his say. Trotter's verbal sparring with the president sparked both praise and criticism among African Americans and outrage among whites—not the least of whom was Woodrow Wilson.

During World War II, President Franklin Roosevelt made some small efforts to court the black press, while he fended off calls from his Justice Department for permission to indict some black editors whose papers ran stories that government lawyers said were biased and hurt the war effort. It was during this time that Harry S. McAlpin, the *Atlanta Daily World* columnist, became the first black White House correspondent. While the number of black journalists covering the White House had not increased significantly by the time Bill Clinton began his campaign for the presidency in 1992, there had been a large growth in the overall number of black print and broadcast journalists who worked for the nation's media organizations.

Clinton understood the power—and influence—of these black journalists better than his opponent. He accepted an invitation to address the annual convention of the National Association of Black Journalists in the summer of 1992; George Bush, the Republican presidential candidate, did not. Clinton was introduced at the gathering of more than 1,500 black journalists by Sidmel Estes-Sumpter, an Atlanta television producer who was the organization's first female president. "The Only Clinton I ever knew before Bill Clinton became a candidate for president was George Clinton," said Sumpter. As the crowd of journalists erupted in laughter, Clinton smiled sheepishly and scribbled some notes on a small piece of paper that he quickly tucked into a pocket of his suit.

Two years later, twelve black columnists, members of The Trotter Group—which took its name from that of the *Boston Guardian* publisher—met with Clinton in the Cabinet Room of the White House. In a planning meeting earlier that day, the columnists discussed how to get the most out of this unprecedented meeting. "Don't telegraph your punch, which is to say, ask the unexpected question," *Newsday* columnist Les Payne said. Several hours later Payne was the first member of the group to hit Clinton with what must have been an unexpected question. He asked the president for three examples of what he would define as racism.

"One, it is racist to affirmatively discriminate against someone on the basis of race, to deny them some opportunity for which they are otherwise qualified or should be considered simply because of their race. That's racism," Clinton said after just a moment of reflection. "Second, it's racist to act or to refrain to act in ways that will cause harm to people, either physical or emotional, simply because of their race. And thirdly, there is a sort of subtle form of racism that we all have to be careful about, and that is, it is a subtle form of racism to have presumptions about what kind of people you're dealing with, what they think, what they feel, and what they are likely to do based solely on the color of their skin, and the absence of any evidence to the contrary. And that sort of subtle racism, I think, still permeates a lot of our social intercourse in America and keeps barriers up between our people."

While Clinton scored big points among the columnists with his answer to Payne's question, he failed badly with the one that Betty Baye of the *Louisville Courier-Journal* asked as the meeting was breaking up. "Did you ever figure out who George Clinton is," she said.

"George Clinton was the governor of New York, the only person in American history to be governor more than eighteen years . . . He served twenty-one years as governor of New York in two different terms, once for seventeen years at a pop—twenty-one years in the late 1700s and the early 1800s," Clinton answered, apparently having gone to some length to research the name of the man Sumpter had introduced him to three years earlier.

"Mr. President, there was another George Clinton," Baye said.

"I bet there's a bunch of them," the president shot back.

"This is the Funkadelic George Clinton," she tried to explain amid some muffled laughter.

"My daughter told me about him," Clinton said as an aide hustled him off to his next meeting.

It's ironic that Bill Clinton didn't know George Clinton of the Funkadelics because the two men have something in common. One of the former president's major undertakings was his "One America" initiative that sought to lower the barriers that separate people along racial, religious, and ethnic lines in this country, the theme song of which could have been George Clinton's hit song, "One Nation Under a Groove."

Interviews

LES PAYNE
COLUMNIST, *NEWSDAY*, LONG ISLAND, NY

The first time I met Bill Clinton was when I went to the White House with The Trotter Group, an organization of African-American columnists. I sensed then that he is a white man who can look you in the eye, and not in a challenging way. His comfort level with blacks was higher than I expected. In fact, it was higher than I would expect from a white man.

I've been in the presence of Nixon and Ronald Reagan, among presidents, so I have a point of comparison. The thing about Clinton is that he was not condescending. You rarely see a white man who can look at a black person and not appear to be condescending. I didn't sense that with Clinton. I didn't pick up that he thought that he was better because he is white, or that I was necessarily worse because I am black. I didn't sense that initially and once we began to talk about issues it was clear he has great intellectual familiarity with black culture.

After that meeting I wrote that I thought he was a person who was probably more comfortable with a group of twelve black columnists sitting in a room with him than certainly any other president—and probably any other white politician. There are several reasons for this.

First, and I need to be careful with this, he's a southerner. I have to be careful because Louis Lomax in a debate with Malcolm X once made the point that LBJ understood African Americans better because he was a southerner. And Malcolm said, "Well, what about . . ." and he named some senators from the South. Now having said that, let me say that Clinton is a fifth generation southerner from Arkansas who lived near, played with, and went to schools with African Americans. He grew up in circumstances in which he was in close touch with black people and I think he has not walked away from those experiences.

When we talked it was certainly clear that he reads black books, that he's read the Toni Morrisons and John Hope Franklins of the world—and maybe even James Baldwin. He's absorbed black culture and I think black folks sense that. I think it's rather rare in America that you have a white person that has that experience. I think blacks sense, whether they are watching him on television or reading about him in a newspaper, that he is not hostile to their ambitions.

I think Clinton knows a great deal more about Jesse Jackson than Michael Dukakis could ever possibly learn about him. He knows more about Jesse Jackson than Mario Cuomo could learn and I think he knows more because of his experience of having grown up in the South with people like Jesse Jackson. So the cumulative facts are that Clinton is not uncomfortable around black folks. He is not ignorant of black culture. He knows not only black authors but also some black music and he knows some black hymns.

But I think history will not judge him in the same way as blacks do. Presidents are judged by the time in which they serve. If it's during a war, a major social upheaval, a time of great migration, dislocation, or some other cataclysmic occurrence, historians would see him differently.

As it is, I think blacks will view him a lot more favorably than historians.

ELMER SMITH

COLUMNIST, *PHILADELPHIA DAILY NEWS,*
PHILADELPHIA, PA

There are a couple of reasons why Bill Clinton's poll numbers have been so high with African Americans. One, his charisma is incredible. He reaches people on a gut level. Black people are not accustomed to being treated with the trappings of respect that they seem to be accorded by Clinton. That's one piece of it. He's a tremendously charismatic individual who is very easy in the company of black people.

I think that has to do with his southern roots. I think that southern people in general are more comfortable, all things being equal, with black people. I think Clinton is a genuinely warm and human kind of guy—and that comes through when you meet him. He is disarming with charm. When The Trotter Group met with him the second time we found it necessary to meet in advance to make sure that we didn't get swayed off course by his gravitational pull.

The precaution was necessary because we knew how good the guy is at making gatherings suit his purpose. I saw him at a couple of NAACP conventions and I felt like calling him "bro." It was unbelievable. He is a guy who is just so comfortable around black people and he exudes genuine warmth. But having said that, I think that is only part of his appeal, and not necessarily the really important part. He could have been as charismatic as he wanted to be, but if he had pushed policies that were anathema to black folks, we would not have accepted him.

I think it's almost a slander of black folks to assume that we can just be won over with a slap on the back and a friendly smile. Bill Clinton's policies ran closer to mainstream black thought than did the policies of the others who were presented to us the two times he was a candidate for the presidency. I think that had a lot to do with it. He was accepted by our leaders, people that we sort of look to for signals. I think it's really important to understand that the Clinton policies, while not perfect, were a good deal closer to where black people were in America at that time. I think his education policy, although it was more or less stillborn, at least reflected an understanding of the importance of urban education, and moved away from the growing reliance on vouchers and things of that nature.

I don't think black people as a whole, certainly the parent-age group, are opposed to vouchers, for instance, at least on an individual level. But I think we understand better than most people do that public schools, certainly urban public schools, are important and necessary and that policies that undermine them do so to our detriment.

I thought his urban policy, if anything, was almost enlightened, at least in principle. In practice I don't know that it was a lot different than the previous policies. But when you consider where the trend was going, at the very least, the status quo ended up being maintained.

The guy is really good. I'm also taken by how quick he is. You know, in any other setting but politics, he would be considered brilliant. And of course he is a brilliant politician, but the word *politics* sort of mitigates brilliance in a sense. When we put questions to him during our White House meeting, his memory was in command of the facts. The way his mind synthesized things was fascinating to me.

I think that Bill Clinton's policies and programs represented the lesser of evils for us at the time of both elections. I thought he was reelected largely on the strength of his stewardship during his first term, the fact that he had done, overall, a pretty good job—a good enough job so that there was no reason to turn him out. I think black people in general were a lot less enthusiastic about his policies early on; then toward the end the feeling about him among blacks started to crescendo. Once those right-wingers went after him, he became a martyr in the black community. So he ended up getting more points from us for taking that public flogging. I don't think white people will ever understand us in that regard and I wouldn't bother to try to explain it.

BETTY BAYE

You can't vote for who's not there. You know what I mean? You have to consider the choices that are on the ballot. I think that Bill Clinton was the best choice we had. The other thing is, we have a thing for people who are in trouble. I think it's reflective of our own situations.

I think what black people feel for Clinton is based on how they think he's treated us. I think that what they perceived was that he had a certain understanding of African Americans and he showed that understanding by the number of black people he put in his cabinet and other jobs throughout his administration. I think a lot of African Americans got governmental experience that they would never get under other presidents. Many of the others had the opportunity to appoint several African Americans but they didn't do it.

But I think there is something else that explains why Clinton was so well liked by our people: he had the right enemies. I think African Americans looked at his enemies and saw the same crew that's been beating up on us.

And also I think what we felt for him had something to do with his early life, with how he grew up. A lot of black folks could identify with his struggle. I mean, in the sense that his mother struggled to raise him and hold her family together as, sadly, so many black women do. He's from Arkansas. He wasn't a part of the American elite. I mean, not even as much as, say, Al Gore—who sort of grew up in Washington. Bill Clinton really was an outsider and I think that's the thing that should not be missed. I had the good fortune to meet Bill Clinton three times privately, twice at the White House, and once when he came here to Louisville. I also had lunch with Hillary Clinton when she was First Lady and another time when she was campaigning for him.

Now, I think the thing that should not be missed is that Bill Clinton is a very smart man, a very intelligent man, and yet when you ask him a question and he has the answer he's not a show-off like

William Buckley or George Will. He doesn't throw around thirty-dollar words when a fifty-cent word would do. I think that people are impressed with that. Black people like this man because he told us our votes meant something to him. And more than that, he acted like he could identify with our lifestyle.

Intellect is not one of his issues. The man is terribly bright. I, quite frankly, was just sort of hypnotized by his intelligence and his quick wit. Hillary Clinton has that same quick wit. Now with George W. Bush in the White House, I think that even people who despise Bill Clinton can see the real difference between somebody who is half an inch deep and someone who goes real deep on a lot of issues. Bill Clinton seems to always know both the minutiae as well as the broad outlines of issues, without coming across as a geek. I think black people are drawn to that kind of duality.

I attended both meetings that The Trotter Group had with Clinton in the White House. The first was in 1995. The second was two years later. I don't know how he managed to do it, but when I walked into that room the second time with all the other black columnists, some who had been at the first meeting and some who hadn't, he looked at me and said "Hi, Betty," like I had just been there yesterday. I don't know how he managed to do that, but this is the president of the United States for God's sake, and there's this sense of intimacy that he creates with black folks that really wins you over. I remember hearing Newt Gingrich say he didn't like talking to Clinton because he'd find himself saying yes. You know I think Clinton seduces everybody in one way or another. He's charming, he's smart, and he's good looking.

But you know, I had some real issues with him over welfare reform and on criminal justice. I had to come to terms with the fact that despite what a lot of people were saying, Clinton was not a black president. He's not black. Not only is he not black, but also Clinton is not a liberal. Bill Clinton is a centrist, at best a moderate. Politically he wouldn't have done as well as he did if he was not perceived in that way by a lot of voters. In politics everything has to be negotiated. We're not the only constituency that Clinton had. Once I understood that, I recognized that there would be issues where we would not agree and there would be many issues where we would agree. So I think we have to give Bill Clinton what we oftentimes give ourselves; and that is that on some issues we are liberal and on others we're conservative. We're not so one-dimensional. He's not one-dimensional.

Black people are practical. We are very astute, practical people even though some people try to paint us as knee-jerk Democrats. People have to remember there was a time when most black folks were Republicans. My grandparents were Republicans. The Republican Party left them. When the Republicans start showing us something other than window dressing, I think a lot of African Americans might give them some attention. Clinton scores high with us because black people understand that we are not going to get everything we want. Even "if we had a black president we probably wouldn't get everything we want. It's like Du Bois said—we have a dual existence, and I think that we cannot be one-issue people, because we can't afford to be. And I hate to use this expression, but you know the thing they say in the community: "You've got to bring some ass, to get some ass." Sometimes you don't get everything you want and I think nobody knows that better than African Americans. Our very existence in this country has been a series of negotiations.

So if you want to know why we still backed Bill Clinton in such great numbers, it's because we sensed that he knew us, that he understood us, and that he was committed to doing some things—not everything, but a lot of things—that made a difference in our lives.

I was at his first inauguration, not as a journalist. Like a lot of other black people, I was there as a guest. I remember wondering how many other presidents are going to have so many African Americans at their inauguration. You should have seen the doormen at those hotels in Washington. It was like a big black holiday. They said they had never seen so many black people, never seen so many black people looking fabulous and dressed up and going to a presidential inaugural ball. The fact that so many of us were invited to the inaugural parties—and then to the State dinners and the other special White House events—and the fact that he put so many of us in his cabinet and on his staff says to me that he didn't take us for granted. We have enough sense to discern friends from enemies. When compared to what the Republicans offer us, Bill Clinton is clearly our friend. I don't think that fifteen million black people can be wrong. I don't think that what I'm saying is what a lot of other people didn't feel.

I think what blacks have always wanted is not for someone to just give us our way, but to give us access. Bill Clinton gave black people access to seats of power that they never had before. James Brown used to say, "Open up the door, I'll get in myself." Once we get the access we know how to turn lemons into lemonade.

It was not unimportant for Bill Clinton to stand up before the cameras and to always have the picture framed by some black people standing around him. These things are important to black folks. They are things the Republicans can't bring themselves to do in the way that Clinton did them.

Now let me just say something about his move to Harlem, the place where I grew up. I think that Clinton will be comfortable in Harlem. I think he'll be safe in Harlem. The fact of the matter is his being there is probably more comforting to him than to the people of Harlem. Black folks like to embrace the underdog. That speaks kindly of us as a people.

GEORGE CURRY
SYNDICATED COLUMNIST, WASHINGTON, D.C.

Bill Clinton's popularity with African Americans has a lot to do with timing. After eight years of Ronald Reagan, and four years of George Bush, David Duke almost would have been popular. People underestimate just how devastating the Reagan years were. So we were eager to have someone come close to representing us in the White House. I think another main ingredient is overlooked. A lot of people see the South as still fighting the Civil War. So when a president from the South enters the White House, he has to prove that he is above all this. Consequently, the best presidents we have had in modern times have been Lyndon Johnson, Jimmy Carter, and Bill Clinton. In each case these are persons who rose above their regions.

We talk about John F. Kennedy having style and the flashiness. He did. But LBJ became the best president we've ever had on social policy issues. The magic of Clinton is after Democrats lost the White House so many times, he had to come up with something different. So he came up with this "double Bubba" strategy. He and Al Gore, two southerners on a ticket. And what he did masterfully was to take away the main issues that the Republican Party had been winning on—welfare and crime. He did that and at the same time convinced people of color that he is our best friend.

Many of Clinton's policies were not good for African Americans, but the practical side of me is saying I don't know how else the Democrats could have won. I mean, you can't go running like a Michael Dukakis simply because you would get stomped, get embarrassed, get humiliated. The challenge was to win back the White House and Clinton figured out how to do that. He managed to do that and still be very strong on affirmative action and put together the most diverse cabinet in history. Even though, that's not enough—we want diverse policy, not just diverse people. So, not all of Clinton's policies were good for African Americans, but some of the ones he adopted enabled him to win the presidency—and that's something Democrats hadn't been doing. So yeah, we could have the perfect candidate go out there and run on the Democratic ticket and go up in flames. That wouldn't help very much.

I think Clinton was a combination of style and substance. He was substantive on affirmative action. He was very substantive on civil rights. He did have a particular style about him. I remember one time going to a party for Democratic donors. I don't give to either party; I was invited there by a friend. I was wearing a silver tuxedo with black trimming. Bill Clinton came across the room and said, "That's a wonderful tux you have on," and we chatted for a while. He has the ability to make you feel as if you are the only person in the room with him. So, he does indeed have a great deal of style.

He did have some substance. And there were some things on balance that he did that were not good for African Americans. But I don't know what white president we can elect who is going to be totally satisfactory to us.

I never bought into this garbage about Bill Clinton being a black president. He is not black, but he was by far a better president for African Americans than either Reagan or Bush, or many other Democrats that were elected president.

DEBORAH MATHIS
SYNDICATED COLUMNIST, WASHINGTON, D.C.

I think Bill Clinton's popularity with African Americans is a victory of personality over policy. His policy was not nearly as liberal friendly and engaging and embracing of black people as his personality was. He is a southern boy. He knows that being nice and being kind and being friendly is the coin of the realm in the South. You can get away with a lot of things and you can get a lot of things done for you if people like you, and southerners like people who are nice. So that was part of it.

In addition to that, I think that because he is a very intelligent man he also understood the foolishness of racism and discrimination. So you put those two together—a real intellectual and emotional understanding of how ugly racial prejudices are and marry that to his kind of southern-born tendency to be nice and outgoing—and you've got a winner in terms of what black people are attracted to.

We like people who like us. We are accustomed to the old days when they used to talk about "a good white man." That meant one who maybe was halfway decent to black people as opposed to a gnarling racist. But Bill Clinton was a different kind of good white man in that he was honestly comfortable in the company of black people. He was not only a white man who came to our churches, but he was also one who clapped on the downbeat. He enjoyed our music, knew a lot of the songs, and had some black hipness about him. I think that won people over. If you can dazzle people enough with that, they can spin for themselves your policy. So they made allowances for Bill Clinton because they thought that his heart was good and it didn't matter that some of his policies were lacking. His heart was good.

I started covering Clinton when he was Arkansas's attorney general. He was a break from the old mold of southern attorney generals and southern governors who were all into states' rights and protecting the status quo, and putting up a resistance to the federal government and maintaining this kind of dual order for blacks and whites. He was lucky in that he was born at the right time for his personality and his intellect.

To some degree I think what Clinton did was courageous because there still are people who truly believe that black people have a place and that place is lower than what white people's place is. And I think that they resented his capitulating to black power and black achievement. I think, to that degree, he was courageous.

I talked about race with Clinton many times. Let me say this, he did some things that were breakthroughs. He named Joycelyn Elders Arkansas's state health director. He put Rodney Slater in as chairman of the State Highway Commission. He made some other appointments to the Board of Trustees of the University of Arkansas. As governor, he just didn't put black people on commissions, he put them in his cabinet at a time when there wasn't all the talk about multiculturalism and diversity.

I have always been struck by how Clinton believes that he understands probably better than any other white in the world what blackness is about. I think he may understand it better than most whites. I don't know if he understands it as well as he thinks he does. I think *he* thinks he really understands it. And again, a large part of this is due to his good mind, because he sees beyond the surface. He knows that when black boys are walking around and writing angry rap, and wearing their hair in a nonAnglo style, and dressing in a nonAnglo style, and maybe not doing well in school, it's not because they're stupid or because they're bad. He knows that, having been ejected from the mainstream, they are trying to carve out some world for themselves. I think he is intelligent enough to understand cause and effect, to understand the linkage between something that may have happened way, way back generations ago and what you see today. He's not superficial in that way. So in that way I think he definitely gets it more than what the average white person seems to, and maybe even some black people.

But of course he can't understand completely what it feels like. I think he thinks he does understand it. And that's always struck me. If you listen to some of the things he said . . . In the very last speech he gave, for example, to the Congressional Black Caucus Foundation dinner—it was a point of pride for him that he made every one of those dinners during his presidency—he exploited the whole Toni Morrison article about his being the first black president.

I really think he believes that. I don't think that's a gimmick. And it's kind of endearing about him that he doesn't mind identifying with black people. And in doing that he's kind of added value to blackness. What we usually hear is what we need to do to try to improve ourselves and measure up, and he's kind of saying, you're already pretty fine in my book. And that is precious to people. That's another way he manages to beguile people—and how much of it is a kind of artfulness and how much of it is sincere, I don't even know if he knows that, because he's such a practiced politician.

I hope and I think that his most important contribution and affect on black America was not necessarily any particular policy. It wasn't "mend it, don't end it" with affirmative action. It wasn't "end welfare as we know it" with welfare reform. It wasn't his education initiative. It wasn't the race initiative. It was that he made black people feel in the game. When Clinton was in the White House black people had access. We mattered. We were at the table. We were able to make demands. We worked deals. We could get powerful positions. We counted. Before Clinton it had been a long time since black people felt we were really a central part of the American thing. Maybe we never did really count, and maybe we didn't even really count with Clinton, but we thought we did. And I think that when you *think* you do, you act like you do. And when you start acting like you do—you do.

And for that we can thank Bill Clinton.

VERNON JARRETT

COLUMNIST, *CHICAGO DEFENDER*, CHICAGO, IL

Most southern black people have had to pass judgment on white people. I grew up in the South and I know the cooks and the houseboys and the yardkeepers and the folks that worked in the hotels spent a lot of time passing judgment on white people. We were good at sizing up white people and observing minutiae about them that made us think that they were not exactly all the same. See, there's a lot of myth to the idea of white people thinking we were all the same, but we made distinctions of them going all the way back to slavery between good white people and bad white people.

Back in 1987—I'm pretty sure that's the year—I was in Washington, D.C., for a celebration of the two hundredth anniversary of the founding of the AME Church. They had distinguished people from across the country there that night and I noticed a rather tall, young white man walk in and get the attention of a lot of blacks who flocked to his side. I asked someone who this guy was and was told, "He's Bill Clinton, the governor of Arkansas."

I remember one lady said to me, "That white boy is really for real about us." It was something about his personality, and he did appear like he belonged, you know. And another person said this, this was an older man, he said, "That guy is going to be president one day." That's what he said, he said, "That guy is going to be president one day, just watch what I tell you." I said this dude will never be president, not coming from Arkansas. That was the first encounter I had with that facet of Bill Clinton's life. He really felt at home with black people and he appeared as enthusiastic about this anniversary as the folks who were sponsoring it. Now, that's one part of it.

Bill Clinton also left the impression by what he tried to do in Arkansas, as I see it, that he was truly an alright guy. "Pretty is as pretty does." That's a cliché among a lot of the southerners. You used to hear people say that about Roosevelt. He never did anything distinctly black except in 1941 when he created the first Fair Employment Practices Commission. But most black people felt that "we got a guy in there that if he could he'd even do more." My parents were dyed-in-the-wool Republicans. They couldn't ever imagine themselves voting for a Democrat because in the South the Ku Klux Klan was the Democratic Party. But my old man secretly voted for Roosevelt and that was a hard one to breach. Clinton may not have been the perfect governor but he left the impression that he was a Roosevelt type of guy. And Clinton did do things for black people. The second time I saw him was at the thirtieth anniversary celebration of the desegregation of Little Rock High School; they were honoring the Little Rock Nine. I went down to Arkansas to witness that event. Clinton got up at that banquet to speak and sounded like he was one of the brothers. He made a hell of a speech. Then when the people started singing the Negro National Anthem, Clinton joined in and sang every verse, from memory. I still have to glance down and read the words, but he stood up there with his head up and sang it right through. He wasn't mumbling like most of us do. He impressed the hell out of me. Clinton sang the song like he wrote the words. There's just something about this guy that makes you say "Hey, this dude here ain't a bad cat."

Black people have had to make some razor-thin political choices all our lives. So, today some black nationalist might say, Clinton isn't any good, but we've had to make many fine decisions when it came to white people. There was warmness about Clinton that I think is real. Just check out some of the things he did for black people while he was governor; it proves that he was for real. I don't know how you judge great personality, but I liked the guy as soon as I met him. My grandfather used to look at white guys like Clinton and say "This old guy, if he had the chance, he'd be colored."

I think he really likes it when people say he's the first black president. I think he likes it a lot.

CHAPTER 6

The Black Elite

"The Negro race, like all races, is going to be saved by its exceptional men," W. E. B. Du Bois wrote in his 1903 tome *The Talented Tenth*. Over the years, the ranks of African Americans have had no shortage of exceptional men and women who have advised and critiqued presidents. From Frederick Douglass to Mary McLeod Bethune, from W. Monroe Trotter to Martin Luther King Jr., from Adam Clayton Powell to Shirley Chisholm, there have always been people among the top ranks of African Americans—members of "The Talented Tenth"—who put the Oval Office occupant under a microscope.

In a little-remembered, but eerily insightful, speech in 1950, Paul Robeson condemned a decision by Harry Truman to supply "arms for the French imperialists to use against the brave Viet-Namese patriots in what the French progressive masses call the 'dirty war' in Indo-China." Forty-one years later, Carl Rowan wrote of Truman in his book *Breaking Barriers* that many African Americans had come to hail the former president "not without justification, as a better friend of the Negro than Roosevelt—or even Lincoln."

Du Bois said "The Talented Tenth of the Negro race must be made leaders of thought and missionaries of culture" for the masses of African Americans. More members of the current generation of the "black elite" have been advisers to and friends of a president than at any other time in this nation's history. Those who did not find their way into his inner circle often probed its members—and their own intellect—for insights on Bill Clinton's great popularity with African Americans.

Interviews

KWEISI MFUME

PRESIDENT AND CEO, NATIONAL ASSOCIATION FOR THE ADVANCEMENT OF COLORED PEOPLE, BALTIMORE, MD

Traditionally American presidents have run away from black people. Bill Clinton is the first president, going beyond even the sort of historical remembrances that some people inaccurately have about Kennedy, who actually ran toward black people. He didn't mind coming into situations and communities and institutions and meetings where there were black people. The interesting thing about that is that you could sense he didn't mind it. There have been presidents that have done that before and there has always been this aura of uncomfortableness about them. With Bill Clinton you just sensed that he was okay and he was comfortable. So whether it was a pulpit, a football game of black high schoolers, or a party that people like Ron Brown and others may have been involved with, and I mean a real party, he was just very comfortable in those moments. Bill Clinton would throw his arm around a black person and shoot the breeze. He had a way of connecting with black folks that most presidents just simply didn't have.

I think Bill Clinton just generally has a fondness for African Americans that grows out of the experiences he had growing up. He often talked to me about how he came out of the old South with all of its taboos, but they didn't exist for him. They didn't exist for him then and so they don't exist for him now. Watching him work a crowd and interact with people was oftentimes fascinating—black people I'm talking about, because it created one of those rare moments. Now, Richard Nixon had one of those "moments" in the minds of some people, with the great Sammy Davis hug. People said "Oh my God, he hugged a black man."

Well Bill Clinton was always reaching out and touching our people in a warm and friendly way. You just came to expect it. He did it quicker oftentimes than some of the black people did. And it did two things. Number one, it took the edge off real quick if you were in the crowd or if you were the person who was the target of his outreach. Secondly, it gave him an ability to connect in a way that made people more receptive to what he had to say, because they thought it was coming from someone who made them feel comfortable.

When Clinton had a state dinner for Nelson Mandela he insisted that Whitney Houston be the entertainment that night. I remember talking to somebody at the White House about the entertainment for that affair and I was told, "If it's not Whitney Houston, it won't be anybody." I said what do you mean? He said the president wants to hear her, he wants her to perform. I asked, what's the problem? He said well, she's got another concert the night before and one the night after and we don't think she's going to get here. But Clinton persisted and she showed up and gave an excellent performance.

When you look at the people who are asked to perform at the White House, and not only people who have performed, but people who've gotten the Presidential Medal of Freedom and you look at the work he's done with the Kennedy Center Performances, it's clear that Clinton recognized talented black people and those who made a real sacrifice for this country.

I've had a lot of conversations with Clinton about racial matters. With him it's easy to get the sense that you're just talking to one of the guys. I mean, you start off talking to the president of the United States and before you know it you're having this conversation like those you experience in a barber shop with a roomful of brothers. I remember one conversation that had more to do with Clinton's belief that if he failed on an issue again, that he would probably be irreparably harmed in terms of how black people thought about him. When he went into office, he went in saying that he was not in favor of repatriating Haitians who risked drowning in the Caribbean trying to get to this country. He said he would give them asylum until the situation in Haiti improved. That was his campaign promise. I was a member of

Congress then and was very concerned about that situation. But when Clinton got into office his administration announced plans to send Haitian refugees picked up at sea back to Port-au-Prince and that infuriated those of us in the Congressional Black Caucus.

I was chairman of the caucus then and that decision really angered me. I announced publicly that the caucus would not go to the White House until the policy changed. We're not going to go up there and pose for any pictures with him, I said, until he keeps his promise. I don't know who advised him on that. He took a real strong hit on it because he had said one thing and immediately did something else. Several months later, it may have been the next year, Haiti blew up again and he had to make a real decision as to whether or not he was going to send troops there. And I remember him calling me one evening.

He said, you know, I'm really wrestling with this Haitian situation. I don't know what I'm going to do, but I got to talk to somebody about it. I was in a Baltimore television station about to tape a show. He said, well think about it and let's talk tomorrow. I realized that what many black people wanted from Clinton was a commitment to send U.S. troops to Haiti to restore the democracy that had been toppled by a coup. I also knew many of my colleagues in Congress, particularly the Republicans, were really against that happening. Some of them were even using the term "banana republic" to describe Haiti, that's how bad it had gotten. And then he and I talked the next night.

I heard on the radio that the president was scheduled to address the nation that evening. I got home and called him. He said you know I got to do what's right here and the right thing is to make sure that we protect life on that island. People should not be murdered because they believe in democracy. He said how can we say we're the bulwark of democracy if we're not prepared to go protect democracy on an island so close to our shores.

I told him I thought he was doing the right thing. The important thing, I told him, was to make an effort to protect human life. We had to show Haiti's dictators that they couldn't pull off a coup like that in our backyard. Clinton told me he had been praying on his decision.

I said, "Mr. President, you just have to do it. It's the right thing to do."
I called him after the speech and asked him how he felt. "I feel like I
did the right thing," he said.

Can you imagine that, the president of the United States calling
me because he needed some counsel on the very issue I had criticized
him on? I mean, I had really beaten him up publicly on the Haiti
issue. Can you imagine any other president having those conversations
with a black man?

When I decided to resign from Congress to take the NAACP
job, I called the president before I announced my decision. I said I
don't want to take up a lot of your time, but this time I need to talk
to you about something. I told him I'd been looking at the way things
had been going in this country and I'd been looking at what's not happening, and I'd been asking myself if I wanted to stay in Congress and
pontificate about what's going wrong in the country or if I really
wanted to do something about these problems. He said it sounds to
me like you know what you want to do, what is it? I told him I had
accepted the offer to be president of the NAACP.

At that point Clinton's whole demeanor changed. He said,
"That's great." "I'm going to hate losing you in the Congress but
everybody else will gain as a result of it," the president told me. We
had a long conversation about the NAACP and the civil rights struggle and he told me about his childhood in the South and what he remembered about the Ku Klux Klan—and when he got his first
NAACP membership card.

Finally, he asked what he could do to help me. I told him I
wanted to take the job with some sense of symbolism. He said, "Well,
I'll be there and I'll make sure the vice president is there." I then asked
him if my installation ceremony could be held in the Hall of Justice at
the Justice Department. That would make a profound statement, I
said, because the NAACP is an organization that exists because it believes in equal justice and the rule of law. Clinton just said, "You got it."

My swearing in was February 15, 1996, and Clinton was there—
and so was the vice president, the attorney general, and several cabinet
members. The president spoke at length. You would have thought that

I had been elected president of a major country or something, because he was just so enamored by it and happy about it. I mean, very happy and wanting to take a role that presidents don't take in something like that. He went, you got to plan it this way, and maybe we ought to do this, and maybe we ought to write so and so. One thing that we did agree upon was that the Morgan State University Choir should perform in the Justice Department that day.

Clinton called me his last full day in office. Why, I have absolutely no idea. I think it was around three in the afternoon, but I'm not sure. I wasn't there at the time. I don't know where I was, but he left a number. I called the number back and low and behold, I got him. He picked up the phone himself. He said, "I was just calling to thank you. I know you are tied up over there doing things, but it's been a good run. It's been a good run," he kept saying. "You stuck in there with me and I'm just trying to reach out to a few people to say 'thank you.' I don't know what tomorrow is going to be like, but we did it well, we fought well and I feel real good about the position that the country is in," he told me.

I told him he had done a great job. Then I said, "I don't know how history is going to record it all. You've had some ups and downs, but you've been a great friend, that's for sure. And you've been sincere. And I wish you Godspeed." And that was the end of it.

Then a few weeks later I gave him my president award at the NAACP Image Awards program in Los Angeles. At the time the right-wingers and some of the media people were really beating Clinton up for the last-minute pardons he gave out. It was affecting him and you could tell it was affecting him, and he didn't have a White House staff to buffer him from some of that. Democrats in Congress were being as spineless as they could be. They were running away from him as if they never knew the guy.

You know the Democratic Party has this terrible business of eating its own sometimes and we do it better than anybody else. So I looked at what he was going through and recognized more than anything else that this was somebody who probably needed someone to reach out to him and say we're still with you. He had been a good friend to black America and to the NAACP and I thought the time was right for me to thank him in some public way.

He didn't have too many friends who were prepared to stand up for him. So I thought it was important that the NAACP do something, because he had been a very good president for black people. That doesn't mean that we agreed with or benefited from everything that he did, but in the aggregate he had been a better president for us than anyone who preceded him in my opinion, including Mr. Lincoln and Mr. Kennedy.

When I told him of my decision to give him the award he said, "Hey, you don't have to do this." I told him it was something I really wanted to do and he said, "You know, I've never been to an Image Award show, but I watch it every year on TV."

Anyway, he came and we worked out a routine with Chris Tucker. Chris was supposed to go into the audience during a commercial break and when the show resumed he was supposed to simply welcome back the viewers and mention that the former president was seated next to him, and everyone was going to applaud, which they did. But then Chris and Clinton started doing this unplanned shtick. Man, it was the funniest thing. They were playing off of one another. The next thing you know, the thing about the first black president came up and Clinton has this great line about how moving his office to Harlem proves he's the first black president.

It was really hilarious.

Finally I went out onstage and talked about my reasons for giving Clinton the award. I talked about his position on affirmative action, his efforts to deal with racial profiling and to end some of the disparity in health care in our communities and his efforts to reach out to historically black colleges and universities and a lot of other things. When he came up to accept the award, everybody leaped to their feet and gave him a sustained applause. And as he stood there with the lights on the entire audience, he could see for the first time people he didn't know were there and they were waving, and, you know, it became a love-in for him. But one thing that it did, though, it gave him a moment of relief from all that was going on. Interestingly enough, his fortune seemed to change after that because the story became less prominent and he was able to get out a different kind of message when he spoke about things. It was just one of those very important moments for him. I knew he needed a friend at that time. Of course, we caught holy hell from the right-wing press.

Listen, Bill Clinton has got his flaws. History is going to record that and we all know what some of them are. But I think that black people responded to him the way we did because he took time to respond to black people. I think that's the bottom line.

MARY FRANCES BERRY

HISTORIAN, LAW PROFESSOR, AND
CIVIL RIGHTS ACTIVIST, WASHINGTON, D.C.

First, I think it's important to say that lots of African Americans didn't like Bill Clinton at all when he was campaigning for the presidency in '92. My point is that looking at it now one would think that the first time black people saw Bill Clinton they all were swooning over him, but that's not really true. After Clinton got elected and it became clear that he was going to make good on his promise to make his cabinet the most diverse in the history of this country—and his closeness to Vernon Jordan—that gave his image a big boost with black people. It was the first time in history that a president of the United States publicly stated that his best friend was an African American.

It was also meaningful for a lot of us that Clinton put people in his cabinet that had a history of emphasizing diversity, and that he put African Americans in jobs we had never held before; this was crucial. So was his willingness as president to talk publicly about race. Probably if one went back to look at Clinton's speeches while he was president, one would find that he mentioned and discussed race or African Americans as an issue or concern more than any recent president. You probably have to go all the way back to Lyndon Johnson to find a president who consciously made some mention of race in his speeches. Clinton wasn't afraid to talk about it. And that is even more extraordinary given the backlash against civil rights that has occurred in this country and Clinton's characterization of himself as a centrist Democrat.

Clinton talked openly and in a deep-felt way about his racial experiences while growing up in Arkansas. The way he grew up, and the positive racial attitudes he developed, gave him a credible background from which to talk about race. His personality and his communication skills are so great that he can find a way to talk about it that is not alienating and that helped him to put race in the forefront of many of the things he talked about. For so long we have had presidents who wanted to downplay the fact that many of us still encounter racial discrimination, or that many of the stresses and strains we have in our daily lives have anything to do with race. It was refreshing that he was willing to talk about these things.

And then of course he started the race initiative, which was not a booming success. Of course no public effort to discuss racial issues can be a booming success because of America's persistent feelings of guilt and its resulting inability to put it behind us. He did have race as an initiative in the White House and people who didn't understand how important that was then may have some idea now that the current president has gotten rid of the White House race initiative and women's initiative offices.

Presidents emphasize what their priorities are—or at least what they want you to think they are—by the things they establish in the White House. Clearly, Clinton wanted Americans to believe solving the race problem was one of his biggest priorities. So that was important, even if his race initiative only had limited impact.

I say all of this to make the point that I think his popularity with black people is the result of a lot of things. It's a matter of style and his experience dealing with black people in Arkansas and his innate communication skills that helped him win over a lot of us. Also, he seemed to be entirely comfortable all the time, inside his own skin and with black people. You know Bill Clinton could sit at a White House dinner party and engage a bunch of black folks just like he was sitting around the dinner table at home.

I remember one night I was sitting next to Clinton at one of those small White House dinner parties. I think it was during black history month. I was sitting at a table with Sharon Pratt Kelly and Anna Devere Smith. The president came over and sat next to me. I jokingly whispered to him that it looked as if he was getting "a little heavy around the middle." He just chuckled, and then he asked me if I knew any good jokes. I said, "I got a good joke I want to tell you." So I whispered it in his ear and he just roared with laughter. Anna was dying to find out what I said to make him laugh, but I didn't tell her because I knew she was likely to put it in one of her plays. The point of this is that Bill Clinton was easy to talk to. Even at a White House dinner he made you feel as if you were sitting at your own dinner table with a group of close friends. I can't imagine any other president who I would tell a joke like that.

I remember the dinner we had in the White House when we were discussing the "mend it, don't end it" speech the president was planning to give on affirmative action. We were all sitting around the table talking about what he might say. Leon Higginbotham was there that night. So was Cornell West. Clinton mostly just listened to us that night. It is really true that as much as he likes to talk he loves to listen to what people have to say.

During a break in our discussion of his speech, Clinton told us some stories about him playing the saxophone and growing up in Hot Springs, Arkansas. Leon Higginbotham played the saxophone, too, so they talked about the glories of saxophone playing. Can you imagine any other president doing that?

Anyway, when Clinton finally gave the speech at the National Archives, we were all invited there to hear him deliver it. His "mend it, don't end it" policy was absolutely wonderful, given the way the courts had been cutting back on affirmative action, especially in the contracting area and higher education. For the Clinton administration to be able to go forward—not as much as it would have wished—but for him to find a way to continue to implement affirmative action was extraordinary.

By the end of the Clinton administration the love that most black people had for him was shown by them during his impeachment. So I think that black people generally like Bill Clinton. The stuff he did on welfare reform was problematic with some of us, but there is a very deep-seated sense in the black community that some people on welfare are cheating anyway.

I also think his appointment of Jesse Jackson as a special envoy to Africa and the trip Clinton made to Africa helped pump up his standing with black people. So I think that on balance while there are some black people who are very critical of Clinton—there are quite a few black intellectuals who are critical of him—I think most blacks believe he did good by them.

Presidents are not really known, and I say this with my historian's hat on, by the policies they implement, but by the tone that they set and by the feelings people have about them. And so when everything is said and done all you can really say is that Bill Clinton connected with black people. That's why the Toni Morrison thing about him being the first black president resonated so much with him, and which is why he went around telling everybody he was the first black president.

ROBERT L. JOHNSON

CEO, BLACK ENTERTAINMENT TELEVISION,
WASHINGTON, D.C.

I think there are a number of reasons why Bill Clinton has been popular with African Americans. I met the president some twenty years
ago—met him at an event that Marian Wright Edelman was hosting
up in Chappaquiddick. He and Hillary were there. We were all part of
a group of people who had been asked to engage in some intellectual
discussions and a little bit of role-playing about what we might do to
improve society. It was basically a little mini-renaissance weekend.

Clinton struck me as an extremely personable person who was
open and easy to communicate with. He was engaging. He talked to
a lot of people. He did a lot of listening. He was easygoing with everybody.

The next time that I met him was when I was invited down to
his Little Rock economic summit after he was elected president. While
we hadn't seen much of each other since that first meeting many years
earlier, we had communicated with each other from a distance. So, I
went up to him and shook his hand and introduced myself. He said,
"I know who you are. I'll bet you I can tell you where we first met—
and that you can't tell me that." He was absolutely right. I had completely forgotten that we met up there at Marian Wright Edelman's
retreat.

The other thing that impressed me about Clinton is that he went
into office with a great feel for how to communicate. Black people by
and large are an oral people. We feel so good about people who can
communicate, whether it's the minister or the people who write lyrics
and sing songs, whether its great deejays on the radio or the street cor-
ner poet. If you can communicate, if you can put words—if you can
say things that make people feel like you care about them—you are
going to win over black folks more than anybody who speaks in a cadence that black people don't relate to. Clinton had that feel. He had
that ability to speak as if he were talking directly to you from an ex-

perience that he knows you had because he was with you when you had it, or because he knows somebody who's like you.

When you add to that his ability to communicate on television—which is the medium that black people gravitate toward—now you have someone who can really connect with African Americans. We watch a lot of television. Television is something that we feel comfortable using as a source of entertainment and so when we see a great communicator talking to us on television, it just adds to our sort of receptivity to that message. Add to that the fact that he came into office by beating a guy who many of us saw as a Republican patrician who was somewhat aloof from what we considered to be our cause, and you can see the roots of Clinton's popularity with black folks.

He ran against somebody that we felt didn't share the same feeling about us that Clinton did, not the kind of guy who we'd see walk into the club and automatically connect with us. He was not the kind of guy we felt could sit up in our church and speak to us in that "amen" cadence, nor the kind of guy that we'd want to have over for a barbecue. So Clinton's personality, his comfortableness with black people, gave him a great advantage with us that George Bush Sr. couldn't match.

During his first campaign, Clinton had a lot of black people from Arkansas, his Little Rock mafia, and some civil rights leaders running interference for him. So he had southern going for him. He had southern Baptist going for him. He had civil rights personas going for him. If you recall when Clinton first sort of started moving forward into the presidential campaign, he didn't have the northern black leadership on his side. He didn't have Charlie Rangel and the guys from New York, but he had William Jefferson from Louisiana. He had John Lewis from Georgia and his Arkansas people, Ernie Green and Lottie Shackleford, singing his praise.

From a political standpoint Clinton had a message that resonated with black people. He had people around him who helped him connect even more with black folks. You go from there—his wife was sophisticated and easygoing with black women. She has pretty much the same kind of feel for black women as he has with men. She didn't seem to be aloof or prissy or looking to do tea. She was Hillary. It wasn't Mrs. Clinton. It was always Hillary and she had a little bit of that confidence that professional black women exhibit and like to be around. They both were nice dressers, nothing real country about them at all, and so you add all of that together, you put all of that in one big nice package—if you were selling them on Madison Avenue you'd have the perfect black product. He was dyed-in-the-wool black in terms of the things that we care about; from his style, to the way he hugged black men, to the way he flirted with black women, he was our kind of guy. He did everything right and then he was also crossover so white folks could relate to him. So we had a guy who we knew was down with us and a guy who we knew could reach over into the white community.

Then when Clinton came into office he said he was going to do some things for us, and he put in a cabinet that looked like America and, so, that boosted his image with black people. Then he did some things that we respected him for, that made us say, you can't push this guy around. He took on Jesse Jackson early on with the Sister Souljah thing. So we said hey, this guy can walk the street, too. He ain't gonna let Jesse bullshit him. We always like it when a guy will go up against another guy—do it in his house or put it in his face. It was like he took it to the hoop and dunked on Jesse on Jesse's own basketball court. Yeah, we got a little pissed off with him for dissin' a brother, but deep down we said, whoa, this guy ain't taking no shit from Jesse. So he did all of those things that made us feel like we had a guy in the big house. We got a guy in the big house that we can call. We got a guy in the big house who will hang out with us late at night. We've got a guy in the big house who will give us some power to come in and talk to him, chat with him, kick it with him, hang out with him, you know. And then when you add that when stuff started going down, when they started coming at him on everything from Whitewater to Monica Lewinsky to impeachment, it was always "hey, he's our guy"—circle the wagons. That just added to Clinton's popularity with us. It allowed us to dismiss a lot of things that he did or didn't do for us.

I'll tell you what else added to his popularity with black people:

the things he said at Ron Brown's funeral. That was just off the charts the way he connected with black folks about a guy that we lauded as a hero and a leader of a new order—not a civil rights leader, not a politician, but a political strategist of the highest order, a power broker of the highest order. When he looked at Brown's casket and said that he wouldn't be president if it hadn't been for Ron Brown, that was something. A white man, the most powerful person in the world, is saying that a black man made him president. I mean all of those things—giving props to black folks for coming out and voting, going to churches saying "you're the reason I'm here and I will always be there for you," the guy could get away with anything. I remember being at the White House with a group that was probably 90 percent black people. Clinton would always have these events where black folks would come to the White House and feel as if the White House was a black house. And he would be there saying "we've got to do this and we've got to do that." If he had said something like "and we've got to go out and pick some cotton," not one black person would have objected. It was just something that they accepted because he had a license. He had a black license. He had a black license to say things and act with us in a way that no other white person has ever had. He was given a black license that said yeah, you can be late to a meeting and we'll wait for you. You can hang out with us and we'll be honored like crazy. You can flirt with our women and pat them on the knee and we're going to say, "Hey, that's just Bill." You can hug us and you can put us on Air Force One and we'll all be sitting there skinnin' and grinnin' and bullshittin' with you. That's what he had and he got that black license because of those things I talked about—that innate ability to relate to black folks on a very visceral level.

CHARLES OGLETREE

LAW PROFESSOR, HARVARD UNIVERSITY,
CAMBRIDGE, MA

I think, quite naturally, Bill Clinton appeals so much to African Americans because as a southerner, as a Democrat, as someone who grew up in segregated Arkansas, he understands the black experience. And unlike any of the other chief executive officers in the last few decades, he is someone who has been confronted with so many of the difficulties that African Americans have experienced. He had an adopted father. His brother has had problems in the criminal justice system. He has always felt in some respects like an underdog. He understands that race plays a pivotal part in everything we do in America.

Clinton also understands that in order to be an effective communicator you can't just relate to the people who are the most powerful and the most successful. You have to be able to relate to the least powerful and those who are often unsuccessful. And so he has that combination of qualities and talents and peculiar abilities that appeal to a group of people who are looking for a leader who really understands the plight of black America.

I also think that his southern tradition is so evident in much of what he says and does. He's very comfortable around people of color. He very much understands how people can have a different experience in America. He is not afraid to admit that there are forms of biases and prejudice in America that are generated by those in the white power structure. And so, he has been someone who I think, whether you accept it or not, is sincere when he says "I feel your pain." On the other hand he had many, many flaws as a president, and I think that even though blacks embraced him warmly and overwhelmingly, it was not that we ignored his flaws, we just put them in perspective in contrast to the qualities that he offered as a chief executive officer.

Clinton made a lot of errors in his presidency, but I don't think they overwhelmed his accomplishments. He was unable to get Dr. Joycelyn Elders confirmed as surgeon general. He denied Lani Guinier the opportunity for a confirmation hearing to be the assistant attorney general for civil rights after she was attacked by right-wing conservatives. He started the process of dismantling affirmative action even though his philosophy of "mend it, don't end it" was seen as sort of updating affirmative action to the twenty-first century. He pioneered this "One America" effort to deal with race and affirmative action, but did not do enough to make it a national issue. And on judicial appointments he did not push hard enough to get qualified people of color on the federal bench. So even though he appealed to both the high and low, big and small, he still failed to accomplish some of the things that needed to get done.

And yet, in my own work and my own experiences, I embraced what he attempted to do, fully recognizing his flaws, because I believe in reconciliation and I believe in forgiveness. I remember when he made a speech on Martha's Vineyard in 1998 at an observance of the thirty-fifth anniversary of the March on Washington. I introduced him and Georgia congressman John Lewis that day. And I credited him with a lot of things that he had done that were helpful: the appointment of blacks to the federal bench, the economy had been changed, his focus on Africa, and his concern about poverty.

I did that even though a lot of people were stepping on him at that time because the Congress was in the middle of its hearing on the Lewinsky matter. My sense was that, like many other people with flaws, he needed to be forgiven. We knew he was a flawed human being, but we would not reject him simply because of his flaws.

Our embrace of him was also a reaction to the attacks on him that came from the media. Sam Donaldson said Clinton wouldn't survive more than a few more days in office. Many pundits thought it was the beginning of the end for Bill Clinton. And yet, quite interestingly, if you watched the polls closely, in some respects his favorability rating went up while the Congress and the media were beating up on him, because people were looking at the economy, looking at national security, looking at his appointments, his programs and priorities, and we could see a lot of positive things happening in the country.

And black folks also knew that we haven't had many leaders in our community who haven't been the subject of attacks, often unwar-

ranted and unjustified. From Malcolm X, to Dr. Martin Luther King
Jr., to Reverend Jesse Jackson, we'd seen this kind of mean-spirited attack before. We have seen our leaders tarred and feathered by both
those who are their antagonists and generally by the press. And we
couldn't always save them. But we worked hard to support and save
Bill Clinton because he was the one person with a position of great
power to do something that would be of great help for black America.

Unlike Franklin Roosevelt or Lyndon Johnson, or any of those
others, Clinton was symbolically and substantively productive. If you
look at his cabinet, you've never seen as many African-American
women and men in significant positions. If you look at the federal
courts, you've never seen anywhere near the number of appointees that
Clinton was able to get confirmed. If you look at the growth of black-
owned businesses and their prosperity, that was unparalleled in its
scope and its depth. And so, we saw him as someone who did things
for us because he felt they were right, not because they were politically
correct. Bill Clinton, unlike any other president other than Abraham
Lincoln, talked explicitly about race and the responsibilities of white
people to understand this issue. And he did it in ways that no other
president of the United States had ever done before, and I doubt that
any president will be as candid and as frank on this subject in the fore-
seeable future.

If there is something that disappoints me about Clinton it is that
I think he could have done more while he was in office about the disparity in the criminal justice system. I think it is shocking and regret-
table that more African Americans were incarcerated on Bill Clinton's
watch than any other president's in the history of the United States. I
think it's shameful in some respects that President Clinton didn't come
out and take a more positive and symbolic approach on the issue of
reparations for slavery. On the other hand, when you look at the symbolic things that he did—you know, by recognizing the travesty for
the blacks in the Tuskegee syphilis experiment, by dealing with the
celebration of the integration of Central High School in Little Rock,
Arkansas, that he did use his bully pulpit more often than anyone else
to deal with the issue of race—I think some of us were convinced that

since he did it so well on these occasions that he should have been able to do it on every other occasion when we thought it was necessary.

We expected much of Bill Clinton and we were simply disappointed that, ultimately, he was just a man with human flaws who could not do all the things that we would have liked to have had done.

But ultimately I think he will rank among the top three presidents for the things he did do for black America. The contrast between him and Ronald Reagan, Richard Nixon, and George Bush is startling. Unless you take a hundred years or more and look at people like Abraham Lincoln and, to a lesser extent, John Kennedy, you aren't going to see a lot of people who were concerned about race in America. You might see people concerned about poverty or disparity and who, through that, might have addressed the issue of race. But you are not going to find another president who explicitly and frequently embraced the issue of race—and who really enjoyed being around black people.

The fact that Bill Clinton has moved to Harlem is not a surprise to most of us who know how much he loves New York, how much he loves Harlem, and how much he loves black people. And what he has done with that simple stroke is what no other president has done, which is to say that "I not only talk the talk, but I walk the walk." It's to say that he can enjoy himself whether it's at Sylvia's having ribs and fried chicken or sitting around listening to some good music, or hanging out with the students at Columbia, or just walking the streets of Harlem. By moving his office to Harlem, Clinton transforms that place from Harlem, New York, to Harlem, USA, a world capital.

RONALD WALTERS

HISTORY PROFESSOR, UNIVERSITY OF MARYLAND,
AND POLITICAL STRATEGIST, COLLEGE PARK, MD

One of the obvious things about the reason for Bill Clinton's appeal with African Americans is that he was a southern governor. I think that some politicians from the South are more familiar with aspects of black culture and black people in general. I think we've seen that certainly in the case of Lyndon Johnson and Jimmy Carter.

I remember during the 1976 presidential campaign that one of the arguments made in favor of Jimmy Carter was that he was from the South and therefore he knew more about black people than his opponent. So I think we have to start with that premise. Then we have to add to that another obvious factor. When Clinton came on the scene with his shades, his like for black religious music and playing the saxophone, a lot of black people said "Oh wow, this guy knows something about black culture." So I think this began to get the attention of black people. Here was a presidential candidate that might be compatible with their interests.

And then the second thing was the nature of his cabinet. It was the most diverse in American history. That I think was a tremendous symbolic signal to the rest of the black community that he might be all right, and that certainly he was on our side.

Now there's a strong factor here that I think gets into why Clinton's approval rating among black people went up during his impeachment. That was the old saying that "the enemy of my enemy is my friend." We cannot discount the very strong sort of political context of this era where blacks have been battling conservative politics that have been defined as Republican. And so I argue that especially during the impeachment era, when after the 1994 elections you had this tremendous upsurge in what I call "white nationalism," it scared the hell out of black people and pushed them further into the arms of Bill Clinton than they would have been. Here you have this scene of Skip Gates and this group on Martha's Vineyard with Clinton. And

Skip Gates turns around and says to the camera, "We're with this president all the way to the wall." What they in essence said was Clinton was fighting the same people that have been kicking our ass. And so we have a political identity with him, it's beyond culture now; we are in the same foxhole. And I think that really accounts for Clinton's high favorable rating with African Americans. It was up in the 90 percent range during that period.

The general public in both the white and black community is not too policy attentive. And so the kinds of things that some of us in Washington would pay attention to like minority contracting, affirmative action, and Clinton's role in welfare reform and the crime bill didn't cause much of a ripple beyond the activist community. Clinton got tremendous support in the black community because he was able to use symbolic politics to overcome the opposition to his policies by a small group of us. He would go to black churches, or he would be seen doing something like giving a medal to some forgotten black person in the White House, and these things won him a lot of support from black people. People saw this on C-SPAN and they said, "Oh, isn't that great? There goes Clinton again. He's our boy." He's honoring the Buffalo Soldiers, or some forgotten black World War II heroes, or whoever, and that stuff played extremely well with black folks. So he played that to the hilt. He invited a whole bunch of black people to the White House. I even went, I don't know how many times. It was an amazing scene for me, too, because I was curious to see people sort of fall over themselves in his presence. I think he has been a master of this art of symbolic politics, and there's some substance in it—just enough to give it credibility. There is another factor for Clinton's strong approval ratings with blacks. We had been shut out of the White House for twelve years and Clinton's presidency was an opportunity for us to get back in. Access politics is one of the currencies of our political system.

Now some of that access produced some real opportunities. Black folks got some money out of the federal government that hadn't come our way before. So a lot of that was very real. I did a project during that period where I trained some South Africans who had just taken over environmental units in their countries. That probably wouldn't happen under the Republicans. So a lot of people got access to resources that otherwise would not have been available to them.

Basically people seemed very satisfied with the fact that here was an American president who went over to Africa, went to this very symbolic place that black people have come to hold sacred, and stood in "the door of no return." Seeing Clinton in that context was very powerful symbolism. And then to hear him when he got over there—I think it was Uganda—come close to an apology for slavery was another thing that, again, I think argued well for him with black folks. I think he rightfully got a lot of credit for that.

He also got a lot of high grades from blacks for his race initiative. Now I don't think that it accomplished anything, but the fact that he was willing to mount the effort went a long way with a lot of our people.

As for his decision to set up his office in Harlem, I don't think people cared very much that Harlem was his second choice, after his attempt to get space in midtown Manhattan fell through. Harlem is the bedrock of black culture, but there is something else here that connects with Clinton's decision to move there: Hillary. Hillary is very popular in the black community, so it wasn't just Bill Clinton. Hillary has a past that connected with the Civil Rights movement and people were not unmindful of that. They remember the pictures of Hillary down in Mississippi as a young attorney in the movement. I mean that's powerful stuff. So it wasn't just him, she has a history of fighting racism, too. I'm sure the connection between a lot of civil rights people and Hillary helped her husband's standing with black folks. Hillary was often the conduit for a lot of gender-related politics during the Clinton administration.

ALVIN POUSSAINT

PROFESSOR OF PSYCHIATRY,
HARVARD MEDICAL SCHOOL, CAMBRIDGE, MA

Bill Clinton did a number of things, behaved in a number of ways, that were probably very different from any other president and that struck a cord with blacks. He was the first president to have a black man, Vernon Jordan, as his best friend and golfing buddy. That was very symbolic. We've never had anything like that before; probably the closest thing that came to that was Jimmy Carter, you know, with Andy Young. They had a close relationship, but not quite in the same way.

The other thing is Clinton seemed so, in some ways, culturally in tune to the black community. He went to black churches. He sang black hymns. When he came into power he appointed a lot of blacks, like Ron Brown, to positions. And I think a lot of people felt these appointees had a real say in his administration.

Clinton was also was very close early in his administration to the black figures who are greatly admired, like Marian Wright Edelman. I think the one screwup was his handling of Lani Guinier, but I think black people interpreted that not as a racial thing but that he couldn't handle the political flack he was going to get if he went ahead with her confirmation hearings. I think her positions were misconstrued by the people attacking her.

During Clinton's first presidential campaign, I was on a show with him; I think it was *Good Morning America*. It was right after he attacked Sister Souljah at the Rainbow Coalition meeting. He attacked her for being antiwhite and kind of suggested that Jesse was promoting this. I was very troubled by that. That was a clear put-down of Jesse at the time. But then Clinton bounced back after he was elected.

He made a lot of black appointments at the cabinet and subcabinet levels and named a lot of black judges. That won a lot of black people over. I mean, sometimes to an extreme. Clinton kind of glorified in the attention and support he got from blacks, even jokingly referring to himself as the first black president. And so he reveled in this identification. And you know, frequently—I'm speaking a bit of psychiatry—sometimes white people who feel rebellious toward the system, sometimes that causes them to identify with blacks more. And Clinton, you know, had this kind of rebellion in him. So in some way he felt like a little bit of an underdog.

His rebellion doesn't necessarily make his closeness to blacks any less genuine, but it may be a motivating force. He considers blacks to be outsiders. He feels a little bit as an outsider and he wanted to do something about it. A lot of black people saw him as an underdog and they saw him as one of their defenders and so were willing to accept him, even when it looked like it wasn't going the way blacks wanted it to. For instance, the welfare reform bill did not have a lot of support among blacks. Also one thing that always puzzled me was his refusal to intervene in the disparate sentencing of crack versus powder cocaine crimes when he knew most of the crack users were black and unfairly being sentenced, compared to the cocaine users who were white. He seemed to just let it go, even though after he got out of office I think he wrote a piece saying this is one of the things that had to change. But he didn't, you know, he didn't change it.

Then when he became closer to Jesse he began mending all his fences with the black community. And I think the other thing is that he stuck with affirmative action and didn't back away from it, even under a lot of pressure. Then he did things like the race initiative that John Hope Franklin ran. That showed that he was trying to keep this issue in the front of white America and that we had racial problems and that they had to be solved. I think he won a lot of support that way.

A lot of black people didn't know how much he was or was not doing. I don't think that made a difference. They felt either he was doing or he was trying to do, you see? So even something like the Lani Guinier thing, they let pass. And when he didn't really go to bat for Joycelyn Elders, the black woman he nominated for surgeon general, they let it pass. Next he nominated a black man for that job who didn't get in. Then Clinton nominated David Satcher and he was confirmed.

So I think blacks felt he was sticking to his guns. He didn't stick with Lani Guinier, because he felt he couldn't win with her.

A lot of black people will say how easy he seems, how warm he is toward them. I remember something he did early on. He had a White House conference to honor all those people who were involved in the Civil Rights movement. I thought that was unusual. So he did all those things—things like being close to Marian Wright Edelman and other leaders. He seemed to be right in touch with what the black struggle was all about. Then after he left office he moved to Harlem. That has to have enormous impact. I mean, an ex-president moves to Harlem and that brings major attention to that community; I think that's hard to surpass.

I think that Clinton's symbolic gesture—not just symbolic, also real—the move to Harlem, is going to have a major effect. A lot of black people think Clinton is hip. He plays the saxophone and he likes jazz and he wears sunglasses.

I think black Americans never had such a friend, even with his shortcomings, in the White House. A lot of Al Gore's positions were similar to Clinton's. When he spoke to the NAACP, when he was running for president, he got a standing ovation. But Gore wouldn't have been as popular as Clinton because he doesn't have Clinton's personal qualities. You wouldn't think of Al Gore as having a close personal friend who was black.

Vernon Jordan used to be head of the National Urban League. So I think Clinton's friendship with Jordan wins him a lot of credits with the civil rights community. The fact that Jordan was part of Clinton's inner circle—a close personal adviser, one of his talking buddies, and you could see pictures in the newspapers of him kissing Hillary Clinton good-bye—that was really significant for a lot of black people. And people like Alexis Herman could get to Clinton almost anytime they wanted to. I don't know any other presidential administration where blacks could do that. And then, even with the scandals, people were impressed that his personal secretary for so long was a black woman. The head of his Secret Service detachment was black. So his administration gave blacks high visibility.

You could see Clinton had a personal regard for blacks. You knew he liked them. So I think all of his associations convinced blacks that Clinton was a different kind of white man—in a way that no other president had been. I think that's why when Toni Morrison called him the first black president, which I thought was a little extreme, a lot of blacks seemed to embrace that. Bill Clinton is probably going to go down in history as the president who identified most closely with the black community.

FARAI CHIDEYA
POLITICAL ANALYST/COMMENTATOR,
NEW YORK, NY

I met Bill Clinton. I was part of a group of young philanthropists and do-gooders who had an occasion to meet with him at the White House. The group was, I'd say, about a third wealthy philanthropists, about a third leaders of foundations, you know, like educational foundations and nonprofits, and a third sort of media types like myself.

It was multiracial. A sizable chunk was black folks; some in the film industry, some in the music industry, some in the media, and some in the nonprofit sector. We were Generation Xers. We had a private dinner, about fifty of us, at the White House and the president gave us a two-hour tour of the private quarters and talked to us about his life. He was incredibly charming.

This was about two years ago and it was on a night I believe when he was giving a speech about bombing raids in Kosovo. It might have been longer than two years ago, but that was sort of the context around the event. That night he was giving this extensive private tour and giving us a lot of background on his life. I think he's always been a person who's pretty generous with his personal life, which is a double-edged sword. I think that politicians today are celebrities. They are expected to completely divulge themselves and then they're punished for doing that. Politicians are expected to be perfect. They're expected to have 2.5 children. Their wives are expected to wear knee-length skirts, peach lipstick, have bobbed hair, perfect nails, and plant petunias. Their daughters are expected to be blond, wear pumps, not drink, and have boyfriends who are varsity captains of the football team.

Bill Clinton is puckish. He has this sort of mischievous sense of humor that is always breaking out and that endears him to some people and gets him into trouble with others. It depends on whether or not you like him. If you like him, it's great. If you don't like him, it's an excuse to tar and feather him and I think that because black Americans have generally liked his policy positions, his puckish sense of humor has been an asset. For people who hate him, for people who funded the Arkansas project, his puckish sense of humor was another reason to try to send him to the gallows.

I have always tried to judge Clinton more on his policies than on his personality. But I think he has a strong personality. He's no Gerald Ford. You know what I'm saying? Clinton has a lot of charisma. He is off the charts. If you like him, you love him; and if you hate him, you are going to just stew. I think black Americans basically think he's a good ol' boy, a good ol' boy who doesn't wave the Dixie flag for racism. He's a good ol' boy who is going to sit down and eat his fried chicken and collard greens with a bunch of black folks, and that is a political animal that we haven't really seen.

I love southern rock. I love the song "Sweet Home Alabama." I don't know exactly why. I mean, I'm from Maryland but I love southern rock. I also know that most of the people who love southern rock don't love me. Bill Clinton is like southern rock without the racism. You know what I mean? So that's kind of why I think black people like him. He's sort of this vision of the new South.

When I think of the Clinton legacy I see the diversity of his cabinet. I see huge gains—huge reductions in teen pregnancy and poverty—but I also see huge losses in how African Americans have fared at the hands of the criminal justice system. Basically it depends on who you talk to how happy people are. Wealthier blacks are happier; poorer blacks are not so happy. The civil rights generation is happier; younger people are not so happy.

On balance, I think his presidency was very successful. It was a triumph of style and substance. I also think there were certain aspects of his presidency that were not successful. But, of course, compared to the presidency of George W. Bush, which has from day one pretty much been an unmitigated disaster, Clinton was very successful.

I think that African Americans have always been pragmatic about leadership because we have always had to be pragmatic about leadership. It's interesting. I've spent a lot of time talking to a black Republican who was a member of Bush's father's administration and he basically said that black Americans have to be the conscience of the country because our lives depend on it. We, more than anyone, will have to bear the brunt of any false moves by the government. White Americans, because of superior income and superior insulation from the whims of government, don't really have to worry that much.

Black Americans don't have much insulation. If government is giving out jobs, we know what that really means to our community. If government is failing to adequately secure civil liberties, we know what that really means. Racial profiling means something to us as opposed to other people. And so what does a sex scandal mean to us as opposed to a drop in the unemployment rate? Why were we talking about sex scandals when we really should have been talking about the government? I personally have very, very deep feelings about sexual conduct, but they have to do with personal feelings. I actually think that members of my generation are deeply, deeply affected by the Clinton sex scandal but in a different way—sort of like, "well that could be my father," because a lot of us have fathers who did mess around and so we're personally very disgusted—but it's on a personal level.

We were chagrined, but that was Clinton's personal business and he needed to work it out with his wife and daughter. I think that part of being a mature citizen is making a differentiation between what is a public action and what is a private action. I think that basically when you look at the Arkansas project for example, that huge privately funded effort to discredit the Clintons at all costs, you know, the right-wing conspiracy, then you can see how sex became just another tool to discredit the president. Again I don't condone his actions in any way but when you look at the number of people who have had sex scandals, like Newt Gingrich, if you tarred and feathered every man in Washington who'd been dipping his wick in someone else's pot, you'd have a lot of people walking around looking like chickens.

JESSE JACKSON JR.
CONGRESSMAN, CHICAGO, IL

Bill Clinton's personal life story greatly identified with the African-American experience: the poor, white southerner. Fifty-three percent of African Americans still live in the South and so his experience as a poor white southerner growing up is comparable to the experiences that poor African Americans in the South have grown up with. So, African Americans identify with Bill Clinton's personal story and personal experience. He ran on that personal story and that personal experience and many baby boomers in the South and throughout the country who are African American identified with that.

As president, his cabinet appointments reflected a spirit of inclusion. He even appointed, for example, my father, Reverend Jackson, to be a special ambassador to Africa. So when you have leaders at the level of Jesse Jackson, and key appointments to ambassadorships around the country, Ron Brown and others in the cabinet, you had African Americans participating as partners in government in ways that we had never done before. He golfed regularly with his best friend, Vernon Jordan. That's against the backdrop of other presidents like Eisenhower and Truman who were known for golfing at all-white, exclusive country clubs; not that Bill Clinton didn't do that. But when he recognized he had played at a racially exclusive club, he refused to go back. That obviously worked in the president's favor. He spoke at, to the best of my knowledge, every Congressional Black Caucus weekend during his presidency. I don't think he missed one.

He spoke at many NAACP conventions, many National Urban League gatherings. And I know that Reverend Jackson tried to get him to come to every Rainbow PUSH gathering and when he didn't come, the vice president or some high-level cabinet representative did show up at the president's request. Clinton did a number of things that African Americans perceived as good. He defended affirmative action. He said "mend it, don't end it." But he did it in part because my father threatened to run against him in 1996 and so he wanted to tighten up his African-American flank. Compared to the Reagan and

Bush presidencies, Clinton was a breath of fresh air for African Americans.

I think African Americans were also very impressed with the idea that Clinton was the first president to take Africa seriously. He visited the continent of Africa, which I thought was great. But he didn't apologize for slavery. He got close, but not quite. I think also African Americans identified with the unfair attacks on Clinton. They perceived them as overreaching and blacks can obviously identify with that. It is in that context that Toni Morrison referred to Clinton as the first black president, which actually reflected some historical ignorance. The first black president was Abraham Lincoln and they referred to him as the black president because the Republican Party of 1860 was increasingly being identified as the party that wanted to stop the expansion of slavery westward. So the Democratic Party referred to the Republican Party as the black Republican Party and referred to Lincoln as the black Republican president.

This is, for me at least, the broad framework: Ron Brown, Alexis Herman, Jesse Jackson, golf with Vernon Jordan, Al Sharpton at the White House, Clinton speaking at the CBC. He was notorious for having blacks at the White House. And so African Americans were impressed with that uncanny, unparalleled access many of our people had to the president. President Clinton had a real comfort level around black people. You could tell by the way he worked the crowds. I was at a number of these events. I remember having cherry pie and coffee with President Clinton in the White House after his first Congressional Black Caucus speech. He invited me, Reverend Jesse, Al Sharpton and my wife, Sandy to the White House. It must have been about midnight when we all arrived. This must have been '93. He took us upstairs to a little sitting room and he went down to the kitchen and got a cherry pie and some plates. And he brought them all himself, no servants or anything like that. We must have talked until 2:00 or 2:30 in the morning.

But I had my disagreements with Clinton. Let me give you a classic example. In San Diego he began an initiative on race and he gave a fantastic speech. That Sunday morning, my father was on

NBC's *Meet the Press* and I was on ABC's *This Week*. On *Meet the Press* my father was arguing what President Clinton had done was the greatest thing since chitlins on rice, and I was on *Meet the Press* saying that I was against President Clinton's race initiative. My father's argument was that no president has ever showed the courage to confront the nation's race problem the way Bill Clinton had done. My argument was that President Clinton began the speech by saying "the economy is doing well; now let us turn to our nations' most difficult problem." I argued that the economy is not doing that well. If it were doing well, the black community, in terms of unemployment, in terms of health care, in terms of housing, would be changing. It was changing for some people, but not for all people.

There are two central issues that have divided our country and been the central part of American history from the very beginning. The issue of how the federal government relates to the states and vice versa, the states to the federal government, and the issue of race. And I argue that the issue of race is a more profound and even deeper issue for understanding America because it predates the federal-state arguments. Race was here before there was a federal government and before the idea of the colonies becoming states became a reality. So both the federal government and states throughout this nation's history have had to wrestle with how to deal with this race question. And both have used state and federal power to either maintain or control this dialogue since the very inception of the nation.

When you look back on who Bill Clinton was and how he will be defined, he must be measured against whether or not he advanced the idea of making the Union more perfect for every American.

WILLIAM H. GRAY, III
PRESIDENT AND CEO,
UNITED NEGRO COLLEGE FUND, FAIRFAX, VA

Bill Clinton demonstrated a very profound understanding of the African-American journey in America, and the continuing problems that African Americans face. And he verbalized that not only in the African-American community but nationally as well. No other president has done this other than Lyndon Baines Johnson. The speech Clinton gave in Texas defending affirmative action was equal to Johnson's "We Shall Overcome" address. And that was the number one reason why he had such a high approval rating among African Americans. Number two, he also appointed more African Americans to his administration in key positions than any other president before him.

But Clinton got off to a rough start in his first term. After criticizing the Bush administration for its policy of interdicting Haitian refugees at sea and returning them to Port-au-Prince, Clinton followed that policy once he became president. That was seen as a significant betrayal by many African Americans. Many people in the black community were harshly critical of Clinton.

It didn't take long for Clinton to realize that his adherence to the Bush policy was a mistake. The president asked me for my views on the situation and how I would solve it. I told him exactly what I thought of his policy, which was that it was a tragic policy, it was a flawed policy. He said, "Bill, will you come and help me?" I asked him if he was really prepared to shape a new policy? Clinton told me, "I want to do what's right and I believe our policy should be changed."

So I agreed to help the president forge a new policy. I reported directly to Clinton and the secretary of state. I don't remember exactly how many days went by before Clinton announced in the Rose Garden he was changing his Haiti policy and that I would be his point man in this effort. Shortly after that I flew to South Africa as part of the U.S. delegation to the swearing in of Nelson Mandela. Colin Powell, who was retired by then, was on the plane, and of course, being his friend and a great admirer of him, I said, "Colin, don't put away the uniform—we gonna need you in Haiti." He laughed and said, "Yeah, right."

Sure enough, four months later he, along with Sam Nunn and Jimmy Carter, went to Haiti to help us get a peaceful end to the coup that had ousted Jean-Bertrand Aristide, Haiti's democratically elected president. I always thought that Colin Powell was the perfect person for that assignment because he was a person of color going to a nation of color, plus his international stature and his military background made him the best candidate to communicate the president's intent to oust Haiti's military junta.

Imagine the significance of that. Clinton put me, a black man, in charge of coming up with a plan to resolve the Haitian problem, and Powell at the head of the delegation he sent to Haiti to give the generals there one last chance for a peaceful resolution of the situation. That's an example of the kind of courage that I saw him demonstrate. But it wasn't the only example. When the coup leaders in Haiti balked at a deal that would return Aristide to power, the president ordered the military to prepare to invade Haiti. I was in the president's office when the decision was made.

That night Clinton said to me, "Bill, you're a minister, how do you feel about this?" I told him I thought he didn't have any other choice. Fortunately, the negotiators Clinton sent to Haiti—Colin Powell, Jimmy Carter, and Sam Nunn—worked out a last-minute agreement that turned the U.S. invasion force into a peacekeeping unit. A few weeks later Aristide returned to Haiti, democracy was restored in that black nation, and Bill Clinton's popularity with African Americans got a big shot in the arm.

CHAPTER 7

The Inner Circle

Since the day Abraham Lincoln first let Frederick Douglass into the White House, every president who followed him into the White House has had at least one black adviser, a person they relied on for advice on black appointments and "Negro issues." For nearly two decades following the end of slavery, Douglass occupied that role. But then as Reconstruction gave way to the Jim Crow era, Douglass was replaced by Booker T. Washington as the leading black adviser to the occupants of the Oval Office.

But for nearly a century the black men and women who counseled this nation's presidents were visitors to the White House who often had great difficulty getting inside "the people's house." Frederick Pryor is thought to be the first African American to gain a foothold in the White House. Pryor had been Franklin Roosevelt's personal assistant in 1915 when Roosevelt was secretary of the navy. When Roosevelt was elected president seventeen years later, Pryor went to the White House with him.

But it wasn't until Dwight Eisenhower added E. Frederick Morrow to his White House staff as an aide, not a manservant, that an African American actually gained regular access to the internal system that fed information to the president. Morrow traveled extensively around the country taking the pulse of black America and giving speeches in support of Eisenhower. Despite this, Morrow was relegated to a minor role in the Eisenhower administration. He had virtually no direct access to the president and little standing with members of the president's inner circle of advisers.

It wasn't until Richard Nixon hired Robert Brown as a special assistant in 1969 and Melvin Bradley as a senior policy adviser in 1981 that African Americans obtained positions in the White House that gave them real access to the president and the policymakers on his staff. Jimmy Carter brought Louis Martin onto his presidential staff as a special assistant and Ronald Reagan named Colin Powell his national security adviser. This trickle became a flood when Bill Clinton took office in 1992. During his eight years in office, Clinton appointed nearly two dozen African Americans to senior White House posts.

Even more impressive, he appointed hundreds of African Americans to jobs throughout the executive branch of government, including seven to cabinet-level positions and more than thirty African Americans to the next tier of jobs—deputy secretaries, undersecretaries, and assistant secretaries. These people comprised the black inner circle of Bill Clinton's presidential appointees—and are among the most vocal defenders of the special relationship he has formed with African Americans.

Interviews

BOB NASH
THE CLINTON ADMINISTRATION'S DIRECTOR
OF WHITE HOUSE PERSONNEL

I remember back in 1976 some friends of mine told me there was this liberal white guy, a law professor, who was going to run for attorney general in Arkansas and asked if I would help him.

I asked them, "Why should I? What has he done?" They told me he had taken a special interest in a lot of his black students. He tutored some of them at night in his apartment and helped them get through law school. And they told me he had made a commitment to appoint the first black assistant attorney generals in Arkansas's history if he got elected. Well, to me, to do that in Arkansas was quite a challenge. So I helped him campaign and when he was elected he did in fact name the state's first African-American assistant attorney generals.

Then he ran for governor in 1978, and after he won, Arkansas had high-ranking African Americans on the governor's staff for the first time. Clinton started putting African Americans on boards and commissions where there had never been African Americans before. He also started inviting African Americans to events, to the governor's mansion, to events at the state capitol. That was new and different for a governor to do. So that's sort of how it started for me with Clinton. I saw all of this, and I said this is a guy who I am going to support and a lot of other African Americans will, too.

In 1965 I went on a field trip to Little Rock, Arkansas. I could not eat in the cafeteria in the state capitol because I was black. That was after the Civil Rights Act of 1964 was passed. They still would not let me eat in that cafeteria. In that same state capitol in January of 1983, under Bill Clinton's administration, I was his senior economic adviser sitting two doors down from his office. So he helped change the state a lot in a relatively short period of time.

Bill Clinton came across as somebody who was comfortable and sincere, not as someone who thought he was an expert on black folks. He was never pretentious, never patronizing. You felt as if he treated you just like everybody else. For example, in Arkansas there had never been an African American on the racing commission, one of the most powerful commissions in the state, before Clinton was elected governor. Well, he put a guy on that commission named George Hammond. A lot of white people were really concerned about that. But Clinton couldn't have given that post to a better qualified person. Hammond had a Ph.D. in chemistry from Harvard University and a master's degree in math from, I think, the University of Arkansas. Because a lot of racing issues had to do with the drugs given to horses and betting, Hammond was well qualified for the job. He did a great job and eventually became chairman. Clinton also put Rodney Slater on the highway and transportation commission. These are some of the reasons I think that black folks are so supportive of Bill Clinton.

And then there are just the personal things that this guy did. My mother was dying of pancreatic cancer. She was about to have surgery and the doctors warned us that she might not live through the operation. I hadn't said anything to Clinton, who was governor at the time. Still he found out about it and called my mother the night before her surgery. He talked to her for a half hour about how he appreciated the work I was doing. He wished her well and told her she was going to make it. My mother told him she would live to see him become president. She didn't survive that long, but she did get through the operation and live another year and a half. There are black people all over Arkansas who can tell you a similar story. I remember we were at a hotel once where he was giving a speech. As he would do from time to time after he finished speaking, Clinton walked through the hotel's kitchen and talked to the black folks who were cooking and washing dishes. One of the kitchen workers, a woman, told him her son had decided to go to college. Clinton talked to her for a while and then we left. A few months later Clinton was back in the hotel to give another speech and on the way out we walked back through the kitchen. He saw the woman and called her by her name. I didn't even remember her name. He referred to her son by his name and asked where did he decide to go to school? This is the kind of guy he is. It wasn't just a perfunctory thing that he was doing, he cared. And this is another example why I think black folks care so much about him.

I remember when Clinton said during the presidential campaign that he wanted an administration that looks like America. No other president in the history of the country had thrown down that kind of gauntlet. He didn't just say it, he made sure that it happened. Clinton found people himself, African Americans who he'd known over the years. He made calls himself to encourage people to come to work for his administration. He was always concerned about it. Everybody understood that when you put together an office you were not going to have a staff of all white males. You just weren't going to do it.

Here's an example of the impact he had. When I was at the Agriculture Department I wanted to make sure that people in the Mississippi Delta and Appalachia, on Indian reservations, and in Hispanic communities along the southern border of the United States got their fair share of dollars for water and sewer, and housing and manufacturing, and telephone and electric services. Those are the kinds of things I worked on, primarily rural development. And because Clinton put me there I was able to increase the number of dollars and attention to the poorest places and the poorest people in this country. That happened all over the administration where we had black assistant secretaries and undersecretaries and deputy secretaries, in addition to black cabinet secretaries deciding how money would be spent and programs would be managed.

Also, Clinton didn't have an event at the White House to which black folk were not invited. No other administration had as many black folks coming to the White House, whether it was for a social event or a policy briefing. I don't care what the issue was or what the event was, black folks were there. And another thing about Clinton, when you are around him you don't get the feeling that he's putting on. Most black folks can tell when someone is trying to do the right thing, say the right thing. Sometimes they try too hard; sometimes they are totally insensitive. This white guy was different. I can't tell you why. I don't know what it is.

Let me tell you how different Clinton is. His presidential library is being built in a black section of Little Rock. There were several sites under consideration, but they settled on one in the black community. Clinton's library will be in a black neighborhood on the other side of the tracks.

Clinton was in Chicago several weeks ago for a DNC fundraiser. This was about six months after Clinton left office. I had taken a job in Chicago and hooked up with him that night. He made several appearances in the city that day and Michael Jordan saw him on TV. Somehow he managed to get a message to Clinton inviting him to come by his club that night for a birthday party Jordan was having for his wife. Clinton thought about it and said to me, "Why don't we go over there?" So we got into the motorcade and went over to Michael Jordan's club. It must have been about 10:30 at night. We walk in and somebody said that's Bill Clinton and the crowd went wild. People mobbed him. Finally somebody in the back said let him through and Clinton went to the back of the restaurant and helped sing happy birthday to Michael's wife. He stayed until midnight.

This is just one more example of why black folks like this guy so much.

MINYON MOORE
BILL CLINTON'S POLITICAL DIRECTOR

I think that Bill Clinton, for whatever reason, either through experience or just true compassion for people, developed a keen sense of awareness for the plight of African Americans. I think he's read a lot about the history of our people. I think he's gone beyond the pages of the book and he's actually tried to build relationships with African Americans that have helped him transcend this whole question of race.

I just think this man has such a deep compassion, let's just say generally, for people and particularly for African Americans. He has somehow been able to absorb some of the feelings of discrimination that we've experienced and he's internalized them in a way that makes him able to empathize with our struggle.

On many occasions while Clinton was president we were called upon to put together lists of people to be invited to various social events or to view a movie in the White House residence with him and the First Lady. If the staff sent him an all-white list Clinton would send it back. "There are no women, there are no African Americans. There are no people of color," he would say. I'm telling you. He has a deep and abiding compassion for an inclusive America. I think he just genuinely finds it a lot more appealing and refreshing to be in racially diverse settings.

I think what he did while president was so profoundly different from anything I've ever experienced. He set the tone. See, discrimination in corporations and organizations can be rooted out very quickly if they know the leader of that entity will not stand for it. Clinton made race relations in the White House tolerable. He made it very easy for us to talk about race. He made it very easy for us to sit at a table and debate our own agenda as well as a collective agenda. He made it very easy for people to talk about the tough issues. Whether you won on those issues or not you at least could put them on the table. That came from him, the man at the top.

I was his political director. That's quite remarkable. I mean that he would entrust in an African-American woman his political care and feeding. I was very loyal to President Clinton. I worked incredibly hard and I was loyal to him because he was not only loyal to me but he was loyal to my people. So I found it very easy to work night and day to do all that I could to make sure that his political health stayed good. I mean I worked behind the scenes building relationships that to this day he doesn't even know.

You know how you can always really tell whether a person is really compassionate or faking it, especially a politician? I remember the first time I observed him, he was at a school and he had a little black child on his lap. That child almost slipped, and you know how when white politicians aren't comfortable being around African Americans you can usually tell. When that child slipped, he caught that child just like it was Chelsea slipping out of his arms and did not miss a beat, and he embraced her like—come on back up here baby. And you never even saw him fumble or look nervous. It was like a father picking his child back up, putting the child back on his lap. He didn't get all upset about it. He didn't look all whacked out like, I just dropped some little black kid. That's when I said, oh yeah. There's something unique in this man.

I remember during his trip to Africa when Clinton went to Goree Island and stood in the "door of no return" through which many Africans were sent into slavery. I think Mrs. Clinton and Chelsea might have been up there with him. Clinton stood there silently looking out at the ocean and his eyes were swollen with tears. I mean, he's a very emotional person and you know just the thought of being at a place where people were just killed for no reason, slaughtered for no reason, taken away from their families for no good reason, you know it just really shook him. And even more importantly when he accompanied Nelson Mandela to the jail cell where Mandela had been imprisoned, the president was obviously really moved.

I have a lot of fond memories of that man. It was a great privilege to work with him. I had the opportunity to spend time riding in a limousine with Clinton, listening to him wax eloquently about some of the things he wanted to do to change America and to make the lives of people of color, especially African Americans, better.

I hadn't joined the White House staff when the Lani Guinier and Joycelyn Elders episodes happened. But I can tell you for a fact that both of those decisions were very troubling for him. The fundamental thing about leadership is that once you make a decision you have to live with it. But I do think there were probably some days that Clinton probably wished he could have done it differently, or that something would have happened differently in both of those decisions.

BEN JOHNSON
DIRECTOR OF THE CLINTON ADMINISTRATION'S
INITIATIVE FOR ONE AMERICA

Bill Clinton was just committed to being fair. I think that speaks volumes for how his administration was put together. When you look at the number of African Americans who were appointed to the highest levels of the administration, I think you can't help but be impressed. What was not widely known is that Bill Clinton not only had six black cabinet secretaries during his eight years in the White House, but at the State Department the number two person was an African American. At HUD, the number two person was an African American, and at HHS, the number two person was an African American.

So there were a lot of black people in the hierarchy of the Clinton administration and the fact that they were there sent a signal to African Americans that we were going to be included in everything that he did. And then you couple that with his White House staff, and then you tie that into the White House staff being able to get large numbers of African Americans to come to the White House as guests, either at State dinners or at other receptions and to come in waves. All of that sent a signal to African Americans that Clinton cared about us in ways that no other president had. And I think his high approval ratings among African Americans was a response to all of this.

Of course Clinton took some hits for some of his decisions. I think he got a bad rap on welfare reform. We fought like hell to make sure that everybody was going to be insured and we thought we had the votes. We knew for a fact that there were welfare mothers who said they wanted jobs, they wanted to come off of welfare. We thought, quite frankly, that we could get enough Democrats elected at the next congressional election to fix the Welfare Reform Bill that Clinton was forced to settle for. Unfortunately that didn't happen.

We also caught hell for the disparity in sentencing for people convicted of crimes involving powder and crack cocaine. We fought that issue in the White House; there was a difference of opinion, you know, among members of the White House staff. Most of the African

Americans believed something had to be done to close the gap. But what a lot of folks didn't know is that Clinton could have decided to change the disparities, but it was going to take the Congress to ratify any change. The president just couldn't say, "We're going to change it." What he did, he kept inching away at it, and we finally got it down to a hundred grams of powder versus five grams of crack. But overall, that's one that we, quite frankly, lost on. I disagreed with the domestic policy people who really were pushing the line that we shouldn't do anything about the disparity because first of all, we're not going to be able to get it through Congress, and we don't need to necessarily have a fight with Congress that we couldn't win.

But let me say, Clinton was probably the fairest white guy in the White House when it came to us, and he had to pull some whites in the White House kicking and screaming, you know, to be fair on the race question.

Clinton was the first president to attend every Congressional Black Caucus dinner during his eight years in office; he went to three or four NAACP conventions. So he spoke directly to thousands of African Americans who could get a feel for what he believed in. And I think they largely approved of much of what he said. I mean, when he talked about education, when he talked about after-school programs, he was talking about things that benefited the black community. I think most black folks understood that Clinton sometimes had to make some tough decisions on issues that concerned us. For example, when we tried to get the crime bill passed there was an outcry from Jesse Jackson and a few other folks, saying that you got these death penalties in here, and African Americans are going to suffer because of the death penalty. But at the same time we had some black ministers telling us that they buried more people who had been shot by drug dealers in a six-month period than had been executed in their state in a hundred years. So while the Crime Bill had some tough penalties, there were people in the black community who backed Clinton's efforts to get it passed because of its strong community policing provision. I think the polls show that most African Americans don't hold that outcome against Clinton.

Clinton was the first president to have a White House conference on Africa and that was so successful. I think it was in '93 or '94. It was so successful that Clinton wanted to go to Africa. So we started planning his Africa trip way back then. Once he got to Africa, I think he was overwhelmed by the enthusiasm that was shown him in Ghana. And that's when more than a million people showed up for his address. He got a warm reception in every country he went to. That sent a signal to African Americans. I think it went a long way toward bolstering Clinton's popularity in the black community and fueled the talk of him being the first black president.

I could see how some people might say that, especially given all the black folks Clinton invited to the White House. I mean, you had black college presidents, you had the United Negro College Fund and its supporters, and you had NAFEO [National Association for Equal Opportunity in Higher Education] and its supporters. African-American clergymen were invited. African-American entertainers were invited. I can remember back to the millennium celebration, you know, New Year's Eve. I looked up and there's Bill Russell, Will Smith, and Muhammad Ali. And these people carried a positive message back to the African-American community about what kind of a guy Clinton is.

There were other times when Clinton would invite a couple of his black aides to ride back from an event in the limousine with him. I've been in his limousine maybe five times. I can remember the night when a couple of us rode back to the White House with him from a Congressional Black Caucus event and he talked about how the Republicans were trying to pressure him into resigning over the Monica Lewinsky affair. He told us point blank, "I'm not resigning."

I used to send the president weekly reports. He would give me feedback by writing notes to me in the margins of those documents. I remember one time I wrote to him that some black folks had expressed concern that while they were pleased to be able to come into the White House, attend receptions and go through all of those famous rooms, they often expressed concern about the lack of African Americans on the walls. And I told him in a report that I think it's time to change that and I think we should find some freedom-fighting African American like Crispus Attucks, Frederick Douglass, or Sojourner Truth to hang on a White House wall. He sent back the report with the words "I agree" scribbled in the margin. After that it wasn't long before a bust of Martin Luther King was placed in the White House.

I think historians are going to remember Clinton fondly. I think they're going to remember him as the president who opened the door wide for blacks to serve in the highest positions in the federal government. I don't think the country can ever go back to the days when you had just one African American in the cabinet. I think Clinton has established a new standard. Not only did black folks around the country give Clinton credit for this, but so did the blacks on his White House staff. When Clinton was facing impeachment it was the black staffers, more than any others, who sprung to his defense and rallied African Americans to his side.

ALEXIS HERMAN
THE CLINTON ADMINISTRATION'S
SECRETARY OF LABOR

The first time I met Bill Clinton was when I went to Little Rock with Ernie Green for a ceremony recognizing the anniversary of the desegregation of Little Rock High School. At the time I was director of the Women's Bureau of the Department of Labor in the Carter administration and Ernie Green was an assistant secretary of Labor.

Clinton was the governor of Arkansas and he decided to have a tribute to the Little Rock Nine, the first black students who integrated Little Rock High School. Ernie had been one of those students. Clinton had just been elected and he wanted to do something to heal his state's old wounds. So he invited Ernie and the others back for this reception at the governor's mansion. I'm from Alabama, George Wallace country. The notion of going back to a southern governor's mansion for a reception to honor some black folks didn't register with me. But Ernie convinced me to go to Little Rock with him for this reception; this was big. So, we went to Little Rock.

It was a wonderful reception. The community poured out for Ernie. We went to the school. Clinton was very personable. I remember thinking here was a guy who had just been elected governor and he didn't have to do this. Nobody has this on their radar screen. Ernie certainly hadn't asked for it. But Clinton thought it was time, he said, to remember the contribution that the Little Rock Nine made to Arkansas and to our nation. But it wasn't just that act by Clinton that impressed me. I was also impressed by what happened when the reception ended.

As people were leaving, Clinton invited a few of us to stay and spend some time with him and Hillary. He called out for barbecue and beer. I never will forget it, we sat at the table that night with a southern governor eating barbecue ribs and drinking beer. That's my first image of Bill Clinton and I became an instant fan. I had no idea he would one day become president, no clue.

Then there was the time in the summer of 1990 when I went to

Mobile, Alabama, for a meeting of Democratic governors. At the time I was working at the Democratic National Committee, which was chaired by Ron Brown. Ron and I went to the Alabama meeting. Clinton was there, too. That night we all got together and we went out to a nightspot in Mobile. Clinton danced—and boy did he have rhythm. And I said, if he ever gets on the campaign trial, he's going to have a secret weapon in the African-American community.

When Clinton became president, we worked hard to help him maintain a real relationship with African Americans. Bill Clinton didn't come into the White House organizing an African-American "strategy." He already had one. He just built upon it. He worked hard to have breakthrough appointments in the White House. We didn't have the traditional African-American office in the White House. Clinton was very clear with me that his would be the first White House with African Americans literally in every office of the White House.

Washington is a town where when you're up, they love you, and when you're down, they scatter quickly. When Clinton was down during his impeachment a lot of people he thought were his friends scattered. But most of us—most of his black appointees—stood with him. We are, and I said this to the president, the children of the Underground Railroad movement. We understand that loyalty is the first criteria, the first thing that holds us together. And you can't talk about a freedom movement, you can't talk about surviving the Underground Railroad if we had been willing to bolt, if we had been willing to cut and run at the first sign of trouble. So, loyalty is very important to us as a people and we understand that. And we also know that we're human, and that we make mistakes. And because of our deep religious convictions, we also know how hypocritical some people can be in condemning others.

We circled the wagons around him, particularly the African-American clergy. I can remember the prayer meeting that we had at the White House one morning during that time period and how the black ministers came in great numbers. They gave testimonials. A surprise guest at that breakfast was Nelson Mandela. He talked about loyalty. He talked about standing with friends. He talked about what a good president Clinton had been. Mandela was reminding all of us not to lose sight of the bigger picture of what the president had done, not just for our country, but for the world. He thanked Clinton for being a good friend to Africa, and of South Africa in particular. So it was as if Mandela was calling all of us to a higher vision, to a higher purpose.

I think everyone at the prayer breakfast went away energized by what Mandela said and committed to doing what we could to protect Clinton from what we knew was a mean-spirited political attack on the best friend African Americans ever had in the White House.

RODNEY SLATER

THE CLINTON ADMINISTRATION'S
SECRETARY OF TRANSPORTATION

In 1982 I was Bill Clinton's deputy manager of his gubernatorial campaign. I was attracted to him in those early years because of his sense of fairness, his vision for the state and his commitment to education and bringing about strong educational standards that would be implemented across the state. I grew up in the Delta Region of Arkansas, which is one of the poorest areas in the nation. I knew the value of education and wanted to devote those early years of my professional career to something that I thought could have significant impact on that problem. So I went to work for Clinton.

Clinton actually had a very difficult campaign that year. He'd lost the governorship in 1980 and was trying to make a comeback in '82, which meant that he had to go through a very difficult primary, then a run off, and then in the general election he had to face the person who defeated him two years earlier. At the time we had two-year terms for the governorship. Anyway, I remember we went to a little town called Forrest City, which is in eastern Arkansas. We went to a little barbecue restaurant there and met with some of the area's African-American leaders.

One of the people at the meeting was John Lee Wilson, the mayor of a little town called Haines, Arkansas. Someone at the meeting said he didn't think they should go with Bill Clinton. You know, something to the effect that he'd had his chance to be governor and lost and that the blacks in that community should look at some other candidates.

Well, this deafening quiet fell over the room. Now, to be sure, this was a time in the campaign when it wasn't clear that Clinton could win. Then John Lee Wilson, the town's mayor, stood up and said, "My little old town is a poor town. Few people even think about my town. And clearly, very few people who are governor, or attorney general, ever come to my town. But when Bill Clinton was governor, I invited him to my town. We had sewage running in the streets and couldn't get any help to fix that problem until Bill Clinton came here and walked those street with us. Now he may not win this election," John Lee said, "but I'm going to stand with him because he stood with me and he stood with my people, and he gave my kids hope. And he may go down, but if he goes down I'm going to go down with him."

It was the most powerful presentation of the whole campaign. Frankly, probably the most powerful that I have ever seen in relation to, you know, the Clinton political ascendancy. And John Lee then sat down and Clinton got the group's support. And as it turned out their endorsement was not about political calculation. It was not about maneuvering. It was not about positioning. It was about where someone had been for them and where they were going to be for that person in his time of need. And in a sense that probably captures the essence of Clinton's relationship with black America and black America's relationship with Bill Clinton.

I think that meeting in Haines, Arkansas, was a defining moment of Clinton's relationship with black America and black America's relationship with him. John Lee Wilson was speaking for a lot of black folks who knew Bill Clinton—or who would come to know him.

TERRY EDMONDS

THE CLINTON ADMINISTRATION'S
DIRECTOR OF PRESIDENTIAL SPEECHWRITING

I think African Americans like Bill Clinton for good reasons. When he was in the White House we knew we had somebody there who really understood our issues and who was willing to stand up for them—and someone who delivered for us. Black unemployment really was at a record low during his time in office. Black income was at a high level. Black homeownership was up and crime was down, educational achievement was up. So a lot of the things that really mattered to African Americans improved under his leadership. The other thing is on a personal level: Bill Clinton just has that certain something that resonates with black people. He is very comfortable around black folks; he's always surrounded himself with a core of black advisers. He appointed more African Americans to senior-level positions than any president in history. And I think the black community recognized and respected that.

For Clinton, black America was not an afterthought. It was a central concern and I think even more so than some of his senior white advisers might have wanted it to be. I'm thinking back to the speech that he gave in Texas on the day of the Million Man March, the one that kicked off his "One America" initiative. He gave hundreds of speeches on a yearly basis, but the speeches that he really cared about he spent a lot of time on personally; doing a lot of writing, rewriting, editing, and consulting with folks to make sure he hit it right. That speech he gave the day of the Million Man March was one of those speeches.

Clinton wanted to use that speech to comment on the march, to praise the objectives of the march. And there was a lot of discussion in the White House about whether or not he should do that. There were those who thought he shouldn't mention the march at all. Their objection centered on Louis Farrakhan's leadership of the march. At some point Clinton had a meeting in his office that I attended in which he basically went around the room and asked people what they thought.

I think I was the only African American in the room that day and he asked us what we thought and I told him that I thought he should definitely praise the objectives of the Million Man March and just stay away from the whole Farrakhan issue because hundreds of thousands of black men would be assembling on the Mall not to worship or follow Farrakhan so much as to make a statement about their commitment to themselves and their families. After some discussion, Clinton agreed with me.

I remember when Clinton gave that speech, I looked on with tears in my eyes. When he came off the stage I gave him a hug. I don't think he said anything but he just gave me that look of brotherhood, you know. He impressed me—and I think he impressed a lot of other black folks—with his concern and affinity for African Americans.

CHAPTER 8

Bill Clinton,
in His Own Words

Much of what is known about this nation's presidents can be found in the many volumes that historians have written about these men. Less readily available are the actual words written or spoken of the Oval Office's occupants, which give a first-person account of their thinking and actions. Probably the greatest and most infamous sources of this material are the 476 hours of conversations about the Watergate break-in that Richard Nixon secretly recorded. On these audiotapes, the nation's thirty-seventh president can be heard ordering a break-in at the Democratic Party headquarters and plotting to derail an FBI investigation of that crime. Less damning, but also revealing, are the 236 hours of audiotapes, also secretly recorded, that have been released by Lyndon Johnson's presidential library. On them, Johnson is heard expressing his doubts about the U. S. involvement in the Vietnam War and his belief that Fidel Castro was the mastermind behind the assassination of John F. Kennedy.

But when it comes to the matter of race, no president has created a larger public record of his views than Bill Clinton. During his eight years in the White House, Clinton often spoke out publicly about this nation's race problems with a candor and insight that far surpassed that of any of the forty-one men who preceded him into the Oval Office. He did so in the first extensive interview he gave on the issue of race seven months after he left office. In this interview, which took place in Harlem where he established his post-presidential office, Clinton offers his thoughts about the reasons for his popularity with African Americans, an assessment of his biggest success in reaching out to African Americans, and an admission of his greatest failure in that relationship.

An Interview with
Bill Clinton

HARLEM, NY
AUGUST 15, 2001

DEWAYNE WICKHAM: Mr. President, why do you think that you have gotten so much support from African Americans over the years?

BILL CLINTON: When I was in public life this question would have been backwards to me because I always thought the more important thing was how I should support African Americans, what I should do to advance civil rights and equal opportunity and to deal with all the challenges that are still out there. I think there are several reasons. I think first of all, while it's important not to generalize about any group of people, I think African Americans have a pretty strong intuitive sense, born of a lifetime of experiences about where people are, not just in their head but in their heart, and I think that there was a sense in the community that I had always been for civil rights and I'd always cared about it on a human level as well as a political issue, and that I tried to follow through when I was president on these things.

I also think they knew I cared about these issues and tried to bring high levels of attention to them, and I think part of it was that I tried to treat African Americans like everybody else and recognize that the challenges that most African Americans face are challenges that other Americans face. And finally, I think this whole idea of building "One America" had particular appeal for obvious reasons to the African-American community. But I think it started with an intuitive sense of where they were and where I was in my heart as well as my head.

DEWAYNE WICKHAM: When I talk to people about you they go back to a much earlier beginning. They talk about your childhood. They talk about your grandfather's store. Someone told me a story about the black kids that you played with when you were growing up in Hope, Arkansas. I'm told that when you went back there years later you were dismayed that while your life had advanced, those young black men you thought were just as bright as you were still stuck in a quagmire that would not release them.

BILL CLINTON: I think there's something to that. That plainly had a lot to do with the kind of person I grew up to be and the things I care about. I remember once in one of the Ohio newspapers—I think it was the Dayton newspaper—there was a column I read, I couldn't believe it, by an African-American woman who said that her father was from Hope and she used to play with me in the back of my grandfather's store. She talked about what her father told her about my grandfather—what kind of man he was and how good he treated black people—so I feel that I owe a lot of this to the experiences I had when I was very young and mostly because of him. He was as good a human being as I've ever known. He and his Spanish wife, my grandmother, and my mother were all basically pro–civil rights, which was fairly unusual among whites of their economic standing in the South, and I think it had a lot to do with personal contact.

DEWAYNE WICKHAM: I'm sure there are a lot white politicians who would say that they, too, have a consciousness born of the civil rights struggle, who still seem to be a little bit uncomfortable at a mostly black event or in a black neighborhood, as opposed to the Gridiron Club Dinner. What makes you different?

BILL CLINTON: I don't know. I don't know the answer to that, but I've always felt that way. I never could understand why white people felt uncomfortable around people of different races and why they always had to be in the majority and why they couldn't see what was always plain to me about what was going on in people's lives. I don't know the reason. I think it is true that I have always felt very much at home in the African-American community, whether it was in the churches or the restaurants or walking the streets. You know, I feel good here. I like being in Harlem, but it's always been that way and I think maybe it is because I always could feel what was going on in the African-American community. I could always feel and understand the reality that was there and I didn't feel threatened by it or repulsed by it. It was always like a magnet to me, always, even when I was a boy.

DEWAYNE WICKHAM: When did you learn the words to the Negro National Anthem?

BILL CLINTON: [Laughs] Oh, I don't know. While I was governor I visited a lot of black churches. When I read the second and third verses to "Lift Every Voice and Sing" they had all these *beautiful*, eloquent phrases: "God of our weary years, God of our silent tears . . . Stony the road we trod, bitter the chastening rod." All those words are just so beautiful and they are the equivalent to me, as an Irish American, to the second verse of "Danny Boy." Everybody can sing the first verse to "Danny Boy"; hardly anybody knows the second verse. The second verse from a literary point of view and from an emotional point of view is overwhelmingly beautiful and powerful. I just loved them both. I thought they were beautiful—the verses— so I tried to learn them.

DEWAYNE WICKHAM: Vernon Jarrett, a columnist with the *Chicago Defender*, told me a story about when you came to Washington, while you were governor, for a celebration of the founding of the AME church. He said it was the first time he'd seen you and he was surprised to see and hear a southern governor sing the Negro National Anthem.

BILL CLINTON: I think more people would know the words if they'd ever been given a chance to sing them and see them. I'm embarrassed to say this—I still have a mental block on some of the words of all but the first verse of the National Anthem. I'd go to Girls State every year in Arkansas when I was governor and they'd always sing the whole thing and I'd always get embarrassed because . . .

DEWAYNE WICKHAM: Girls State?

BILL CLINTON: Girls State. You know that picture of me and Kennedy. I was there at Boys Night. That's sort of what it is. At our Girls State they would sing all the verses and I would never

159

know them and they just used to hoot and holler and make fun of me and I tried to learn them and I literally had a mental block because to me they were nowhere near as good as the first verse of "Lift Every Voice and Sing" and "Danny Boy." It seems a shame to not know them and embrace them. I always loved them.

DEWAYNE WICKHAM: Mr. President, your approval ratings among African Americans throughout your administration were remarkably high, remarkably so because there were times when you had some public clashes with black leaders. The Sister Souljah event that occurred before the election; the issue of Lani Guinier; some people say you weren't forceful enough in supporting Joycelyn Elders; the welfare reform legislation and the disparity between sentencing for crimes involving powder and crack cocaine—in all of these areas you were sharply criticized by a number of black leaders. Even so your support among African Americans remained strong. To what do you attribute this?

BILL CLINTON: I think most African Americans thought I was pulling for them and trying to really be helpful.

DEWAYNE WICKHAM: Even when you were in the eye of the storm?

BILL CLINTON: Yeah, that's what I think. First of all, any president who's an active person and who has challenges or crises will have so many tough decisions to make. There's no way that every single one of them can be right, and even if right, can be agreed with by the majority of any given constituency. I think that's what the answer is. On the welfare thing, I actually believe that a majority of African Americans agreed with what I was trying to do.

There was a study that came out last week showing that there's been a rise in two-parent households among minority communities in America and among lower-income working people. But I have to be completely candid and say that we won't know for sure how well the welfare reform effort worked until there is either a sustained downturn in the economy, or at least the states run out of money, because I don't think the states all spent their money the way we intended for them to spend it. But I do believe that we put more money into education and training and job placement and child care and transportation, and that by requiring able-bodied people to go to work, but by insisting that their children still have the food and medical guarantees from the old welfare reform law, I think it's on balance worked quite well. But I think that most of the people who disagreed with me understood—particularly after I had vetoed the first two, more harsh versions the Republicans passed and finally got it more or less where I wanted it—that I was trying to do something that would be good. I still believe that we did the right thing and I think most people thought that, and even if they disagreed with me, they thought I thought I was doing the right thing.

DEWAYNE WICKHAM: And the polls seem to suggest that as well.

BILL CLINTON: Yeah.

DEWAYNE WICKHAM: And what about the disparity between crack and powder cocaine?

BILL CLINTON: On the disparity between crack and powder cocaine, I just don't agree with that. We urged the Congress to reduce it. They said—well there's more violence associated with crack than with powder cocaine. So we said okay, then don't eliminate it, just reduce it. It doesn't have to be ten to one. Cut it down to two to one. And I remember Senator Hatch saying that Congress would cut the disparity by raising the penalties on powder cocaine. It was very frustrating to me.

I don't blame people in the African-American community for being disappointed that I didn't do a better job of closing that gap. I had the Congress to deal with. By the time we got to this issue, the Republicans were in majority and we just couldn't do it.

DEWAYNE WICKHAM: You were the first U.S. president to make an official visit to sub-Saharan Africa. What was that like for you?

BILL CLINTON: Well, first of all, it was wonderful. It was an amazing experience to be there with a half million people in the city square in Accra, Ghana, or to go out into the desert in Senegal and see villages where Dorothy Height and the National Council of Negro Women had helped to build a well. We gave them microcredit loans and they turned this desert patch into a green, vibrant village. It was exciting to go into the little villages in Uganda and see the schoolchildren and to go to South Africa and to be there with Mandela and then to be in Senegal at the "Door of No Return." It was personally a great trip for me, but I also thought it was very important for America.

My basic premise about the twenty-first century is that it is the age of the greatest interdependence among people across the globe and within countries in all of human history. So the great question in the early decades of the twenty-first century is whether on balance this greater interdependence among people is going to be a positive or a negative force. In order for it to be a positive force for American citizens, Africa has to do better. We have to do something about AIDS and TB and malaria, about the fact that a billion and a half people never get any safe water and a billion people there live on less than a dollar a day. I saw Africa as an enormous opportunity, not a problem, and so I thought it was crazy that America never had a sustained African policy. So I went there and tried to get it started, and to be fair we had some good bipartisan support for this. There were some really committed Republicans who supported the Africa-Caribbean Basin Trade Initiative, which passed the Congress in my last year as president.

So I always thought it was kind of like this big hole in America's foreign policy—and it was really crazy since African Americans had been so much an important part of the United States, and the whole history of slavery was integral to who we are for good or ill, or a little bit of both—that we didn't have any kind of meaningful African policy. So now we do and I must say it appears to me that Secretary of State Powell has succeeded in convincing the administration that we should continue on with that goal. I think that's very good. I'd like it not to be a partisan issue.

DEWAYNE WICKHAM: Eight of this country's first fifteen presidents were slaveholders. Most, virtually all, of the presidents who preceded Abraham Lincoln into office supported slavery in one fashion or another. Most of the presidents who followed Abraham Lincoln in office turned a blind eye to the legal and de facto oppression of African Americans. It wasn't until Lyndon Johnson that a president saw fit to add a black to his cabinet and then from that point until your administration, the unspoken rule was that there be only one black in a president's cabinet.

BILL CLINTON: We had seven.

DEWAYNE WICKHAM: Were you conscious of this history when you came into office and opened the door so widely to African Americans in your administration?

BILL CLINTON: Absolutely. First of all I don't think a president can preach at people about what they ought to do in a given area if his own actions are inconsistent, unless he admits he's wrong. I mean, I've had to admit I was wrong about a thing or two, and then that frees you up to go on and advocate what you believe. When I was governor of Arkansas I had appointed more African Americans to high positions in government than all my predecessors in the history of our state. They were people like Rodney Slater and Bob Nash. They were good. They were gifted. They enriched the life of all of our state. No one can claim, the way the right-wing attacks were made on affirmative action, that their appointments diluted the quality of work and all that. I always thought that was a bunch of bull. So when I became president I realized that because of my age and my contacts, and because of work that others before me had done in giving young African Americans educational and career opportunities, I had a bigger pool to draw on and I owed it to the United States, not just African Americans, to try to prove that we could build a twenty-first-century community that was truly diverse and committed to excellence. To me that was a very important part of the job of being president. So I did it deliberately, and I wish I could have done more. I don't think there's any question that it changed the rules, not just for us but for the Republicans. I mean look at President Bush. He's got the most diverse Republican administration in history. There was no question that among the crowd he had to choose from that Colin Powell and Condoleezza Rice were as well, and probably better, qualified as anybody else. They got those jobs on their merits and people now think that's the way it ought to be. So you just have to keep pushing this, and I think this is going to be very important to keep working this all the way through until we have a sense that we live in a country where people are not forgetting about their ethnic or racial or religious heritage, but in fact they're celebrating it. And they can do so because we live in a country where common humanity is more important. It's not enough for people to just say, we have to manifest it in our actions. I hope I did a good job of that. I certainly tried— and I think what I did will stand up pretty well in history.

DEWAYNE WICKHAM: Given your commitment to the inclusion of African Americans in your administration, what would you say was your greatest success in terms of reaching out to African Americans and what would you now consider your greatest failure?

BILL CLINTON: Well, I think the greatest success was making African Americans feel like they are full partners in twenty-first-century America, that they were part of my vision and that I was committed to fair treatment and real progress for them. I think they could see this in all the numbers: in lower unemployment, in greater job creation, in the number of new businesses owned by African Americans, in the increase in single female African-American unemployment, in the decline in African-American poverty and the decline in poverty among African-American children. I think there was this feeling that, it's not just that we've got people in the cabinet, we're a part of this deal.

I think the biggest failure, and there were lots of them, but the biggest failure that I see was in the criminal justice area. You mentioned one, that we didn't reduce the disparity between crack and powder cocaine. But in general there is a grossly disproportionate percentage of African Americans behind bars, particularly young African-American men. Some of them did commit violent acts, they hurt people and they should do time and they shouldn't be out there hurting other people. They are more likely to hurt African Americans than they are other Americans. But a lot of African Americans who are in prison are there for nonviolent offenses, many of them related to drugs and if they stay a long time it's going to have an enormous impact on our social fabric. When they get out are they going to be able to make a living? Are they going to be able to establish stable families? Are they going to be treated fairly and without prejudice? Will their voting rights be returned?

The last message I sent to Congress was basically the unfinished business of building "One America," and I think in almost every other area, whether it's child health or education or economics or representation in the government, we made real strides. But I think that we still haven't found the right balance in having a tough and fair and effective criminal justice system and not having the kind of racial disparity and warehousing of people that we're going to pay for many times over when these young people get out of prison. So I would say that was my greatest failure.

DEWAYNE WICKHAM: And finally, Mr. President, There have been several books written about the relationship between presidents and African Americans. What would you hope historians will say about your relationships with African Americans?

BILL CLINTON: That first of all, for me, it was an affair of the heart and not just the mind. That it was about my personal values and convictions, and not just the politics of the late twentieth century. And that the relationship had enormously positive consequences for African Americans without regard to their income, gender, or their age, and that I helped to build a broader sense of community of which they were fully a part. One of the great tests of America at every period is change—we've gone through about five periods of real sweeping change in our country. Every one of them so far has resulted in an expanded vision of who is a member of our community. I think when people look back on this period they will say that not just for African Americans but for all minorities—the disabled, the gay community, and women—that this was a period in which we expanded the meaning of membership in the American community. I think that even my severest critics would give me pretty good marks for helping to make this happen. But for me it all started with the African-American community. It all started in the little town where I was born and it was always more an affair of the heart than it was of the mind.

CHAPTER 9

Trotter's Return

When William Monroe Trotter took a second delegation of African Americans to meet with President Woodrow Wilson on November 12, 1914, the mood between the two men was noticeably less cordial than during their first White House meeting a year earlier. During that earlier meeting Trotter beseeched Wilson to reverse a decision that was made shortly after he took office to increase the racial segregation of federal workers in the nation's capital.

This expanded segregation of federal workers was especially troubling for Trotter, who was a leading member of a group of black Republicans who supported Wilson, a Democrat, in the 1912 presidential campaign. Wilson wooed Trotter and the others with promises of equal treatment. But once in office, the Georgia-born Wilson increased the "separate but equal" segregation of federal workers in Washington—a decision that forced more black federal employees into grossly unequal working conditions.

During his first meeting with Wilson, Trotter assumed that the president knew little of the changed working conditions and was encouraged by the president's assurance that he would look into the matter. But Trotter labored under no such misconception when he made his way into the White House for his second meeting with Wilson.

"One year ago we presented a national petition, signed by Afro-Americans in thirty-eight states, protesting against the segregation of employees of the National government whose ancestry could be traced in whole or part to Africa, as instituted under your administration in the treasury and post-office," Trotter said, according to a transcript of the meeting. "We then appealed to you to undo this race segregation in accord with your duty as president and with your pre-election pledges. We stated that there could be no freedom, no respect from others, and no equality of citizenship under segregation of races, especially when applied to but one of the many racial elements in the government employ. For such placement of employees means a charge by the government of physical indecency or infection, or of being a lower order of beings, or a subjection to the prejudices of other citizens, which constitutes inferiority of status. We protested such segregation as to working positions, eating tables, dressing rooms, rest rooms, lockers and especially public toilets in government buildings. We stated that such segregation was a public humiliation and degradation, entirely unmerited, and far-reaching in its injurious effects, a gratuitous blow against ever-loyal citizens and against those many of whom aided and supported your elevation to the presidency of our common country."

Trotter's words had a sharp edge and his demeanor, though respectful, was far from cordial. Harvard's first black Phi Beta Kappa graduate, Trotter was a man of great intellect and enormous race pride. He'd joined with W. E. B. Du Bois in leading a defection of black Republicans to Wilson's campaign because he believed African Americans had gotten little for their decades of overwhelming support for GOP presidential candidates. So when Trotter returned to the White House in the fall of 1914 he had grown impatient with Wilson's failure to roll back the racial segregation his administration had imposed on federal workers in the capital.

"Only two years ago you were heralded as perhaps the second Lincoln, and now the Afro-American leaders who supported you are hounded as false leaders and traitors to their race," Trotter lectured Wilson. "What a change segregation has wrought."

"If this organization wishes to approach me again," Wilson said testily, "it must choose another spokesperson. I have enjoyed listening to those other gentlemen. They have shown a spirit in the matter that I have appreciated, but your tone, sir, offends me," he said to Trotter, who was the publisher of the Boston *Guardian*, a leading black newspaper during the early years of the twentieth century. Trotter was never allowed back inside the White House.

Eighty-one years later a dozen black columnists met with President Bill Clinton in the cabinet room of the White House. The journalists were members of The Trotter Group, an organization of African-American columnists that takes its name from the fiery black publisher and race man. The never-before-published transcripts of that ninety-minute meeting and a second one that was held in the White House two years later appear on the following pages.

Bill Clinton and the
Trotter Group

THE WHITE HOUSE CABINET ROOM
NOVEMBER 1, 1995

QUESTION: Mr. President, you had a chance to meet us informally, but if you would allow me to, I'd like to introduce us formally. And I'll begin in my favorite direction, to the left. [Laughter]

BILL CLINTON: The country's coming back to the political center. [Laughter]

QUESTION: I'll begin by introducing Barbara Robinson of the *Las Vegas Review Journal*; Derrick Jackson of *The Boston Globe*; Norm Lockman of the *Wilmington News Journal*; Adrienne Washington from *The Washington Times*; Charlise Lyles with the *Virginian-Pilot*; Dwight Lewis of the *Nashville Tennessean*; Peggy Peterman, the *St. Petersburg Times*; Nichele Hoskins is with the *Ft. Worth Star-Telegram*; Les Payne with *Newsday*; Gregory Freeman, he's with the *St. Louis Post-Dispatch*; and Betty Baye with the *Louisville Courier-Journal*, a Gannett paper. We like her a lot.

We appreciate the opportunity that you've provided to us to come in to talk to you. We have a lot of issues on our plate, but none more important than the one we'd like to discuss with you today, which revolves basically around the question of race relations. We're very mindful of the speech that you gave in Austin. In fact, we were in a meeting in St. Petersburg, Florida, at a retreat of African-American columnists, when you gave that speech. And so we paid some attention to it, as we did to the Million Man March.

And we noticed in your remarks that you talked about the fact that black Americans and white Americans often view the world in different ways—in fact, I think you said "dramatically

169

different ways." And we come here today to represent the interests and concerns of those readers that we write to directly, African Americans, and to give voice to the different views that African Americans bring to many of the important domestic and international questions of the day.

So we'd like to begin our discussion with you, if I may, by asking you a question that I'm sure you have anticipated, and that is, why did you reject the Federal Sentencing Commission recommendation, and also the opinion of our own attorney general, that sentencing, sentencing for possession of crack and powder cocaine ought to be equalized?

BILL CLINTON: The bill did a lot more than that. The bill did much more than that, and I'd like to mention just two things in particular. First, one that got almost no attention, but it's very important that you understand how important it is to me. One provision of the Sentencing Commission's recommendations that was disapproved by this legislation would have lowered penalties for money laundering to the penalties for other possession of property in wrongful ways.

And I very much opposed that because money laundering and our ability to reach it is at the heart of a lot of what is done in international drug trafficking and organized crime and terrorism. I put that in my statement. Almost nobody knew that, but that was a part of the omnibus—you know, the way this works, you accept or reject their—the Congress didn't modify it; they accept it or reject it in the package of recommendations. And that's a very important thing.

The second thing is, I examined who had actually been convicted and sentenced under the trafficking, the crack trafficking provisions. And almost all of them were repeat serious offenders with—and their—that had an average, I think, of something like 109 grams of crack—they had large volumes. Their average age—60 percent of them were over twenty-six years old. They weren't young people. And I don't believe that we should lower the penalties for trafficking in crack. I think there ought to—the disparity is entirely too great. I think they should raise the penalty for trafficking in cocaine.

The third thing is, for the people who are young, nonviolent first offenders, in the crime bill last year, we passed a provision called "the safety valve," which we took a lot of grief for, which expressly give judges the right to ignore the sentencing guidelines or not follow the sentencing guidelines of younger, first-time offenders. If you look at the profile of some people who have been sentenced, we only have the profile through '94 now, so '95 is the first year the safety valve has been in effect. But that's another thing that I feel very strongly about—that we've got the safety valve in there to keep the law at the lower—to keep the guidelines at the lower levels from being abused.

So, in sum, I don't want to lower the penalties for money laundering. I don't want to lower the penalties for crack trafficking. I think the penalties for cocaine trafficking should be raised. And there is a safety valve which, for trafficking and possession, permits young people who are first offenders without weapons to, in effect, to get out from under the sentencing guidelines.

QUESTION: Well, would you raise the penalty for powder cocaine?

BILL CLINTON: That's what I would do—yes. Oh, no, I have no quarrel with the fact that the disparity is entirely too great. You could make an argument for some disparity based on the level of violence associated with the crack trade. But I think that everybody— If you look at the connection between the disparity of the prison population and the disparity of the crimes—racial disparity—the crimes that are committed, there's no question that the disparity is entirely too great in the sentencing.

And I think when it comes to trafficking, they should raise the cocaine trafficking penalties. And keep in mind that then you would have the same option there—young, first-time offenders who didn't use weapons under cocaine would still be affected by the safety valve there as well. But I think—my own view is, that is the proper way to handle it.

So this rule that they have to either accept or reject had all those elements in it, which is why I decided I should not sign the legislation. But there should definitely be some changes made, and we sent it back and asked them to make some changes.

Next question?

QUESTION: Mr. President, I'd like to ask you—Health and Human Services produced a report pointing out that more than a million children would be in poverty under the Senate welfare bill, and I know that you sent that back for additional analysis. My question is, if the analysis comes back with a report similar to that of the Health and Human Services report, would you veto that legislation?

BILL CLINTON: I asked some questions about it. Let me say, first of all, I think this is important to put out there. I gave no one any instructions to conceal this memorandum from anybody. I know that was the implication. When I got it, it was sort of in the form of a quick study by the people at the Department of Human Services, and they recognized, as I recall—I haven't seen it in several weeks—but they recognized, as I recall, that there were several assumptions in the work they were doing, including what the job growth would be, our ability to place people in jobs, and some other things that they recognized might or might not be true, and they said it was just a quick review of what was in the Senate bill. So what I asked them to do was to consider some other factors as well and just look at it again in greater depth and come back to me with a report.

The first thing I'll tell you is if I get any definitive conclusions out of it, I'll certainly make them available to the public. There was no intent on my part, and as far as I know on the part of anyone in the White House, to not talk about this, because I went over a lot of these very same issues with the senators. The House members didn't ask us for our opinion, they just rolled out a bill. But there was an attempt to have a dialogue in the Senate, which I very much appreciated.

My belief is that we ought to have a welfare reform bill that is both pro-family and pro-work, that promotes work, that has the possibility of ending welfare after a certain length of time if people have a job that they can take, that gives the states more flexibility in the way they run their welfare programs, but that fundamentally protects little children. That's what I believe we ought to be doing.

So if I'm convinced that this will do a lot of harm to innocent children, then I'll have a very difficult time going along with it. But I think there are a lot of things in the Senate bill that—I think first of all, on balance, it is far superior to the House bill in virtually every way. I think there was one provision, and I can't remember what it is now—but even the welfare rights advocates thought the House bill was better than the Senate bill, but only one. And I'm trying to get a welfare reform bill that will build on what I've done the last three years.

Basically, I've gone about this in a state-by-state way. We've given over forty waivers from federal rules and regulations—I think forty-one or forty-two now—to thirty-five separate states to try to reshape welfare. And we've done some very interesting things. For example, Oregon now has permission to give employers the cash value of the welfare check and the food stamp check if the employer will pay more than that to the welfare recipient and promise to hire the recipient for a certain amount of time and give job training, so that even if there is a reversion to welfare, you have somebody that builds a résumé, acquires job skills and always winds up ahead by working. That's the kind of thing that we try to do.

I think that and the fact that we passed the earned income tax credit, doubled it in 1993—so that we basically are trying to achieve the principle that if you work for a living and you have children in the home, you won't be in poverty, the tax system will put you out, not put you into poverty—is one of the reasons that we have seen a decline in the poverty rate.

So the answer to your question is, I would be very reluctant to sign a bill that I thought was really bad for children. I'm trying to do something that I think is good for children, and if the study comes back wrong, then I will try to achieve the changes that I think are needed in the Senate bill before it comes to my desk.

QUESTION: So we're clear, Mr. President, if I might follow up—are you saying that if your study comes back and confirms the findings of HHS, that the Senate bill then would be unacceptable to you in its present form?

BILL CLINTON: Well, let me just say this. I want to say it the way I said it for the simple reason that—[laughter]—and I'll tell you, because I do not know the person who is doing the study, I don't know if I will agree with the study. But I was concerned enough by what came out that I sent them back to do some more work on it. If I'm convinced that it's going to hurt children, I'm not going to go along with it. But I don't want to wed myself to the findings of a study I haven't read yet; done by someone I don't know. That's the only thing I was—but I was very concerned by the findings. I asked them questions, I sent it back, and we're going to make an honest, good-faith effort. And when we get it done, we'll show you and you can also make your own judgments.

QUESTION: I'm not trying pin you down on the measure of the pain. You say if it hurts children—the study, I think, talked about a million children.

BILL CLINTON: The study speculated, as I recall—I wish I could have gotten it and read it again. It wasn't a study; it was a memo, a two- or three-page memo. It speculated that over a course of seven years, if all these things were passed together, that is, if you had the welfare reform bill plus what you're trying to do in Medicaid—this is my recollection anyway.

Keep in mind, I have not read it in several weeks, and I've done a thing or two—but if my recollection is right, what the HHS people try to do is to say if this welfare reform bill is passed and the Medicaid bill is passed—which I'm strongly opposed to, by the way; I think it's in some ways the worst part of the budget—and they block grant the school lunch program and food stamps and all that; then all these things together, unless there is a dramatic increase in employment among people on welfare, could wind up after seven years putting another million kids in poverty.

And it was quite plausible with all this stuff—so one of the things I was trying to do was to break down these component parts, because I'm very much hoping that if we have a decent welfare reform bill, it will be separate from, not in, that big budget bill. They could do it either way, by the way.

The other thing you need to know, as I remember, this is one thing I'm quite sure of, another reason that they thought that more children would be in poverty is because the Republican budget drastically cuts aid to immigrant children, not just illegal children. And they seem determined to do that independent of the welfare issue. And so we're working on that.

For example, I'm quite concerned about the extent to which aid to disabled children is cut. You can make some case that our definition of disability has been too loose and there's been some abuse of it, and we've really worked hard to try to tighten it up. But I think anybody who's ever had a family—who's been friends with a family with a disabled child in it—understands that by and large most people with disabled children really do need some of the help that the federal government provides.

So the point I'm trying to make, to be perfectly—the reason I'm being somewhat careful is, if my recollection is they read the terms of the welfare reform bill with the cuts—the across-the-board cuts in aid to immigrants, which affected immigrant children; but it's different from the terms of the welfare bill; and with the Medicaid changes—but I may be wrong, because I really believe that if the Medicaid changes go in the way they are, you'll have a whole lot more kids than a million in poverty because they're going to jerk—we estimate that that Medicaid bill would jerk medical care from 4.4 million children.

So again, I'm not trying to be evasive, I'm just trying to make full disclosure here. My concern is, I want a bill that is tough when it comes to work and responsibility, but is good for children.

What is our objective, after all? What is our objective here? It's kind of like what the Million Man March was about. Our objective—I mean, you may want to ask me some questions about that, but our objective is to allow people to take greater responsibility for themselves and their families and to build a stronger community.

In a world in which most nonpoor people are working, who also have children, our whole focus as a nation ought to be on how we can strengthen families and strengthen work. How can we help people to succeed as workers and as parents? And so whether I sign or veto that welfare reform bill will depend upon whether I believe that cavalierly putting a bunch of kids back below the poverty line is not my idea of doing that. We've got the poverty rate coming down, you know. And the African-American poverty rate, I think, is the lowest it's been in fifteen or sixteen years now.

And I think the earned income tax credit had a lot to do with it. I think the expanding economy had a lot to do with it. If we would raise the minimum wage like I'm trying to get Congress to do so it doesn't go to its lowest level in forty years next year, we could cure a huge amount of poverty overnight and we could have a big drop in the poverty rate. That's the background I look at in this welfare debate.

QUESTION: I was hoping at some point for us to be able to talk about race, as you suggest—talk about race and perceptions of race while we have a chance and to spin it into the Million Man March. It was surprising to me to note that in the survey that Howard University did of about a thousand men, they found a substantial number of men with college education—38 percent, something like that; they found about 77 percent of the men they talked to make over $25,000 a year; they found that about 41 percent made more than $50,000 a year. Did the middle-class nature of that surprise you?

BILL CLINTON: You mean that the perceptions were different, even though they were probably middle-class people?

QUESTION: I'm wondering if it surprised you at all to discover that the middle-class black male would show up here for that event.

BILL CLINTON: No.

QUESTION: Does it suggest—

BILL CLINTON: No, but I had a different—

QUESTION: —you can do anything different as president?

BILL CLINTON: Well, I've been asking myself that question ever since about a week before the march because I had a feeling, of, two or three weeks out—I remember I was talking about the time of the Congressional Black Caucus dinner. How long was that before the march?

QUESTION: That was September twenty-third, twenty-fourth, that weekend.

BILL CLINTON: And when was the march?

QUESTION: The sixteenth of October.

BILL CLINTON: So it was about three weeks ahead, three and a half? I remember talking to Reverend Jackson and two or three other people that weekend about this march and I just had a feeling that it was liable to catch on like wildfire because I thought it was— and I never thought it was basically about Mr. Farrakhan. I just never did. I never thought it was basically about white folks. I thought it was about people determined to make a certain statement about how they wish to live and what they wish to be, how they wish to be identified and what they want to do. And then having said, all right, I'm going to assume greater responsibility for myself, my family, and my community, then that basically was I'm also going to exercise more power as a citizen through voting; and I expect you, the rest of America, to respond accordingly. That's the message I got out of that march.

And I must say, I didn't really focus on it until about a week or ten days beforehand, but Alexis [Herman] and I, every time we went someplace, she would go up and ask everybody she saw if they were going to march. And everybody—everybody she asked said yes. Then she'd come back and tell me. [Laughter]

I remember we were down at Colonial Williamsburg, you know, hardly a hotbed of radicalism, and Alexis went up to the young man behind the counter at the Williamsburg Inn, and he said, "Yes ma'am, I'm going. We've got three busloads going." He said, "Now the other folks here don't know it yet, and they won't understand, but we're all going. There's not going to be many people here Monday."

And I thought it was a very important thing. And maybe you can help me. I got a memo from my friend William Julius Wilson yesterday saying what he thought we should do to follow up on it. But I've been out actively soliciting opinions from people about what next; what can I do as president beyond what I said at the University of Texas?

QUESTION: Did the fact that it was fundamentally conservative make you stop and think about any of your perceptions about black men?

BILL CLINTON: No, because I knew it anyway. I was going around for three weeks telling everybody what I thought was going to happen. I mean, I've spent a lot more time with African Americans than most politicians have—most white politicians. It didn't; none of that surprised me. I'm, frankly, surprised it didn't happen earlier. And I thought it was a very positive thing. I liked it. It had a good feeling to it.

QUESTION: How can you translate that for most white Americans that didn't understand?

BILL CLINTON: Well, that's what I tried to do a little bit in my speech. And that's what I'm looking for more opportunities to do.

You see, I basically think a lot of people think they have acquaintances and even friendly relationships with people of different races. But they still—all the deep waters in their lives, they kind of pass like ships in the night. They don't really still tell each other what they think, which is why when I talked in Texas, I tried to talk about black pain and white fears as both legitimate forces and how we could bridge that gap. Because I think the different perceptions of reality that all those surveys showed after the Simpson trial reflect different ways people experience reality. And I just think the only way to bridge that is for people to really get to the point where they can stand in other people's shoes. And I just think most people don't sit around and just not—maybe even when they work together, maybe they don't have enough time to do that, but I just don't think people are as straight with each other as they need to be about how they feel. And I think—

QUESTION: Do you have some initial thoughts on—you said—I'm sorry—where you said as president you wonder what you should do since the march? Do you have any initial thought on one or two things that you should do?

BILL CLINTON: I do, but I'm not ready to talk about it yet. I don't want to raise a lot of false hopes. As you know, some members of Congress in both parties of different races have urged that I appoint a successor commission to the current commission. I think if that commission has a specific mission—for example, organizing some sort of dialogue—maybe that would be a thing to do.

The last thing I want to do is to study a problem that we already know about, and to give any of us, including the president, an excuse for inaction. I don't want an excuse for inaction; I like to do things, and I like to see things move. So, now, that doesn't mean I won't do it because, I mean, John Lewis signed a letter, for example, to me. But I just wonder, before we do something like that, I want to know what is the mission? What are we going to do? What do we expect to see? And if we did it, it would have to be that, plus something else. I just think we need some action here.

If I can get to the real point, I think there need to be—and this is a point Reverend Jackson made in his, I think he made it in his speech—there needs to be both a personal response and a policy response. That is, I want to know what my job is. I've got some ideas. I think I'm helping with a lot of these fights I'm fighting in the budget. I think a lot of the things I'm trying to get done in an affirmative way, in terms of an urban policy—I think these things are important. So I want to focus on that. And I also would like to think about how the power of the presidency can be used to generate the kind of energy and affirmative impression that was created at that march all across America. Is there some way to organize the kind of dialogue that we need to have? Is there some way to do that? So those are the general areas I'm looking at.

QUESTION: —asking questions about the definitions of racism. And this is a good time to ask that question.

Well, that's what I wanted to ask about specifically, in relation to your speech on race. As we were sitting there in Florida looking at it, one of the things that occurred to me is that you went through a list of things—and I have them here—of what racism is not. And I think a part of the divide may be a debate about what racism is. And so I want to ask you, if you told the nation what it is not, what are at least three things that you think it is, and what might be some examples of this? Because now we're talking perception.

You say, for example, it isn't racist for a parent to pull his child close when walking through a high-crime neighborhood, or to wish to stay away from certain neighborhoods. It isn't racist to recoil in disgust when people read about—so I guess what I'm saying is, what is racism, from your perception?

BILL CLINTON: I think you asked, can I give you three definitions or three components—

QUESTION: I said at least three. [Laughter]

BILL CLINTON: One, it is racist to affirmatively discriminate against someone on the basis of race, to deny them some opportunity for which they are otherwise qualified or should be considered simply because of their race. That's racism.

Second, it's racist to act or to refrain to act in ways that will cause harm to people, either physical or emotional, simply because of their race. And thirdly, there is a sort of subtle form of racism that we all have to be careful about, and that is, it is a subtle form of racism to have presumptions about what kind of people you're dealing with, what they think, what they feel, and what they are likely to do based solely on the color of their skin, and the absence of any evidence to the contrary. And that sort of subtle form of racism, I think, still permeates a lot of our social intercourse in America and keeps barriers up between our people.

You see, it's very interesting. I'll give you some examples of all of that, but some of them are obvious. What happened to the federal agents at Denny's; what happened to the people in Vidor, Texas; but what happened when people said automatically, jurists vote in a certain way just because of their race. But it's also what happens in millions of occasions every day when we encounter each other across a racial divide and we tippy-toe around and don't say what it is we're really thinking of one another because we don't think the other would listen, and we just presuppose how people are.

I mean, one of the things that Norman [Lockman] used to tell people all the time in '92 was that most victimized people of crime in America were African Americans. The bravest people in America for my money are the people who live in all of those tough high-rises, who work forty hours a week for very low wages and obey the law, pay their taxes or the best they can. They don't get good law enforcement. They don't often have good schools. They're doing their best to take care of their kids, and nobody is helping them with child care, and they're still playing by the rules.

So these preconceptions that somehow African Americans don't share our same values—when, in fact, so many African Americans have to go the extra mile to embrace and live by the values that it's easy for the rest of us to spout off about—I think are a mistake. So, I mean, those are just some examples.

QUESTION: Because, essentially, I hear what you're saying, that African Americans are probably victimized by crime more than anybody, but is it fair, then, to tell white people that they should be afraid, when, in fact, the reality doesn't bear that out? I mean, it builds them up as the victims as opposed to who the victims are.

BILL CLINTON: No, because there are plenty of white criminals, too. When I have more time to talk about this—you know, I always talk about that—the level of violence and crime is too high without regard to race. I'll give you another example.

The level of out-of-wedlock pregnancy is growing faster among whites than blacks. Instead of saying there's something racially indigenous to this, we know now what happened is that the economic and social structures that bound the black community together at the end of World War II disintegrated over thirty years. And it was very well documented in Bill Wilson's book *The Truly Disadvantaged* what happened. And it didn't have anything to do with race, except that black people were disproportionately impacted by economic and social change and by—and he says— by the fact that the civil rights laws made it possible for people who didn't want to lie in unpleasant circumstances in cities could move other places, so we left people ghettoized and that's what happened.

But if you look at what's happening now, the out-of-wedlock birth rate among young white women is growing faster than any other group, and it's often related to changes in their economic and social circumstances that closely mirror what happened to young African-American women twenty-five to thirty years ago. It's quite interesting to see.

At the end of World War II, there was no difference in the out-of-wedlock birth rate, in the divorce rates, among the races in America, even though there were dramatic differences in income. Why? Because the economy was moving in the right direction, there was a certain social structure that operated, and when the economic structure and the social structure both collapsed, you had the sort of thing that we see.

So I'm just—I think those are the kinds of things that I would like America to know. What's that black woman's name who wrote—she had written a book about the myths. Do you know what I'm saying? There was a young journalist who wrote a book about the myths. Do you know what I'm saying?

QUESTION: Not Gwelinda Burton? [phonetic]

QUESTION: The young woman who wrote—

BILL CLINTON: There was a young journalist who wrote a book about racial myths. It's a great book. It gives you a lot of factual data about what's really going on out there. Anyway, I gave it to my wife, so I don't have it. I wish I had it.

QUESTION: Mr. President, you said in your Texas speech that Lyndon Johnson addressed the great divide, and his Commission on Civil Disorders specifically called for two million jobs in three years and six million housing units. A few months ago, you said that you have ideas, but you don't want to say them because you don't want to promise. Is that a way of saying that the political climate has made it impossible to promise specific goals to reduce the disparate unemployment situation?

BILL CLINTON: No, I don't believe that. No, what I'm saying is, I like to work through a problem and then decide how I'm going to present it and have all of its component parts ready to go; that's all I meant.

I'll give you one example of something I know we ought to do. Look at what is now happening in Detroit as a result of the empowerment zone proposal where we passed this empowerment zone program through the last Congress and Dennis Archer and the other people of Detroit went out and got $2 billion in private-sector commitments to invest in downtown Detroit to create jobs there for people who live there, as well as to deal with a lot of other problems. That's just an example.

Well, what I had hoped we were going to do with the empowerment zone concept was, we got as much as we could through the Congress in '93. What I wanted to do was to go around and empower mayors like Dennis Archer, Bill Campbell down in Atlanta, and the other cities involved—Michael White in Cleveland has got a big part of one of those, and there are other examples—to go out and get people to invest and say, okay, if you don't want us to spend tax money putting people to work on the public payroll, you have to invest in these cities. You have to invest in these abandoned rural areas.

If you look at the money we've spent trying to help create opportunities in Central and South America—I don't begrudge that; I'm for that, because they are a big part of our future. There will soon be a billion people living to our south, and they're a big part of our market for the future. But the biggest underdeveloped market in America is the American city. The largest number of underutilized resources in America is the people who live there.

So I think one of the things we ought to do, if we're going to have a tax cut program, part of that tax cut program ought to be directed strictly at getting people incentives to invest in the inner cities. Now, we did it in two ways, in a limited way in '93. One was through the empowerment zones, the other was through the community financial institutions. We provided seed money to set up more funds like the South Shore Development Bank in Chicago and other development banks.

Now, I think we need to do much, much more of that. I think we've only scratched the surface. If you look at the progress that Mayor White has made in Cleveland, just to use one example, without very much help—if we gave a lot of these mayors the tools they need to work with the private sector and put people back to work and clean up a lot of these neighborhoods and put people to work building good, new houses and renovating houses and bringing new industries in, I think we can make a huge difference.

I think unless we do something about the job situation, the rest of it will not work.

QUESTION: Let me just follow on that for a second. Your own administration just dropped "rule of two"—the Department of Defense, which jeopardizes $1 billion of federal contracts. You've said that you want to mend affirmative action, but not end it. But is this not an action that ends a piece of affirmative action without mending it?

BILL CLINTON: No. First of all, the rule of two comprises about 12 percent of the total contract value that goes to disadvantaged business from the Department of Defense. Deval Patrick, who is an ardent supporter of affirmative action, studied it and found that it complied with the Supreme Court's Adarand decision, so we've got some of the contractors in now meeting with us. I just saw a couple of them, before I came to meet with you, talking about what we can do to comply with the Adarand decision, which we have to do, and still continue to have an aggressive outreach program that gives minority businesspeople a chance to do business with the Department of Defense.

But a lot of these programs will have to be reconfigured under that Supreme Court decision, and that's all we did. That rule was suspended because our review at the Justice Department reached the conclusion that the present program, as constituted, doesn't comply with the Supreme Court. But I believe in these economic development programs. I like to see them expanded. I'd like to see more affirmative action in areas where there are disproportionate numbers of really low income people so that we can merge the business interests with the economic interests of the communities. And we're working very hard on an initiative not to replace affirmative action, but to add that to our other efforts.

QUESTION: Mr. President, I'd like to return to the mandatory drug sentencing. I mean, I listened to you very carefully on that, because—

BILL CLINTON: Wait a minute. George is my affirmative—

GEORGE STEPHANOPOULOS (CLINTON AIDE): Let me just add one other thing as well—on the track of the review, there was also an important timing issue. That rule of two was being challenged in court. We had gotten an extension for several weeks, but we could not get any more extensions on the court, so we had to make a cutoff—on the day in the court. We had no choice but to make a cutoff on that day, and that was the only reason that the full alternative is not yet in place. We're working very aggressively now in both DOD [Department of Defense] and Justice to make sure we reach the goals—

BILL CLINTON: But the objective that the rule of two had will not be abandoned. We won't just get rid of that much money. We're working on a substitute for it.

QUESTION: The other thing is that we are looking at the program through other subcontracting opportunities, through the incentives that we give to crime—and that's not been reported very much.

BILL CLINTON: Yes, let me just say this: I believe that one of the great victories we have won in the aftermath of the affirmative action speech I gave is that there have been no wholesale repeals of affirmative action statutes and no affirmative bans placed by this Congress.

My view is that we've gone a long way toward reestablishing broad-based political support for responsible affirmative action programs, and I'm committed to them.

QUESTION: Do you credit your speech with that?

BILL CLINTON: I think it had a lot to do with it. I think the other thing it had a lot to do with is, I think that the Republicans decided that they knew I would veto it if they did it, and they didn't want to do any more to alienate the minority community. And, after all, they've got two African-American Republican congressmen now. You know, I think they thought, they've hung that string out enough. I think that some of their leaders didn't want to do it, but I think the speech had something—well, we know from the evidence, actually, later, that the speech had something to do with changing public opinion about it. The American people paid close attention to it; closer attention than I would have thought. They were interested.

QUESTION: Mr. President, I'd like to, if I may, return to the sentencing bill that you signed, because criminal justice is one of the most explosive issues in the black community, and there is some misunderstanding here. I listen to you carefully, we can get a transcript and take a look at it. But I want to hear you on this point. I know the bill does other things that you've cited, but one of the things that is of key concern is the first-time offenders, I mean, with no prior record, for possession—forget dealing now—for people who are caught with crack cocaine, five grams or more, mandatory five years now with no prior record.

When you signed that bill, there was a great deal of disappointment and now, even confusion. And I think we probably should take the time—a more important thing we'll take back and try to explain, but I want to make sure we understand it. Is it your view that—you said that you think that the disparate relations, racial a hundred to one or whatever it is, that's too great.

BILL CLINTON: Much too great.

QUESTION: You said that this bill will turn over to the discretion of judges more than it did before. But, no—

BILL CLINTON: I'll clarify that. Go ahead.

QUESTION: Right. And the problem—on the streets and as Reverend Jackson was saying, in the suites—that there is still the understanding that this bill is a terrible bill that allows and contributes to the incarceration of African-American males, disproportionately unfair and unjustly, and that there is no relief that this will provide to those accused or arrested for possession, and that the discretion that may be placed—taken out of the hands of prosecutors who go before a grand jury and indict—to the discretion of judges still isn't sufficient.

BILL CLINTON: Okay. Let me go back. I want to make sure I'm very clear on this. This bill does not provide any relief. But the crime bill that I supported last year that was passed provided a safety valve from the sentencing guidelines for the first-time, nonviolent offenders covered by this law, number one. Number two, what I objected to about this was that the Sentencing Commission took money laundering, trafficking, and possession and they lowered them all to the next nearest offense. Okay?

So what we did was, we sent this back—the only effect of this law was to send it back to the commission and ask them to find another way to deal with the disparity that couldn't be interpreted as encouraging trafficking in crack, but should be interpreted as discouraging trafficking in cocaine, and that dealt with this money-laundering issue, which is a big deal for me for other reasons that I think the African-American community would fully support. And nobody's noticed that, that this was a big part of the deal. But it's a huge deal for what we're trying to do in the work we're doing with Colombia and a lot of other places.

So that's what I said. I want to see what the Sentencing Commission comes out with. I think the Sentencing Commission was trying to respond to some things that were wrong, but we do have the escape hatch in the form of a safety valve. And we do have the evidence that for trafficking, the overwhelming number of people, way over 90 percent, were repeat offenders with substantial offenses, and that those people convicted of trafficking tended to be older, and that they tended to have much, much, much bigger volumes than the minimum prescribed in the statute.

So what I want to do is give the Sentencing Commission a chance to take a look at all of this and come back with another proposal. And I'm not ruling out anything; I want to see what they do.

QUESTION: Mr. President, let me go back to the Million Man March. On October 16, we listened to your speech that you gave in Austin, Texas. Here in Washington, Louis Farrakhan gave a speech. Have you studied it or listened to it or looked at it and analyzed it, or did you pay any attention to it?

BILL CLINTON: No, I have not studied it and analyzed it. I saw a little bit of it, but I was traveling that day, so I could see only a little bit of it. But I did see a little bit. You know where I am—basically, where I am with him is that I think—not with him, but on the issue, I think that the emphasis in the Black Muslim community on personal and family responsibility and upright conduct and self-help is a very fine thing. I think that anything that divides people instead of unites them or that characterizes people by their own race or ethnic background in a generic way is a bad thing to do. So I'm hoping that this Million Man March will change Mr. Farrakhan some, too.

You know, the most encouraging thing you said before the march was that if they could do something in the Middle East, maybe we could do something here.

QUESTION: But wouldn't it be important to find out what he said? Maybe he didn't talk about separation—

BILL CLINTON: I've read all of the news reports of what he said, and I didn't agree with everything he said. And, of course, he commented extensively on what I said. But I just—[laughter]—what

I want to say to you is that I believe that march, as much as any public event I have seen in a very long time, was not about the readers, it was about the people that showed up. And I believe that when something like that happens and when there's something real deep running through the society—and it's good and it's wholesome and it's being manifested like that—the job of leaders is to give voice to it and not to get in the way of it, and then to figure out how to give energy and direction and life to it, and not to turn it in one way or another.

And so, I think that it's not only the president that has the responsibility that we discussed earlier, but it's also leaders in the African-American communities and others. And I've been encouraged. You know, I think—didn't they have a march in Detroit just the other night on Devil's Night. I mean, some good things have come out of this already. But America said something, I think, that was basically, profoundly good in the faces, in the lives, in the commitment of the people that showed up at that march. And to me, that was the overwhelming story.

QUESTION: Along that line, Colin Powell, to ask a political question—[Laughter]

BILL CLINTON: Yes, it's about that time.

QUESTION: —he's a war hero, he has moderate, white Republicans who are supporting him. He is a kind of politician, black politician, who so far has not turned off large amounts of the black population as, say, an Alan Keyes would, or Clarence Thomas, who is not running for office, of course.

Now, my question is, if he should get the Republican nomination, do you consider him to be your worst possible opponent? And the other question is, part two to that, given his view on the death penalty, given his view on affirmative action, why should African Americans vote for you as opposed to General Powell?

BILL CLINTON: Well, first of all, we have to see, obviously, whether he runs—whether he runs and what he says. You know, he has a lot of admirable qualities, and I think all Americans sense that his is a compelling life story.

But what I will say to the African-American community is that there is no president in modern times who has done more to address the legitimate concerns of African Americans, to try to make real changes that will affect the lives of African Americans, and to try to involve at every level much larger numbers of African Americans in the decision-making life of this country, whether it's federal judges, or in the cabinet, or you name it. There is no approximate record of this and I would like to be judged on the basis of my record, my commitment, and the quality and the substance of my policies, of my advocacy.

Most of the things I've done I had to fight the Republicans in Congress to do. Not just the assault weapons ban, but what about the rest of the crime bill? The Republicans led the fight against the crime bill. What about all of the community programs, all the prevention programs? What about the Family and Medical Leave Law? What about the fact that we did double the family tax credit, which helped African-American families disproportionately because—what about all of that? And that counts for something. And I had to fight the Republicans to do every bit of that. So voters will just have to evaluate that.

And it depends—I said, it really depends on what happens. I have no idea what's going to happen. All I can do as president is to get up every day and do my job as best I can and put my case to the people, and I have no control over what anybody else does.

QUESTION: You have a formidable candidate right now if—I'll just ask the hypothetical question.

BILL CLINTON: Well, you can draw your own conclusions about that; all you have to do is read the *Post.* [Laughter] But I have—let me remind you of something. On June 6, 1992, when I was nominated by the Democratic Party, I was the first Democrat ever to defeat anybody whose last name was Brown in the California Democratic primary. And the entire story was taking exit polls of the people who were so disappointed in their choices—what they really wanted to do was have Ross Perot be president. I was running third. Six weeks later, I ran first and stayed there.

Nobody knows that's happening. This is a crazy world. One of the things I try to tell everybody who works here is that we're living in the most profound time of change in the way we work, live, and relate to the rest of the world, that we've lived through in a very long time—maybe in a hundred years, maybe since we became an industrial society. And at a time like this, it is absolute folly to try to predict what will be popular a month from now, much less a year from now. And I have to do a lot of things that alienate a lot of interest groups.

I'm gratified when somebody comes along after the fact and says they think I did the right thing to ban assault weapons, but it was pretty lonely when we were out there fighting to do it. We did it by only two votes. And when we took on the tobacco companies or I sent the forces into Haiti to restore Aristide, or any of the number of things I've done that were unpopular, you just have to think about what's going to be right ten, twenty, thirty years from now and hope the politics will take care of themselves.

I literally have no control over what anybody else does. So, believe it or not, I think that the best political thing for me to do is to try to be a good president and let everyone else make the decisions that they want to make.

QUESTION: Mr. President, allow me to play traffic cop. We've got a couple of questions over here that we're trying to get in.

QUESTION: You ask what you can do in terms of policy in response to the Million Man March. I've heard that your administration has been exploring all-black male schools from K through third or K through sixth. Do you think that's a good idea? Why? And would it be a platform item in '96?

BILL CLINTON: You know, I'm not aware of that. Let me—I'm just sitting here thinking as you ask the question, and I hate to speculate. My folks beat me up for a year and told me to stop thinking out loud. [Laughter]

As you know, the federal government doesn't run any schools. I think what my answer to you will have to be; I need to find out if we've had any such proposals and whether we should get back to you. But let me tell you how this might have come to us.

We passed Goals 2000 legislation and the Chapter 1 programs, which provide extra funds for poor kids and poor school districts, under circumstances which would permit much more flexibility to local schools and school districts that try experiments if they're committed and tied to a plan to raise student achievement.

Among the things we've done, for example, is to give such funds to the state of California for the establishment, through the superintendent of education, out there of charter schools, where—and I visited one in San Diego the other day—where a group of teachers will organize a school, and it will be part of the school district, but it will be outside the bureaucracy. And they'll have certain performance goals, and if they meet them they get to keep running their school that way, the way they please.

As you know, there's been a lot of speculation about whether or not—not only for young boys, but what would be good for young girls who grow up, who are in poor areas—to have all-girl schools or all-boy schools for a certain period of time. It may be that we have such a proposal that the secretary of education has something like that under consideration, but I am unaware of it at the time. So I will look into it and I'll get back to you.

QUESTION: In your own backyard, you were talking about what you need to do for mayors. Right here in your own backyard, the Speaker of the House has made a laboratory of the District of Columbia, with the Republicans' agenda. And you are seen as just not here, not a player, but a sort of persona non grata. The budget that is about to be passed is going to seriously cripple this city, and serve as a barometer of what will happen in other cities. So my question is, why haven't you been more of a player? And do you intend to be more of a player?

BILL CLINTON: First of all, I have been. I mean, we have—I think I'm the only president—I think I've been out in the neighborhoods in Washington, D.C., since I've been president more than any of my predecessors. When Washington got in trouble, I established a cabinet-level task force to, first of all, collect everything we had already done for Washington, D.C., and to see what we could do to intensify our efforts to help the city, first of all, to get out of its financial crisis or to manage its way through it and to deal with the housing issues, the homeless issues, the drug issues. It must have been no more than two weeks ago that Eleanor Holmes Norton was here with a number of others, and I had several cabinet members here and we went through this exhaustive laundry list of all the things that we have done.

And we haven't publicized it a great deal—perhaps we should have—but I instructed our folks to draw up a report that we could issue to the people of Washington, D.C., which would chronicle the efforts of the last year or so, and then talk about the things we could do in the future. I think in light of the vote Congress just took on the budget of Washington, D.C., nobody seriously believes the Speaker has it as a laboratory anymore because of what they're doing on the budget.

But I think that we do need to up our profile. But I want to assure you we have done a lot of work on this. And I have had several meetings that I have personally supervised where I go through department after department after department; they tell me what they're doing, what we're trying to do to help.

Not everything in Washington, D.C., is bad. There are some very successful public schools here. Some of the police precincts are quite effective. The thing that has always frustrated me about Washington is that there's a sort of unevenness about it. I mean, one of the things that we had hoped to do in helping set up this Control Board was that we would be able to provide some sort of support that would enable the good things and all the talent of the people that lived here to somehow be channeled into a uniform assault on the cities problems, taking advantage of its opportunities.

I've also had a couple of kind of interesting conversations with Speaker Gingrich about what we might do. I still think we might be able to get him to help us in the budget in the end to give some financial incentives to private sector people to invest in Washington. And I'm still hopeful that that's one place where we'll have agreement on it. But, meanwhile, I'm going to try to get some changes in the budget. I thought the budget was too harsh. I do think it's a legitimate criticism that in the last year my profile on this has been too low. But we have spent an enormous amount of time working on it. And I'm going to try to lift the visibility of it.

QUESTION: Mr. President, you asked in Texas for white people to clean their house of racism. In the past, during your presidency, you've gone to black churches to talk about black and white crime, and what Dr. King would have thought. Now, the *Washington Post* did a survey, and they said 58 percent of white Americans believe that black people, the average African American, has a better job, better education, better housing than the average white American.

BILL CLINTON: I missed that. Was that in the survey?

QUESTION: Yes.

BILL CLINTON: Wow. I missed that.

QUESTION: How do you use your presidency to be a reality check to white Americans? It's very clear that during your presidency there has been sort of a reality check to black Americans.

BILL CLINTON: Well, that's one of the reasons I said some of the things I did in that speech. I said some pretty tough things to white Americans in that speech, especially about the way the legal system has treated black Americans over time. But I think—you may be right. I'll go back and look at that.

That's one of the elements that I want to—that I have encouraged our people to give me some ideas about, because I do think most—even white Americans that do not support me otherwise, because they're Republicans or they're mad at me or whatever—I think most of them believe that I've tried to be fair on the question of race. And they know it's a very important issue to me. And that gives me a higher responsibility to talk to them about it.

I think there are a lot of misconceptions out there, though— I think, in the white community. That's why I'm—I think the

Million Man March, one of the reasons that I liked it is that I urged all my friends in the news media to try to report it at least as two stories instead of just about whether—what Farrakhan said or what that was—

QUESTION: They didn't hear you. [Laughter]

BILL CLINTON: I pleaded with them. I mean, because I think that white folks could learn a lot about African Americans just by looking at the faces of the people in the march.

QUESTION: But let me just question for one second, as a follow-up—direct follow-up. You've found very symbolic places to deal with—talk with—black people about "their problems."

BILL CLINTON: And you're suggesting it might be a good thing to find a similarly symbolic place to talk to white people about racism—

QUESTION: What kind of place would you imagine that would be?

BILL CLINTON: I don't know. I hadn't thought about a symbolic place. But I have thought a lot about it, I talk a lot about it. When I go to predominantly white audiences, I always try to talk a lot about what I consider to be—I think that—you know, of course, you would expect me to say this, but I think the information—the evidence supports it. My view is that we're going in the right direction economically, but we obviously have problems we need to address. We're coming back together as a society around mainstream values, but we still have problems we need to address. And one of the big questions is whether we really are going to treat each other as if we're a community or not; whether we're going to be a winner-take-all society or a society where everybody has a chance to win; whether we're going to be a society where we really think we're going up or down together, or where we think people should be left on their own.

And the management of our diversity—which starts with the relationships between white America and African Americans and then goes through this incredible kaleidoscope of other racial and ethnic and religious groups in our country—I think will have as much to do with where we are as a country thirty years from now as any other factor, because if you look at it objectively, it is a god-send. What once was viewed as a burden in America is a godsend. Our racial and ethnic diversity is a godsend for the global village.

And so I will look for—I will think about—the symbolism issue. And if you get any good ideas and you want to drop me a note, feel free. [Laughter]

QUESTION: One of the frustrations of the black community along that line, Mr. President, is that whereas there is almost unilateral agreement that there's a lot of white racism, but no one seems to know any. I mean, David Duke and Mark Fuhrman came along. Yet in New York, where I'm from and work, and with the Bob Grants and the talk radio all the time, if you ask who is a racist or who is an anti-Semitic—Jesse, Jesse Jackson, Farrakhan, Michael Jackson maybe, Johnnie Cochran certainly, maybe even Nelson Mandela for embracing Castro and Arafat or somebody. And the question is that it doesn't have a face on it.

And whereas it really is a serious problem, when we write about these issues, I think all of us as columnists who write issues and all our mail—comes back saying we're racists for raising these issues. Jesse Jackson is a racist—

BILL CLINTON: I don't agree with that.

QUESTION: Yet, on the white side of it, there are no names or faces associated. Yes, you say racism exists, but where are they? In New York, if you say Bob Grant, who is a radio hate—is racist, no, everyone comes to his defense. All of the disc jockeys come to his defense. Yet, African Americans are called upon increasingly to de-nounce Jesse Jackson. We went through this for eight years. Al Sharpton is a racist—all of these "leaders of racism," they're sin-gled out, they're badgered, they're hounded, we're hounded. The question is, on the other side of that, where are the faces and the names to this racism that you and your speech editors, what you have again reinforced here as—issues than any other president I'm aware of. And that's why I ask the question.

BILL CLINTON: But, look. You know, Fuhrman put a big face on it.

QUESTION: Fuhrman?

BILL CLINTON: And it had a big impact on America. And it was inescapable. But people may forget about him, but the point is, it will stay in people's consciousness. When Henry Cisneros made a big issue of the housing situation in Vidor, Texas, it wasn't because—Vidor, Texas, was a little, bitty town. He did it because it was an injustice, but also because he knew it stood for things that were happening elsewhere that were not so obvious.

You know, my own view—I understand the importance of your question, and I think some black leaders have been unfairly criticized on that regard, particularly some of those you mentioned. But I think the issue is not to try to find somebody that white people can hate just like some black leaders are made the object of hate or disdain in the white community; the issue is to try to force people who do that to come down off their high horse and talk about the real issues and the real problems.

QUESTION: But not so much—

BILL CLINTON: And, you know, let me say what I said in the '92 campaign to whites a lot, which is that white people who are frustrated by their own condition, by stagnant wages, by job insecurity, by not thinking they're going to be able to educate their own children, what they need to do is to get with the rest of America. We all need to get together and figure out how to solve their legitimate problems. And it's counterproductive to try to look for somebody else to blame for that circumstance. I think that's where a lot of this misinformation has come out of.

You know, a lot of political leaders, for their own benefit, have tried to deflect what would be the legitimate frustrations, the legitimate concerns of white Americans to think that because blacks are getting a special deal, or Hispanics are getting a special deal, or women are getting a special—somebody else is getting a special deal—that's why they're in the fix they're in, when the truth is that the issues are bigger and more complex. But by dividing us, it may benefit a politician or two in the short run, but all it does is hurt America in the long run. So rather than make sure we have a face on white racism to go with somebody's face on black racism, especially if the black face is unfair, I think the thing we need to do is to try to take advantage of the permission that the Million Man March gave to white Americans to say these black folks share my values; now, why don't we see the world the same way, and what are their problems, and maybe I can tell them mine and maybe we can be honest for a change and create some constructive action on that in every community in this country. That's what I think we need to do.

We've got to change; in order to change people's perception we have got to change their experience. Most of us—some of us have very highly developed imaginations. Almost all of you do because you have to write. [Laughter] I don't mean that you have to make it up. You know what I'm saying. I mean, sometimes I think you're imagining things about me—but what I mean is, you do five different columns a week, or you read different kinds—you have to cultivate an imagination. Not everything you see and hear is sufficient for what it is you want to say. It's not self-evident. So you are living in a business where words come out of somebody else's mouth, they go into your ear, they rattle around in your brain. You have to write something down on paper. You have to cultivate an imagination. And you have to be able to think of things that you do not personally experience.

But if you think about it, most Americans, whatever their race, it's all they can do to keep body and soul together. They're up to their ears in alligators. They're trying to figure out how to pay the bills and get the kids to school, and do all that. And it's not that they don't have the powers of empathy and imagination, but they don't have the opportunity you and I do to imagine that.

And one of the things that we have to do, those of us who do have some measure of empathy and the time and resources to develop it, we've got to get people who get diverted too easily into circumstances in which they can relate to other people—because they can only change their attitudes as their experiences change. They can't just imagine themselves out of this. Most people can't. They have to experience themselves out of it.

QUESTION: Mr. President, I'm told that our time is up.

BILL CLINTON: Did anybody not get a question?

QUESTION: You mentioned Haiti briefly. And I'm wondering if you would intervene if President Aristide is convinced to stay in office for three more years and, as a follow-up to that, how would you navigate barriers to providing Haiti with aid—financial aid—in order to maintain the democracy that you helped to restore?

BILL CLINTON: Well, first of all, I have no reason to believe that. We'll have to deal with conditions in Haiti like we do in every other country we don't control as they come up. But President Aristide right now is trying to plan for elections, and we'll just see what happens. But that's what I expect to occur.

I also think that the people of Haiti see him as their predominant leader, and even if someone else is elected president, which I expect to happen, I think he will be a very strong voice in the public affairs of Haiti. And I think that is a good thing. I think he is a positive influence and a good man.

A lot of the people in the Congress, as you know, in the congressional majority, never supported my policy in Haiti, didn't want me to do what I did. It makes it more difficult for me to get the aid that we need for them. But what we've done is to work very hard through the AID [Agency for International Development] program and through the multinational programs to try to get more resources down there. And we've tried to do things that could have an immediate impact.

I've also done my best to encourage the businesses that were there before to go back and reopen now—the ones that we all shut down with the embargo. I'm trying to get them back up. And I've been quite disappointed, there's another, I think, almost thirty thousand factory jobs that would have to be restored just to go back to the level that existed when he was deposed.

But I keep telling everybody, whether it's in Haiti or the Middle East, we've got to prove that these poor people can get some benefits from peace. When people do the right thing, the United States ought to be out there hitting it trying to reward them. Just like I think we ought to reward people who live in the inner city. Most people who live in the inner city don't break the law. Most people do work for a living. Most people have children that are there. I mean, we need to do that, and I feel very strongly about that for Haiti.

But as a practical matter, given the budget cutting that's going on, given the general unpopularity of foreign aid, and given the specific opposition to my Haiti policy by people who are in positions of influence, most of what I'm going to be able to do with Haiti—for Haiti—I will have to do through multinational channels, where the United States contributes and, therefore, has influence.

QUESTION: My question is, given the Republican control of Congress and the recent heightened racism, would you be willing to issue an executive order to make the penalties for people and companies that discriminate harsher, and make the victim's burden to prove discrimination easier, as it was before?

BILL CLINTON: Before when?

QUESTION: Well, the last five years they've taken away a lot of it, have made it much more difficult for victims to prove—

BILL CLINTON: Let me ask you this way—

QUESTION: Those are the poorest people and they don't have the money.

BILL CLINTON: We have substantially increased civil rights enforcement since I've been president—through the Civil Rights Division and through a lot of the other departments of the federal government.

I don't know enough about the facts to know how to answer your question. But I do know—I've seen the statistics—I know how much we've increased civil rights enforcement. And I am committed to that. And if you can make a case that this is the only way to continue to fight discrimination, then I will certainly have to seriously entertain it. But I don't know—I'm embarrassed to tell you, I don't know enough about the evidence underlying your question to give you an answer. But I can only tell you, we've increased civil rights enforcement. And whenever I find evidence of discrimination, I try to go against it, and I will continue to do that.

QUESTION: I wanted to ask a question. Block grants are going to be with us. It looks like it's going to happen, and people are very frightened—African Americans, poor people. In those very poor states, like Mississippi, where single mothers get $140 a month with two children, what have you, the human services people are upset because there is already bickering among the handicapped children as opposed to the poor children. And they're saying that we're putting too much credence and reliance on local and state officials, and they're scared. Is there anything the administration plans to do to—

BILL CLINTON: Absolutely.

QUESTION: —monitor what's going to happen, what local officials are—

BILL CLINTON: Absolutely. Well, first of all, I believe in all those block grant programs there ought to be a performance standard. And if I can't get Congress to go along with a performance standard, then we'll monitor them with the executive branch and at least confront them with the evidence as time goes on, because there ought to be.

Secondly, I'm not so concerned about some form of block grant for welfare if there are protections for it, because in effect, the welfare programs have been turned over to the states already. And the best evidence of that is that the monthly benefit in Vermont is five times the monthly benefit or four times the monthly benefit in Mississippi right now. In other words, there's this wide disparity under present law.

So the most important thing in welfare was to make sure that there had to be a reasonable maintenance of effort by the state. You see, at the rate the Republicans originally proposed for the welfare bill, the states would get a check from the federal government, but now they have to put up half the money, at least. They didn't have to put up any money anymore. So we now have maintenance of effort tied to the 1994 state effort, which was the highest year, I think, on record. Anyway, it was '93 or '94, whichever one was the higher, we tied the maintenance of effort to 80 percent of that so that with the welfare caseloads coming down, and projected to stay down for sometime, that will guarantee you that the state effort will be there.

The real tragedy would occur if you cut Medicaid as much as they want to cut it and turned it into a block grant. So you have welfare and Medicaid. And then they cut aid to education. And keep in mind, Medicaid, one-third of it goes to poor children and their mothers, 70 percent of it goes to poor older people in nursing homes and to disabled children and disabled adults in nursing homes and home care.

So here's what's going to happen. I was a governor for twelve years. I'm stunned that any Republican governors would support this. I've just described just what you said. Here's what's going to happen. If you block-grant welfare, and you block-grant food stamps and the school lunch program, and you block-grant Medicaid, and you cut down what would otherwise go to the states, you tell me what's going to happen.

Then the next year, January shows up, state legislature convenes, and you look outside your door, and the nursing home lobby is standing there; and the hospital lobby is standing there; and the medical association is standing there that's been providing care under Medicaid—not getting what they're entitled to right now; and then the teachers' lobby is standing there; the principals' lobby is standing there; the school board lobby is standing there. Right? And then there's a group of nice community people; then there's the people who represent the developmentally disabled— they're standing there. And then there's a group of nice community workers who represent all these poor little children. Now, you tell me who's going to get the shaft.

QUESTION: It's already happened.

BILL CLINTON: It's bad enough as it is because in the last several years health care inflation and states spending more money on prisons have taken money away from education and human services. Now you will have nursing homes, hospitals, education, and organized human services against the generalized needs of poor children. That's what I'm telling you; we'll lose at least 4.5 million kids from the health care rolls if this budget passes.

That's what I'm very upset about. I'm strongly opposed to this block-granting of the Medicaid program and cutting it this much. It is wrong. That's where the damage to the poor children is. It's wrong. And I'm going to do everything I can to beat it.

QUESTION: Thank you, Mr. President.

BILL CLINTON: I enjoyed this very much. You asked me questions I couldn't answer, but I enjoyed it. [Laughter]

QUESTION: We want you to come to Nashville this year to speak at the NABJ [National Association of Black Journalists] convention. We'd love for you to do it.

BILL CLINTON: Would you invite me?

QUESTION: Yes, we'll do that.

QUESTION: The question is did you ever figure out who George Clinton is? Do you remember that? [Laughter] When you came to the NABJ convention as a candidate and our president introduced you and said that the only Clinton she knew before you became a candidate was George Clinton. And I saw you taking notes and wondered if you ever went out and figured out—

BILL CLINTON: Oh, you know who George Clinton was—Henry Clinton was the guy that built the Erie Canal. [Laughter]—Clinton built the Erie Canal; Henry Clinton was a cousin of his; George Clinton was the governor of New York, the only person in American history to be governor more than eighteen years. George Clinton was the longest-serving governor in American history. He served twenty-one years as governor of New York in two different terms, once for seventeen years at a pop—twenty-one years in the late 1700s and the early 1800s.

QUESTION: Any relation?

BILL CLINTON: I don't think so. [Laughter] I claimed him. His electability far surpasses mine—twenty-one years he served as governor of New York. And I believe also he was the vice president with somebody, and he died early—a presidential nominee to someone. But he was—twenty-one years.

It was interesting, because if I had served another term as governor and served eighteen years, if I'd finished the term I was in and served another one, then the two longest serving governors in American history would have had the same last name. [Laughter] A little trivia there.

QUESTION: Mr. President, there's another George Clinton. [Laughter]

BILL CLINTON: I bet there's a bunch of them. [Laughter]

QUESTION: This is the Funkadelic George Clinton. [Laughter]— Rock and Roll Hall of Fame George Clinton.

BILL CLINTON: My daughter told me about him.

Bill Clinton and the
Trotter Group

THE WHITE HOUSE CABINET ROOM
JUNE 11, 1997

BILL CLINTON: Well, I'm glad to see you all. Let me just briefly say, by way of opening—and then we'll go around the room however you want to do the questions—the initiative that I am going to announce in San Diego is basically an effort to look at what America is going to be like as we enter a new century as the first truly multiracial democracy in history, to examine what is still defining us in terms of our traditional dynamic between black and white Americans and how that will be overtaken over time as we become ever more multiracial and multiethnic.

But there are, I think, two distinct questions there. I want to do it at this time because I think that—because we don't have any burning social upheaval as we did when President Johnson established the Kerner Commission, because we have the lowest unemployment rate in twenty-four years and the crime rates and welfare rolls are coming down and we see that maybe we can solve some of our problems—we ought to be free to look at what we really have to do to deal with this incredible diversity of ours, and also honest enough to know that under the surface we still have a lot of significant problems that could flare up and undermine our progress and get in our way.

So that's basically what I'm doing and why. And I think it's the right thing to do at the right time.

QUESTION: Mr. President, when we were last here, in response to a question you gave a very clear and concise definition of racism. Can you give us an equally clear and concise statement about what

it is you are attempting to do? What is the problem that you're trying to tackle here?

BILL CLINTON: I am trying to get America to focus on what we will
have to do to create a genuinely unified, multiracial country in the
twenty-first century. We know what we're going to look like, and
we know that it won't be long before, in most states, all of us will
be members of minority groups. The question is, what are we
going to be like? And that's what I'm trying to get us to do.

In that connection, I want to do three things. I want to foster a dialogue, I want to foster—I want to get—I want to promote
education; that is, I want to explicitly expose myths that aren't true
and salient realities that are. And I want us to have concrete actions that come out of this endeavor.

But in the end, the important thing is that we demonstrate
to the world that America is still capable of rising to a new challenge. This will—arguably along with our founding, which was an
act of genius, where we took the ideals of the French Revolution
without its excesses and created a system of stable democracy, and
the freeing of the slaves in Civil War and the long Civil Rights
movement—this will arguably be the third great revolution of
America if we can prove that we can, that we literally can, live
without in effect having a dominant European culture. Are we
going to become a multiracial, multiethnic society? And that we're
not going to disintegrate in the face of it, but we're actually going
to be more unified by learning how to respect our differences and
celebrate them, but be bound by common values. It is a huge challenge. And you see it in what's happening in the rest of the world.

QUESTION: The recent Gallup Poll that was just printed today—

BILL CLINTON: It's fascinating, isn't it?

QUESTION: Yes, it really is. One of the things that poll did is that it,
as you know, it broke down the components to black and white—
Hispanics, for instance, had to choose sides. I mean, you're black
or white; they didn't factor out for Hispanics. And one of the
things that came out in that poll—many of them came up—but
one of them was that 59 percent of whites in America said essen-

tially that the federal government had done enough. Fifty-nine percent, almost the same exact number, of African Americans said that the federal government need yet to do some more.

Now, obviously, in trying to get your initiative moved you'd run against this with whites probably saying that you're offering a prescription for which there is no ailment, essentially, if we are to believe those polls.

But more specifically, though, one of blacks' concerns—and I think this from my experience of making the rounds—is that they believe that we have not yet arrived at a position where what gains that were made—and there have been quite a lot and your administration has been responsible for some—but that they're not irreversible, which is to say they fear now that some of these gains are being rolled back.

And one specific—if you take not just [Proposition] 209 out in California, but the fact that the law schools both at—the two law schools, University of California at Berkeley and Los Angeles, as well as University of Texas Law School, 80 percent drop in enrollment. How can your initiative, or how can the federal government, be brought into play when there is that resistance among the vast majority of people who are white, and this anxiety on the part of African Americans?

BILL CLINTON: Well, let me make two points there. Have all of you looked at the Gallup Poll findings? I mean, to me, it was fascinating. Some of it was discouraging, but some of it was quite hopeful, I thought. It was very much a mixed bag.

The first thing I think we have to do is to recognize that those poll findings may be rooted in deeply held convictions, but they also may be rooted in assumptions about the evidence that are not true. For example, if we would have had another three weeks, I think we could have beat 209 in California. You know, we worked hard against it; I think we could have beat it in three more weeks.

I believe, even though it's a chilling development, it may in the end redound to the favor of sensible affirmative action policies that these enrollment figures in California and Texas are as disturbing as they are. Why? Because they show something to white America that those of us who have been active in this area knew, but *they* didn't know and didn't believe.

So I think the first thing—I agree with you, the biggest—in a way the biggest practical divide—you ask, how is this going to change people's lives. The biggest practical divide in the Gallup Poll was the difference in blacks and whites over whether the government should do more. But evidence is the cure for that.

One of the things that I hope I can do with this advisory board and having hearings around the country is to put out some very salient—here are myths about our racial divide in America and here are realities. And I think if we do that we can find a way to have a sensible affirmative action policy.

You know, it would be tragic indeed if you go all the way back to Brown against Board of Education and you look at what we tried to do, if the only education institutions that could promote affirmative action were private ones. I mean, you know, my daughter's class had 120 people in it and I'll bet you there were thirty different groups represented. I mean, it was an amazing thing, one of the most diverse classes I've ever seen.

Public higher education has been the—I've supported strongly the historically black colleges and universities, but we have always wanted more affirmative action, and we have seen that as a way of moving our country forward.

Secondly, just availability of education. I think it is fair to say that the—I think the unemployment rate among black high school graduates is triple what it is among black college graduates. So this is a huge issue—facts.

Now, let me give you another sort of nonthreatening thing. One of the stunning things that came out of the Gallup Poll is that both blacks and whites were wrong about the percentage of the American population that is black. Did you see that? The biggest plurality in both—the biggest group—about 40 percent of each said, when asked to check a box—was it less than 10, 10 to

20, 20 to 50, or over 50—the biggest block checked 20 to 49—both.

So we got to say—one of the things that I've got to try to do in this endeavor is say, hey, you got to be willing to call time out here, and let's realize there are certain facts not subject to argument. And you'd be better off if you had them. And we can still disagree, but let's get that. And that's one of the things that we have to do there.

I was amazed by that.

QUESTION: Mr. President, how will your initiative address the tone that's being set by 209? That's one of the concerns because, as you know, California is a precursor of many of the national trends. And we, of course, have 10 percent of the votes cast from that state. And I'm just wondering how you'll go about it. Would you, for example, directly criticize Wilson and some of the proponents of 209? What would you do to—

BILL CLINTON: Well, first of all, my relationship with California has been rather interesting because they voted for me twice now, and they know I really care about the state. And the state's gone through all kinds of turmoil and terrible economic problems and all those natural disasters. And I came out against what they did on immigration, and I came out against what they did on affirmative action; and they still voted for me. It was interesting.

But I think that going to California to give this speech at a campus that is very much a multiracial, multiethnic society—interestingly enough a campus that has produced twelve Nobel Prize winners from nine different countries and America—and restating my position on affirmative action, the people of California get that. I mean, they're very sophisticated about this.

And we made a lot of headway from 1994 with the immigration position to 1996 with Proposition 209. It didn't win by that much. And if we'd had a little more time, I think we could have beat it. And I think now they have evidence that they didn't have then. And I personally believe that we can turn this around in California. I think time is on our side there. So I'm very hopeful about it.

But that's one of the reasons I wanted to go out there—because it is on the cutting edge, and that's why the last time I gave the affirmative action speech, I went to the Archives. I thought it was the right place to do it, around our founding documents. But this race speech should be given in California because it's about the future and because of 209.

QUESTION: What are you going to say, Mr. President? What do you want to say?

BILL CLINTON: Well, I'm going to say on affirmative action what I've always said—that we don't need to get rid of it; that I have tried to comply with the Supreme Court standings; and I have tried to improve some of the government's programs; but that every American has a vested interest in seeing that people who live all over this country have a chance to get a good education and have a chance to get into business, have a chance to do business with the federal government, have a chance to build the fabric of opportunity that is a precondition of a stable society; and that we would all be better off if that happened.

So, I'm going to restate my position about it. And I'm going to ask people to think about it in terms of the way they want America to look twenty years from now.

See, I think, in a funny way, because there's not the level of economic anxiety that existed in much of the '80s, we can get people to think about this in a more clear-headed way. But to go back to what you say, we've got to go back and make sure they've got the facts to start with.

And I think the facts of the enrollment figures at the law schools will be very helpful to this debate. I think it will be shocking. I do not believe that white Americans will be happy about that, nor do I believe they will be reinforced. I think they will be surprised, and I think it will bother them.

QUESTION: Mr. President, what myths of white Americans do you hope to expose or explode? For instance, in the last thirty years, regardless of the state of the economy, African-American unemployment has always remained twice that of white Americans. In the era of affirmative action, black male college-degree holders make only 76 percent of what white males do. And one relatively not-touched fact by many people is that white women have zoomed past black women in valued job positions under affirmative action to the point where, despite all the myths—despite the myths—most of the job shifting that has happened with white males has been simply to white women.

So the question to you is, how do you account for the continuing disparity despite bust or boom? And how do you use your office to begin to deal with that problem?

BILL CLINTON: I think there are three reasons for it. One is, I think there is some continuing discrimination that would be identifiable as such under the law.

The second is, I think that there is still a cultural divide that doesn't rise to the level of illegal discrimination, but because you don't have as many independent economic centers in the African-American community, I think it's been harder for people to catch up.

And the third is—and this is why I'm so upset about 209—the levels of educational attainment past high school have not been equalized yet, including more subtle things like opportunities for continuing education in corporations and things of that kind.

So I think all three of those things are there. And again I will say, but I think there are more allies now. In the context of looking to the future, this is going to become a bigger problem for Hispanics than for blacks. In the last three or four years, only Hispanics have failed to make gains as a group. That doesn't mean that within the group there haven't been some blacks who still have declining incomes or unemployment, but as a group only Hispanics are not better off. And the reason is that in the past decade African-American high school graduation rates have risen almost to the level of whites. So that in a boom economy, where people at the margins get picked up, everybody kind of goes forward. That, plus the minimum wage, plus the earned income tax credit and some of the other things have tended to lift, in the last four years, blacks as a group, along with whites.

Hispanics have for—well, I've only looked at the figures going back thirty-five or forty years—always had bigger drop-out rates from high school than blacks, but used to have more coherent family structures, where everybody worked, lived together, minimized cost so their family incomes were higher. Now poor Hispanic family structure is beginning to look like poor white and poor black family structure, but the drop-out rate is still the same. So they are now going to face this same sort of problem. And I think many of the same kind of solutions will be required.

But I'll give you an example in terms of the law. When I became president—I can't remember how many—there was this huge backlog of EEOC [Equal Employment Opportunity Commission] cases—just to give you one example—which sets a tone for the whole country as they get resolved, in terms of opportunity. We've handled all the current cases and cleared out about 25 percent of the backlog. And we should have cleared, in four years, over half of the backlog, but we couldn't get the Congress to give us the money to clear the backlog. We've also increased the awards.

So one of the things that I'm going to argue hard for in the context of this endeavor is that even the conservative Republicans who don't agree with affirmative action always said they were against discrimination. And if they really are, give us the money to do the job at the EEOC, and in the other areas of the federal government to enforce the law.

QUESTION: One of the forms of discrimination that many people feel that your administration has abetted, if not directly participated in, is when you signed the Crime Bill in '94 you maintained the hundred to one crack sentencing ratio. As one concrete sign of your administration's effort to end discrimination—as you may know, a recent study, one from Minnesota, says that there's no medical basis—many people are saying there's not medical basis to have a hundred—at most, two to one, three to one. Are you prepared to begin to change that and eliminate that one hundred to one sentencing ratio?

BILL CLINTON: Yes. Keep in mind, the only choice we were given last time was, I thought, a Hobson's choice, and the wrong one, which was simply to lower the crack penalties to the cocaine penalties without asking whether or not—not only *was* any disparity justified, but if they were going to be made equal should there be at least some marginal lifting of the cocaine penalties. And the situation that exists is unfair, unjustifiable, and should be changed. And I'm going to do what I can to eliminate a huge percentage of the disparity this time.

QUESTION: In what way?

BILL CLINTON: Well, we're going to get a recommendation from the Sentencing Commission; then we're going to try to implement it. Whatever we can do by executive action, we will. Whatever we have to do through congressional action, I will try to get passed through the Congress.

I'm saying this out of some ignorance now. I'm not sure, given the present posture of the issue, what I can do by executive action and what has to be done through the Congress, but there is coming to me a recommendation for a drastic reduction in the disparity, and I intend to support a drastic reduction in the disparity. I think it's not a sustainable thing.

And if we did it, particularly because of the rules in federal prison, where parole is rare and we have much more strict guidelines about how long you have to serve—I don't know if parole is rare, but you have to serve a higher percentage of your sentence—it would go a long way toward, I think, at least eliminating one of the real reasons that blacks feel that there is a disparity in the criminal justice system.

QUESTION: Mr. Clinton, I think it's always a real, you know, tricky issue, and I'm sure it's tricky for you, in particular, but in this speech will you talk about, or is there an opportunity to talk about, the unique relationship, I think, between white and black Americans as a dysfunctional family? I mean, it's sort of like it's not just the numerical numbers, where the numbers of African Americans are expanding. But that particular relationship—it seems to me that every time we try to deal with these other, broader issues, we always get back to that issue between blacks and whites in America.

And how do you help other minority groups understand that it's more than a numbers thing, numerically, but that particular institution, that particular relationship that almost makes us brothers and sisters in the same household in a way that others have not been in that house.

And is this an opportunity for you to do that? Or do you see yourself trying to help—when we deal with mythologies and all of these arguments, it's often cast as a numbers thing—there are going to be more Hispanics than blacks, but no one I think has had this particular relationship. And it seems to me that it stymies us as we try to deal with these others, because this one is so big and so—

BILL CLINTON: Well, first of all, I agree with that. I had a group in here yesterday, and we were talking about whether—how you said, how I would say that the issue is how we build a multiracial society, but there's still unfinished business between blacks and whites in America that without resolving we can't ever get to the next stage. So that you have to see these two things together and not one or the other. Maybe the way you suggested is the right way to say it.

But I think it's true. It's the same thing that—I mean, I'm sure because South Africa is the richest country in Africa now, unless the Nigerians can really pull together, that it will become more multiethnic and multiracial because people will want to go there and be there. But they'll still have to deal with the legacy of 350 years of oppression. It will never be out of their character, at least not for quite a long while.

And it's the same thing here. It's just different because blacks were brought to our shores against their will as slaves, subject to institutionalized oppression. It is different in that—and the legacy of that and how we lived as families in the beginning on farms, often really living as families, is a unique part of what makes us how we are.

That's a rhetorical question as much as anything else. I've tried to imagine how to think about it and haven't approved any final language for the talk yet.

QUESTION: And in a way I guess what I'm thinking—you know, I don't want to tell you what to say—but in a way that makes it nonthreatening and not—you know, because that's always how it's cast. It's either "us" or "them," and I don't think that African Americans generally want that or can afford it. But, you know, it's just our family.

BILL CLINTON: It's amazing how many people have—you know, I've heard of many discussions—it was the first time in a long time about what really causes racism and why people are prejudiced. And you look at Bosnia, for example, where there is no biological difference between the three warring groups and where they lived together in harmony in Sarajevo for decades. And I mean, in a matter of weeks they were shooting each other.

Some of this is learned behavior. But a lot of it goes back to the vulnerability people have to defining their greatness in terms of their ability to look down on somebody, beat up on somebody else, feel that someone else is inferior to them. And a lot of what will shape America in the future is whether we can find a way to— all of us—define our own individual aspirations as well as our nation's greatness in terms that are nonoppressive, that don't require us to be pushing down on each other or someone else.

QUESTION: Mr. President, in Bosnia and in the Congo, the thing that was missing as ethnic groups decided to kill each other was a policy structure to prevent it. So I'm kind of interested in what your commission is going to be doing. What's the product going to be? Are we talking about new policies? Are we just talking about moving around the country doing—

BILL CLINTON: No, there will be new policies. There will be some new policies at the end of the day and there will be some in between.

215

QUESTION: What's the goal—I guess that's what I'm asking.

BILL CLINTON: The goal is twofold. The goal is to produce a report in about a year—maybe a little more, but not much more, sometime next year—that will encapsulate what we learned during the year about how we can create one America in the twenty-first century; what policies do we need to change, what perceptions do we need to change, and how can we institutionalize a level of not only dialogue, but common action, that will prevent us in times of stress from disintegrating into our version of what has bedeviled so many other countries and what has bedeviled us in the past.

That is the goal, so there will be a heavy policy component. And these other things, as well.

QUESTION: Who are they going to be? Do we know yet? Do you know yet?

BILL CLINTON: Sure. Well, I'll tell you three people I'm going to put on the commission. I've got to save something for tomorrow. [Laughter]

QUESTION: We won't tell. [Laughter]

BILL CLINTON: John Hope Franklin, whom all of you know, and for obvious reasons, he's still in great shape—I mean, he's not a young man, but he's very sharp, and he's very much attuned to this. I'm going to appoint Bill Werner, who was formally governor of Mississippi, and he's been a friend of mine for twenty years and been very, very active in the racial activities in not only Mississippi, but throughout the country. And I'm going to appoint a young woman named Angela Oh, who's a Korean-American lawyer in Los Angeles, who's been very active in the Korean community there and in developing the relationships between the Korean community and the African-American community and other communities there. I thought it was really important to have somebody from Los Angeles County there since it's the biggest county in the country and has people from 150-plus racial and ethnic groups in it. And there will be—probably three or four more. I'm not going to have a great big commission. I don't want a big group.

QUESTION: Is there any concern about having somebody on the commission, though, who can speak for those people in the black community particularly who are alienated, who are angry and alienated and some of whom hate white people?

BILL CLINTON: No, because we're going to go see them. We're going to give them a chance to speak for themselves.

QUESTION: Okay.

BILL CLINTON: I mean, one of the things that I did not want to do is—I don't want a big group. I don't want people to think this commission somehow is there—I want this to be an advisory board to me. I want this to be something where I can have no distance from this, so I can't just say it's something I did, and then if I choose to take the recommendations, fine; if I don't, fine. I don't want that sort of a deal. I'm not looking for a way out here; I'm looking for a way in.

And so I have consciously chosen to stick with a small number—six or seven people—small. And what I want to do is go give those people who feel angry and alienated their chance to tell me and them what they expect and what's not working and what we still have to do. And I want us then to be able to use that to get a lot of those things done.

I still believe that there's a serious economic component to all this and that we've got to create a climate in the country for continuing that.

This whole welfare business—I'm really not worried about our capacity to create enough jobs for the people on welfare before their time runs out. I'm not worried about that. I know a lot of people are; I'm not. I'm confident we can do that. What I'm worried about are all these young, single men who were never on welfare in the first place, who are out there on the street corners of the country, still having trouble putting their life together.

QUESTION: One of them asked me for money on the way in.

BILL CLINTON: One of them asked you for money on the way in— yes?

QUESTION: Mr. President, this commission is going to hold town hall meetings and so forth throughout the country. How do you get those alienated folk to come to this kind of a meeting? These are people that don't show up to town hall meetings and government things.

BILL CLINTON: But if we go to them, I think we will. And if we hold town hall meetings and they're not all in fancy neighborhoods and they're in places that are accessible to folks like that—and also, there are community groups in this country now full of former gang members, full of people who work in these communities, who live with these problems. And I want this to be their forum. I want to give this to them.

That's actually one of the most encouraging social developments in America today, is all these community groups with former gang members in them, going back committed to trying to rescue their own neighborhoods and the kids they grew up with and the people that they live with. I just was with one of them today over at Georgetown at a Justice Department program on juvenile justice and rescuing children.

So if we go out there and give them a chance, I think they'll show up. I've found that a lot of these people are not the least bit shy about telling you what we need to do.

QUESTION: So, you're going to go to real grass roots?

BILL CLINTON: Yes, that's what I want to do. That's what I intend to do.

QUESTION: Mr. President, when we were last here, you told us that you believe that you know more about black folks than most white politicians do.

BILL CLINTON: That's not arrogant, that's just the fact of my life as opposed to other politicians.

QUESTION: I wasn't trying to characterize it.

BILL CLINTON: It might be, but I think it's true. [Laughter]

QUESTION: But you said that, which leads me to ask you this question. In undertaking this effort, do you begin with an idea of where you want to end? And is this a process, then, simply to teach or one in which you hope to learn something about the relationship between blacks and whites in this country?

BILL CLINTON: Well, yes, I begin with an idea of where I want to end because I think where I want to end is the only sensible place for us to end up. That is—let me say again, I can give every one of you right now a little handout that will tell you what America will look like twenty years from now, and barring some totally unforeseeable outbreak of disease or some massive immigration pattern different from anything that's ever happened or some total change in birth rates, that's pretty much what we're going to look like twenty years from now.

QUESTION: Demographically?

BILL CLINTON: Demographically. But what I cannot tell you for certain is what we're going to be like twenty years from now. So what I want us to do is—what do we look like now? What are we like now? What are the myths and realities? Here's what we're going to look like twenty years from now. I want us to be one America.

Now, I have an idea about where I want to go. And I also have an idea about some specific things that I think we have to deal with, like affirmative action, like genuine economic opportunities, like discrimination where it still exists—through the EEOC and other mechanisms. But I also expect to learn quite a lot. I expect to learn quite a lot about it.

QUESTION: Mr. President, when you go back and read the Kerner Commission, which was released thirty years ago next year, it talks about some of the underlying problems of race relations—poverty, problems in inner cities; the Kerner Commission called them ghettos for the most part. And today we still—some politicians, some journalists—not all of us—see some of the areas and there are a lot of problems. Is that what we want America to be like? Or how do we get rid of those?

BILL CLINTON: Well, for one thing, I think a lot of the things the Kerner Commission said are still relevant. Someone told me the other day when we went back and read the whole thing that we had actually done some things in the first year of my presidency that were recommended in the Kerner Commission report. So I think that we shouldn't be ashamed to say that we have not solved all the problems that the Kerner Commission identified three decades ago.

Now, one of the things that I think we ought to say—and I've heard Reverend Jackson, among others, say this for years, but I firmly believe it's true—is that, with America at a national unemployment rate of 4.8 percent—that's actually quite a misnomer, isn't it. Nebraska has an unemployment rate of, like, 2.3 percent. There are five or six or seven states with unemployment rates at 2.5 percent or below, which all economists will tell you is a functional labor shortage. Anytime you get below 3 percent, there's serious labor shortage because you've got that many people just kind of moving around all the time—changing their lives and doing things.

So what that means is, that because we didn't do what the Kerner Commission said we should do as a country, because we have huge chunks of people who have not moved into the economic mainstream, that is not in the self-interest of the rest of us. How can we keep the American economy going without inflation? We have to have new markets and new workers. Where are the nearest new markets and the readiest new workers? In those places in America that are still too poor and too underemployed and too underinvested.

So, I mean, I think that that part of the Kerner Commission report is relevant today, and we need to be—that's one of the reasons that in this budget deal I fought so hard for trying to create an investment framework that would naturally flow more capital into those areas than we've had in the past. I think it's terribly important.

QUESTION: Mr. President, you have a reputation for being sort of a student of history. And I wonder if you have in your mind any historic precedent for a situation where the president of the United States was able to exert the kind of leadership to bring about what you're talking about, which is to have the American people confront the future, to create a consensus for what that future ought to be, and get them to move forward on it—other than in a time of crisis, like war.

BILL CLINTON: On this issue there isn't such a precedent. But I'll tell you, the nearest precedents don't relate to this issue. But the nearest precedents would be the progressive things that Theodore Roosevelt and Woodrow Wilson did as we moved into the—as we became a more industrialized, more urbanized country. And they said in their different ways, hey, you've got to look at child labor; you've got to look at resource conservation, as well as resource use: you've got to look at the regulation of monopolies.

Theodore Roosevelt passed the Railroad Act, and called for the Hepburn Act. It was the first example in American history of the president going out and rallying popular opinion against the institutional interest that controlled Congress, and actually getting Congress to change its position on whether the Interstate Commerce Commission should be able to regulate how much the railroads can gouge the common people to ride around on, or could gouge the people to carry things back and forth on the railroads that could only be carried on railroads. It had never happened before.

But anyway, Wilson and Roosevelt were, in essence, trying to involve the American people as a massive group in a way they had never before been involved and explain to them what the Industrial Revolution was all about and how we're going to make it so everybody could be a part of it.

The only other time that is even kind of close to this—that is, when there's not a crisis—was the period between Thomas Jefferson becoming president and the War of 1812, which presented us with a crisis. And during that period and then after it settled down right afterward, we still were being governed by a founding father when the existence of the country was not at issue. And they were trying to figure out whether we were going to continue to become a continental country, were we going to expand, what did it mean to be an American, were we just going to be these thirteen little colonies or were we going to do something else?

And they had the same sort of debates. They fundamentally changed the country without a crisis. And the same thing happened—much more relevant to the present day—with Roosevelt and Wilson. I don't think there is any other historic parallel.

QUESTION: Mr. President, is there a country or a place that you would point to or hold up as a guide of where we ought to be headed, multiculturally?

BILL CLINTON: No, because they're having problems everywhere. You know, India is the biggest democracy but they have their problems with the Sikhs, for example. The Russians have about as many different ethnic groups in their far reaches as we do, and linguistic groups, but they all live segregated; they're not living together. Even the Chinese are, in ways that are mystifying to Americans. How could they be afraid of the Tibetans? Why would they crush the Tibetan culture? If the Dalai Lama is willing to admit Tibet is part of China, so there's not a big territorial deal, why in the world would they not want that culture to flourish? They're even separate from them. So no one has really succeeded in building this kind of culture.

And, interestingly enough, our friends in Great Britain are facing similar challenges now, but not to this extent. They have different racial issues and different historical problems that they have to deal with. But it's very interesting to see. You know, the Europeans are by and large much tighter on immigration than we are. And they're concerned about it.

But no one has ever tried to do this. But if you consider the problem in the Middle East and you consider in America we have Jewish Americans, Palestinian Americans, Jordanian Americans, Syrian Americans, Iraqi Americans, and Iranian Americans; we have Croatians, Serbians, and Muslims from the Bosnia area in the United States; we have Greeks and Turks in the United States; we have Irish Catholics and Irish Protestants with roots in Northern

Ireland in the United States; we have people from every African country and every tribal group in Africa in the United States.

So in a funny way, because we haven't cut out anybody, we may have a better chance than anybody else does to get this right. But I do agree, to go back to what Betty said, we have to recognize that there's something unique here, and always will be, about the black-white dimension of this and we have to recognize that we have an obligation to create this multiethnic society.

QUESTION: Mr. President, you mentioned before that one of the biggest problems is a cultural bias that does not quite make legal discrimination, which I think most of us in this room think is actually the fundamental problem right now.

BILL CLINTON: But it still exists, doesn't it? Every one of you has sensed it, haven't you, at some time in your life.

QUESTION: Correct.

QUESTION: Today. [Laughter]

QUESTION: Well, how do you, given that on the administrative side you had to back off of health care, you had to back off of the pledge to end the ban on gays and lesbians in the military—given that there is no precedence for attacking a problem like this, where is your moral capital? What is it that you are bringing to the table, particularly with white Americans, that somehow you are going to rise up over some of your past failures to succeed on this issue?

BILL CLINTON: Well, first of all, I think most white Americans, even those who don't vote for me, believe that my conviction here is genuine, that this is something I really care about and that it's something I know more about than most of them do. I believe that, and there is a lot of polling data that supports that.

Secondly, there is some evidence now after five years that when we follow policies that I advocate, things get better—economic policies and crime policies. There is some evidence here that I ought to be given the benefit of the doubt on.

Thirdly, I don't quit trying when I'm first defeated. Look, in this budget agreement we didn't win the health care debate; but as a result of the health care debate, health inflation dropped because a lot of the things we were advocating were happening anyway. And the cost of health care stopped going up so much and now we've got money in the budget to insure half of the uninsured kids in the country, and I think we'll get the rest of them before we're done. So we will have a big victory in health care.

We didn't win the victory on gays in the military, and I think I was right on that, but there are a lot more gay Americans serving in the federal government without fear of prejudice or of censure. We've repealed a lot of other discriminatory provisions in terms of government service that affect gays. I have supported the Employment Nondiscrimination Act and basically, if you look at the record of this administration on behalf of gays and lesbians and compare it to anybody else, it pales in comparison.

So to talk about the fact that we didn't win the gays in the military, which was the most visible and most controversial one where we had the weakest hand to play and where we had a veto-proof margin in both Houses against us, that's really why we lost—when there was a vote in the Senate sixty-eight to thirty-two against my policy and we knew we were stronger in the Senate than the House, that's the only reason we had to pack it in.

I think the fact that I've fought the fights that I've fought and then I could keep coming back and making what progress I can should be reassuring to people, not discouraging. They shouldn't—nobody should want an advocate that only picks fights they always win.

QUESTION: Mr. President, from New Orleans to Sioux City, Iowa, there is a group called ERACISM, which basically meets once a week, or once a month—it's a multiracial group, and it deals just with conversations where whites and blacks sit down at the table and discuss racial issues. How do you get America to just talk about race, and just to look at the issues.

BILL CLINTON: For one thing, I want to highlight groups like that. To us, I know it's because we're all here and we're focused on all of this policy stuff, I know it's easy to minimize the impact of that. But keep in mind, most Americans live somewhere else, and most

Americans live beyond the reach of a lot of these policies. And most Americans would be really incredibly better off if they had a chance to participate in a thing like this and if they would figure out how to solve some of their problems without my help or yours. That's not an excuse for me to evade responsibility; it's just a fact of life that if people get together, they figure out how to take care of a lot of their own business.

So I think one of the central objectives of this whole endeavor should be to get people in every neighborhood in America to have that kind of cross-racial dialogue.

QUESTION: When you talk about the grass roots, I think one of the things that we, who are polite journalists who don't get into a lot, keep running into is the criminal justice system and I've noticed that when you begin to deal with race, you inevitably, because it is a continuing problem, you go back and you deal with the past. You talk about the syphilis issue, you talk about the Medals of Honor that were not given, you talk about things that have happened in the past and force the country to confront it.

On the issue of criminal justice, you're going to California. The Geronimo–Pratt case, not so much as an individual case, but as a case that—it has been charged that this represents a reminder to us, like the government prosecutor—an unjust war, perhaps, in the view of some—in the view of a lot of blacks of the era, to include myself, they felt that the Justice Department pursued an unwise and ill-advised campaign against blacks who were trying to win rights. Geronimo–Pratt may very well have been caught up in that. What are your views on Geronimo–Pratt; and what are your views, broader than just Geronimo–Pratt, on that era of the '60s in which there were people who were caught up and in some cases prosecuted?

BILL CLINTON: I don't know enough about the Pratt case to have an informed opinion. In the turmoil of the '60s, both in the streets in America and in the controversies over the war in Vietnam, I think there were a lot of people who got hurt who shouldn't have. And I think we all know that. This sort of picture that gets painted of the '60s now, mostly by people on the right, that it was all just a bunch of amoral, self-indulgent people smoking dope and having irresponsible sex and not caring about their obligations—I find that to be a horribly disfiguring characterization of the decade in which there were probably more people who tried to seriously ask and answer what their moral responsibilities were as citizens to make this country a better country and to deal with our responsibilities at home and abroad than at any other time.

Often, they disagreed with one another, but it'll be a long time before we remove the scars of all of the people who got hurt, who were just kind of standing there trying to do what they thought was right.

QUESTION: When you look at—like the situation in California with [Proposition] 209—when you look at those situations, who do you see as the enemy? Who are the enemies?

BILL CLINTON: Well, in racism, I always think the number one enemy is ignorance and fear; there's always somebody trying to take advantage of it for political purposes. But you look at what Hitler did with—

QUESTION: Would you care to name them, Mr. President? [Laughter]

BILL CLINTON: You look at what Hitler did with the Jews. Now, Hitler used racism to build a power base to achieve his own sort of grandiose objectives, but he could not have done it if the people who were voting for him did not at least have some predisposition to define themselves in terms of their superiority to the Jews and to believe that somehow they were right to be afraid of the Jews, they presented a threat, and they had to do all these terrible things.

So I still think the enemy is largely within here. We can handle all the politicians trying to take unfair advantage of the race deal. We can handle people who—it's not in our economic self-interest to do so anymore—we've been talking about that. No serious person can claim that discrimination is in the economic self-interest of anybody in America—or of any substantial block of people. It is undermining our capacity to keep beating the business cycle here and keep growing.

So the enemy here, I still believe, is learned behavior, and even prior to learned behavior, there's either fear of people who are different from us or our inability to define ourselves in positive ways as opposed to negative ways. That is, we always got to figure there's some good in us because we're better than somebody and that somebody else we're better than is different from us. I still believe that is the central problem.

QUESTION: A follow-up to that. We were talking about myths and the need to dispel bad ones and the assumption had been made that white people harbor bad myths about black people. Are there any myths—do you think there're any myths that black people harbor wrongly about white people? And if so, what would they be and what do we need to do to get rid of them.

BILL CLINTON: Well, if you look at the Gallup Poll, the evidence is that—I think that if there is a myth, I think it is that black people think a majority of white people actually know the bad stuff that's happening to them and it's kind of all right with them as long as they don't have to deal with it directly. And I'm not sure that's true. I think that most people in this country confronted with the facts will do the right thing, not the wrong thing.

That's why I think—to go back to what you said about that—what did you call it—all these conversations occurred. That's why I think one of the things it's important for us to do is to go out and puncture every myth we can find because I—

QUESTION: The media—

BILL CLINTON: No—I really do believe that the most important difference in perception and reality right now in blacks and whites—I'm not talking about other racial groups—is this whole law enforcement business.

So I think that if there's a myth—I would just say to the black community, if we can get a hold of most white people and they actually know what the truth is, I think they will do the right thing.

227

I don't think they really believe—just like this government thing—I think they're wrong that we don't need more policy, but I think they honestly believe that. I think if they knew the facts— that's why I think you're going to be amazed at how much we can move white opinion on the facts in California and Texas now. That's what I believe.

QUESTION: The media is one of those conveyors, of course, of impressions in this attack—we are part of it here in this attack constantly, as you know.

A substantive point is, in addition to the rollbacks and the reversals that have happened in the enrollments of the law schools in Texas and California, there is also the problem of black ownership, which is in a free fall now because of the removal of the tax incentive in 1995. The tax incentive for black ownership of TV and radio stations was removed in 1995. There has been a reduction over the last year of 10 percent, and it is going down steeply.

The FCC says that they are studying the issue again to see if they should restore incentives. There is no will among the Republicans in Congress to do anything about this. What can your administration do in the area of black ownership of media?

BILL CLINTON: First of all, I have to share some of the responsibility for that. I signed the bill and I said I would support that. We were in part trying to stop an even bigger encroachment on affirmative action, but I have to take my fair share of responsibility for this.

What we underestimated was the coincident effect of removing the tax credit with the structural changes that were going to happen in media anyway because of the telecommunications law and just economics.

So that if you're sitting out here and you have one of these certificates and you're an African American and you own a radio station or a television station or whatever the heck you own, and one of these big conglomerates comes along—Mr. Redstone, Mr. Murdoch, Mr. Somebody Else—and they offer you five times what you've got in this thing, and you've got three kids to send to college, it's pretty hard for you not to take the deal.

Now, under the old system, because of the way the tax certificate thing worked, you could almost always guarantee that there would be some kind of replacement or some sort of joint deal or something would come up. And I think when I signed that legislation, I totally underestimated the extent to which people who had properties wouldn't hold on to them or pass them on to other minorities and really, economically, almost couldn't because of what was happening.

So the short answer to your question is, I have asked the FCC what our options are and whether we can we do anything short of going back to Congress. But I wouldn't even be too sure that we couldn't get this Republican Congress to do something because the facts are so stark. It is breathtaking what's happened.

QUESTION: Mr. President, let me quickly ask you about welfare, which you mentioned briefly. The bill that, of course, you signed was not exactly what you proposed in the beginning. And a key component of it was that it ended the federal guarantee of assistance to kids, even to families that might even play by the rules, try to get work and that kind of stuff.

BILL CLINTON: Let's talk about it. Let me just say what it did do and what it didn't. It ended the federal guarantee of the monthly check. It kept the federal guarantee for food stamps and Medicaid, basically food and nutrition and anything else that people were eligible for, like housing—it kept those guarantees.

However, we also did give the states—the block grant we gave to states was based on the population—their money that they were entitled to when the welfare population was at its all-time high in early 1994. That means that today, forty states have huge windfalls, and they have to spend all that money on poor people. Among other things, let me just say that they can spend the money paying people to take community service jobs; they can spend the money to send people back to college; they can spend the money on extra child care.

And we got in this bill a restoration of most of the benefits to legal immigrants and a commitment for $3 billion more for the highest unemployment areas of the country to create opportunities for work, including the ability of cities to hire people to do community service jobs. And we now have several hundred businesses that have agreed to participate in this.

And the real trick now is, I think, to get the states to do things that make sense to create job opportunities for people. If they do that, these people will be alright. The people that I still have not been able to help are the people that weren't getting helped in the first place, and those are the young, single men who never were on welfare in the first place and therefore we can't give their welfare check to any employer as a job subsidy; we can't do anything. That is something that I expect to be a big focus of this endeavor here.

QUESTION: Mr. President, when we were here in November, you were gracious enough to say that you would have us back. We appreciate that and we hope that you will have us back again. Thank you very much.

BILL CLINTON: I will.

QUESTION: Your wife is here from Chicago. I'm north from Nashville and Al came down to our convention last year, but he promised that you would be in Chicago this year.

BILL CLINTON: When are you going to meet in Chicago?

QUESTION: It's July sixteenth through the twentieth.

QUESTION: We also have a golf tournament there this year. [Laughter]

BILL CLINTON: Where are you going to play?

QUESTION: I'm not sure.

BILL CLINTON: You know the oldest eighteen-hole golf course in America is in Chicago?

QUESTION: Is that right?

QUESTION: I'm sure we'd love to have you there.

BILL CLINTON: July sixteenth through twentieth?

QUESTION: Yes.

QUESTION: We're also having an election, so be careful which day you come. [Laughter]

QUESTION: Mr. President, you said you wanted to use facts. What three facts, off the top of your head, would you use to try to explode the myths that white Americans have of African Americans? Is there any that come to mind, if you had to pick three?

BILL CLINTON: Most people on welfare are white, not black. Most black people work. Most poor people work. And I would—there's a lot of things. There was a young journalist—or a scholar—who wrote a whole book on myths about black America. Do you remember that book?

QUESTION: Oh, yes.

BILL CLINTON: Sabrina Young. I got that—it's a fabulous book. I want to start with that. It's terrific. But one of the things that we know is that public opinion is impervious to evidence, but not necessarily because of bigotry. [Laughter]

No, no, let me give you an example. One of the reasons we lost the Congress in '94 is the public bought two myths. One was my 1993 economic plan raised everybody's income taxes, which it didn't. It raised income taxes on only the top 1.2 percent of the American people. The people believe politicians always raise taxes on everybody. Two was that nothing good was happening in the economy, which was also untrue. We'd also had big, heavy growth in '93 and good growth in '94. But it took more than a year and a half of that kind of growth for people to feel it. So that by mid '95—two and a half years later—everybody was saying, yes, Clinton's doing a good job on the economy. Meanwhile, we had all these people who lost their seats in Congress because the perception didn't catch up to the reality.

I'll give you another example. We just had the biggest drop in crime in thirty-six years reported for 1995—or 1996. If you took a poll, I would bet you my child's college education that if you asked people, did the crime rate go down or up last year, 55 to 65 percent of the people would say, it went up. And no more than 20 percent of the people would say it went down. That does not mean that people are stupid. They're not stupid, but they don't live by statistics. We all live by perceptions, by our feelings, by our own apprehension.

So one of the things that we can do at this convention is we can jump-start—we can save lots of time for millions of Americans. If they really will focus on this and trust this, we can get rid of a lot of these misperceptions in a much quicker time frame than we could if we had to do it coffee table by coffee table. We can, in that sense, reinforce what all these groups you talked about are doing.

You know, it's not all about race. If you took a crime poll, I bet you anything that's what people would say.

QUESTION: Thank you very much.

CHAPTER 10

A Race Man in the White House

Bill Clinton was not the first black president. That title properly belongs to the first man or woman of African descent who someday manages to rise to this nation's highest political office. The chance of that happening any time soon is not very good. Race still matters in this country largely in ways that are subtle, but no less venomous to the threadbare proposition that we live in a colorblind society.

Since it is, of course, no accident of history that all forty-three of this nation's presidents have been white men, it would be a grievous mistake to misidentify any of them—no matter their closeness to African Americans—as being a person of color. The mere suggestion that a white man could be considered even an "honorary" black must cause the earth around James Baldwin's casket to tremble like a volcano about to erupt.

"I have often wondered, and it is not a pleasant wonder, just what white Americans talk about with one another," Baldwin wrote in a 1965 article for *Ebony* magazine that was reprinted in his book *The Price of the Ticket*. "I wonder this because they do not, after all, seem to find very much to say to me, and I concluded long ago that they found the color of my skin inhibiting. This color seems to operate as a most disagreeable mirror, and a great deal of one's energy is expended in reassuring white Americans that they do not see what they see.

"This is utterly futile, of course, since they do see what they see.

233

And what they see is an appallingly oppressive and bloody history known all over the world. What they see is a disastrous, continuing, present condition which menaces them, and for which they bear an inescapable responsibility. But since in the main they seem to lack the energy to change this condition they would rather not be reminded of it," Baldwin wrote.

What impresses me about Bill Clinton is that he does not view black skin as a "disagreeable mirror." More to the point, he has shown a greater willingness than any other president to look African Americans in the eye not with condescension, as Les Payne points out, but with an uncommon sense of fairness. Any black person who spends time with Clinton notices a palpable absence of the discomfort far too many whites display when they have more than a fleeting conversation with an African American.

Clinton seems to relish such talks. In the three lengthy conversations that I've had with him—twice in the White House and once in the Harlem office he moved to after he left the presidency—Clinton extended the meetings beyond their scheduled ending and dove into discussions about this nation's racial problems. In each of these exchanges, he listened as much as he talked—and he seemed to give as much weight to the ideas expressed by African Americans as he did his own views. While this might strike some as a common courtesy, it is actually rare behavior for many white public officials and rarer still for occupants of the Oval Office.

Bill Clinton not only opened his mind, but also his administration, to black people. He confronted this nation's most intractable problem—that of equal opportunity—head on by naming an unprecedented number of African Americans to senior positions in the executive branch of government. No president before or after him has come close to empowering so many black folks. And no other president has claimed a black man as his best friend, as Clinton does Vernon Jordan.

Clinton's harshest black critics view him in a vacuum. They judge him against little more than a wish list of black goals and objectives. Seen in this way, he is vulnerable to sharp attack for the welfare reform and crime bills he signed into law, for his conflicting positions on the disparate treatment of persons convicted of crack and powder cocaine offenses and for not standing by Lani Guinier when she came under attack by conservative Republicans. But when viewed in the context of a broader array of issues—and the political backdrop of the 1990s— Clinton is catapulted onto the short list of the best presidents for African Americans. And that is exactly where he belongs.

Clinton deserves to be ranked alongside Abraham Lincoln and Lyndon Johnson as a president who advanced the standing of African Americans more than any of this nation's other chief executives. Lincoln's Emancipation Proclamation, while it freed virtually no slaves, set the stage for the Thirteenth Amendment that ended slavery. In the 1960s, a decade defined largely by violent resistance to the push by African Americans for civil rights, Johnson won passage of the most important civil rights legislation in a century.

By the time Clinton took office the campaign for legal recognition of the claim by African Americans for racial equality had been won. But the fight to turn that legal right into an everyday reality was stuck in second gear. In the 1990s some of this nation's largest corporations reached out-of-court settlements of lawsuits that accused them of racial discrimination against their black employees or customers. The nation's public schools were nearly as racially divided by choice as they had been by law before the Supreme Court's 1954 decision that outlawed school segregation. The widespread housing discrimination of the 1960s had given way to mortgage redlining and predatory lending practices that created new barriers to black homeownership. It was against this backdrop that Clinton entered the presidency in 1992. He not only talked racial equality, he practiced it. He named six African Americans to his cabinet. His predecessor had one; his successor has just two.

Clinton transformed the look of official Washington. He named African Americans to top positions in virtually every federal agency; appointed more black judges than Richard Nixon, Ronald Reagan, and George Bush combined. When he was in the White House, social events at 1600 Pennsylvania Avenue had the look of a racial melting pot.

Clinton's appointment of African Americans to key positions and his high-profile inclusion of them in the social life of his administration won him widespread support in black America—and over-shadowed his failures. While his job approval rating among whites fluctuated between 48 and 70 percent between November 1997 and January 2001, it ranged from a low of 78 percent to a high of 97 percent among African Americans during that same period, according to polls done by the Gallup Organization

Clinton's black critics say this strong show of black support was due more to style than substance. They argue that while he was naming record numbers of African Americans to positions in his administration, the number of blacks in the criminal justice system grew at a far greater rate. This was due in large measure to the Crime Bill he signed in 1994, they contend. That legislation expanded the use of the death penalty for federal offenses, it instituted a "three strikes" law that mandated a life sentence for people convicted for three felonies and authorized nearly $10 billion for prison construction. But as harsh as the law was, it had little impact on the growth in this nation's prison population during Clinton's presidency. For example, between 1993 and 1997, the last year for which this data is available, the number of African Americans who were under control of the criminal justice system (incarcerated, on probation, parole or supervised release) climbed from 2,011,600 million to 2,149,900. But the vast majority of these people were under the supervision of state and local corrections officials, not the federal government. They were arrested, tried, and convicted for violations of state laws, not provisions of the federal crime bill. Just 43,844 African Americans were federal prisoners in 1997.

The 1996 Welfare Reform Act that Clinton signed is more problematic. Since its passage the nation's welfare rolls have been cut from twelve to six million people. Three-fourths of the women questioned in 1999 as part of a tracking sample of former welfare recipients had incomes below the federal poverty line. "The longer they had been off welfare, the less likely they were to have health insurance for themselves or their children," Harvard professor William Julius Wilson and Professor Andrew J. Cherlin, of Johns Hopkins University, wrote in a July 2001 article in the *New York Times*.

The welfare bill Clinton signed in the summer of 1996 was the third one the Republican dominated Congress sent him. He vetoed the first two and expressed some misgivings about the one that he eventually signed. "I want to be clear, some parts of this bill still go too far and I am determined to see that those areas are corrected," Clinton said at a press conference shortly before he signed the welfare reform bill. His decision to do so was no doubt rooted as much in presidential politics as in his tug-of-war with the Republican-controlled Congress. Three months after Clinton signed the welfare reform bill he was elected to a second term. In 1992 he campaigned as a centrist Democrat. Four years later his appeal to middle-of-the-road voters was strengthened by the welfare reform and crime bills.

While some, but by no means most, African Americans consider those laws anathema to their interests, many seem to understand, as Betty Baye said, that the very existence of African Americans in this country "has been a series of negotiations" and this legislation was part of the "give and take" of the political process. During the twelve years that Republicans held the presidency prior to Clinton's election, the political process in Washington was nearly all "take" and no "give" for African Americans.

Had Clinton campaigned for the presidency in 1992 on the liberal platform that many of his black critics advocated, George Bush almost certainly would have been reelected. Had Clinton run on those issues in 1996 there's a good chance he would have been defeated by Bob Dole. Either outcome would have been a bigger disaster for African Americans than the crime and welfare bills.

With Clinton in the White House the Republican assault on affirmative action was turned back, more than sixty African Americans received lifetime appointments as federal judges, black unemployment fell sharply, black homeownership and the number of black-owned businesses rose to record levels. Even more important, African Americans got to play the game of Washington politics as never before. By naming so many African Americans to positions in his administration, Clinton moved black folks off of the sidelines and onto the playing field. He also did more than any other president to keep black issues on the nation's radar scope.

"In recent weeks, every one of us has been made aware of a simple truth—white America and black America often see the same world in drastically different ways," Clinton said in a speech he gave on October 16, 1995, the day of the Million Man March. "The two worlds we see now each contain both truth and distortion. Both black and white Americans must face this, for honesty is the only gateway to the many acts of reconciliation that will unite our worlds at last into one America.

"White America must understand and acknowledge the roots of black pain. It began with unequal treatment first in law and later in fact. African Americans indeed have lived too long with a justice system that in too many cases has been and continues to be less than just. The record of abuses extends from lynchings and trumped up charges to false arrests and police brutality. The tragedies of Emmett Till and Rodney King are bloody markers on the very same road," Clinton said.

Two years later in another major address on race Clinton again talked frankly about that which most of his predecessors tried mightily to duck: this nation's gnawing race problem.

"The ideals that bind us together are as old as our nation, but so are the forces that pull us apart," he said in a June 14, 1997, commencement address at the University of California at San Diego. "Our founders sought to form a more perfect union; the humility and hope of that phrase is the story of America and it is our mission today.

"Consider this: We were born with a Declaration of Independence which asserted that we were all created equal and a Constitution that enshrined slavery. We fought a bloody civil war to abolish slavery and preserve the union, but we remained a house divided and unequal by law for another century."

It was in this speech that Clinton announced his "One America" initiative, which he said would be "an unprecedented conversation about race." Clinton hoped his initiative, which was chaired by John Hope Franklin, a distinguished black scholar and historian, would tear down the wall of misunderstanding between whites and African Americans and build bridges of understanding. That didn't happen for a lot of reasons, not the least of which were the deeply ingrained and starkly different views that black and white Americans have on racial issues.

A 1996 survey by the National Opinion Research Center found that while two-thirds of African Americans believed the federal government was spending too little money on assistance to needy blacks, less than one in five whites agreed. Five years later that gap persisted. The *Washington Post* reported in July 2001 that 52 percent of whites believe that too much attention is paid to racial issues, while 64 percent of African Americans said just the opposite. This result was gleaned from a survey by the *Post*, the Henry J. Kaiser Family Foundation, and Harvard University, which also found that 40 to 60 percent of whites think blacks are faring as well as whites in the areas of education, income, employment, and access to health care. In fact, the *Post* reported, although some progress has been made, African Americans lag far behind whites in all of these areas.

As much as he tried Clinton couldn't overcome this perceptual barrier to racial progress. But the fact remains that he made an effort. Given the history of how this nation's presidents have dealt with African Americans—and how they distanced themselves from black issues—Clinton deserves both praise and credit for what he attempted to get done with his race initiative.

When viewed in context, Clinton's presidency was the best of times for African Americans. He did more for us than every president but Lyndon Johnson. He did more with us than any of the forty-two other white men who made it into the Oval Office. It's understandable that some people would look at what Clinton did for African Americans during his presidency and brand him a "blue-eyed soul brother." But that actually diminishes the significance of his efforts. Clinton is a white man unlike any other who has risen to the highest position of power in this country. He understands the roots of America's racial problems like few others do—and he tried harder than any other president to make race less of a factor in our lives.

Bill Clinton was not the first black president, but in the long line of white men who ascended to this nation's presidency, he was the next best thing.

CHAPTER 11

A Drum Major for Change

Presidents are often remembered, if not defined, by a speech. George Washington's farewell address signaled the willingness of this nation's first head of state to permit a peaceful transfer of power—a practice that has made our political system the envy of much of the rest of the world. Abraham Lincoln's Gettysburg Address, which was scribbled on the back of an envelope and delivered in less than five minutes, has become a moving testament to his great sense of humanity and his strongly held belief in a "government of the people, by the people, for the people."

As World War I drew to an end, Woodrow Wilson's "Fourteen Points" speech to a joint session of Congress on January 8, 1918, laid out a broad range of principles about relations between nations that became the basic tenets of international relations—and disputes—during the twentieth century. But it is probably best remembered for its call for the creation of "a general association of nations" that came to be known as the League of Nations, the forerunner of the United Nations. Twenty-three years later Franklin Delano Roosevelt addressed a joint session of Congress a day after the Japanese attacked Pearl Harbor on December 7, 1941—which he called "a date which will live in infamy." Both that tragic event and his defiant speech helped etch Roosevelt's presidency into the annals of history.

In the spring of 1965, a week after Alabama state troopers and sheriff's deputies attacked Civil Rights demonstrators in Selma, Alabama, Lyndon Johnson went before a joint session of Congress and urged the federal lawmakers to pass the Voting Rights Act to help African Americans realize the right to vote.

"Their cause must be our cause too, because it is not just Negroes, but really it is all of us, who must overcome the crippling legacy of bigotry and injustice. And we shall overcome," Johnson said, invoking the mantra of the Civil Rights movement. His speech, and the public support it generated for the legislation, helped win passage of the Voting Rights Act and endeared Johnson to millions of African Americans.

On August 8, 1974, Richard Nixon gave a televised address from the White House to announce his resignation in the wake of revelations that he tried to cover up the role of Republican Party operatives in the break-in of the Democratic National Committee's office during the 1972 presidential campaign. Nixon's resignation speech was as affirming for this nation's democracy as was the one George Washington gave 178 years earlier.

During the eight years he spent in the White House, Bill Clinton gave hundreds of speeches. Four of them appear on the following pages. These addresses are a window onto Clinton's thinking about race: his embrace of affirmative action, his shame for the abuses of the Jim Crow era and his hope for a time when this nation will be defined more by people's willingness to work for the common good than by the racial problems that have plagued it for nearly four hundred years.

Clinton Speeches and Administration Black Appointees

On Affirmative Action

My fellow Americans: In recent weeks I have began a conversation with the American people about our fate and our duty to prepare our nation not only to meet the new century, but to live and lead in a world transformed to a degree seldom seen in all of our history. Much of this change is good, but it is not all good, and all of us are affected by it. Therefore, we must reach beyond our fears and our divisions to a new time of great and common purpose.

Our challenge is twofold: first, to restore the American dream of opportunity and the American value of responsibility; and second, to bring our country together amid all our diversity into a stronger community, so that we can find common ground: and move forward as one.

More than ever these two endeavors are inseparable. I am absolutely convinced we cannot restore economic opportunity or solve our social problems unless we find a way to bring the American people together. To bring our people together we must openly and honestly deal with the issues that divide us. Today I want to discuss one of those issues: affirmative action.

It is, in a way, ironic that this issue should be divisive today, because affirmative action began twenty-five years ago by a Republican president with bipartisan support. It began simply as a means to an end of enduring national purpose: equal opportunity for all Americans.

So let us today trace the roots of affirmative action in our never-ending search for equal opportunity. Let us determine what it is and what it isn't. Let us see where it's worked and where it hasn't, and ask ourselves what we need to do now. Along the way, let us remember always that finding common ground as we move toward the twenty-first century depends fundamentally on our shared commitment to equal opportunity for all Americans. It is a moral imperative, a constitutional mandate, and a legal necessity.

There could be no better place for this discussion than the National Archives, for within these walls are America's bedrocks of our common ground: the Declaration of Independence, the Constitution, the Bill of Rights. No paper is as lasting as the words these documents contain. So we put them in these special cases to protect the parchment from the elements. No building is as solid as the principles these documents embody, but we sure tried to build one with these metal doors eleven inches thick to keep them safe, for these documents are America's only crown jewels. But the best place of all to hold these words and these principles is the one place in which they can never fade and never grow old—in the stronger chambers of our hearts.

Beyond all else, our country is a set of convictions: We hold these truths to be self-evident that all men are created equal; that they are endowed by their Creator with certain inalienable rights; that among these are life, liberty, and the pursuit of happiness.

Our whole history can be seen first as an effort to preserve these rights, and then as an effort to make them real in the lives of all our citizens. We know that from the beginning, there was a great gap between the plain meaning of our creed and the meaner reality of our daily lives. Back then, only white male property owners could vote. Black slaves were not even counted as whole people, and Native Americans were regarded as little more than an obstacle to our great national progress. No wonder Thomas Jefferson, reflecting on slavery, said he trembled to think God is just.

On the two hundredth anniversary of our great Constitution, Justice Thurgood Marshall, the grandson of a slave, said, "The government our founders devised was defective from the start, requiring several amendments, a civil war, and momentous social transformation to attain the system of constitutional government and its respect for the individual freedoms and human rights we hold as fundamental today."

Emancipation, women's suffrage, civil rights, voting rights, equal rights, the struggle for the rights of the disabled—all these and other struggles are milestones on America's often rocky, but fundamentally righteous journey to close the gap between the ideals enshrined in these treasures here in the National Archives and the reality of our daily lives.

I first came to this very spot where I'm standing today thirty-two years ago this month. I was a sixteen-year-old delegate to the American Legion Boys Nation. Now, that summer was a high-water mark for our national journey. That was the summer that President Kennedy ordered Alabama National Guardsmen to enforce a court order to allow two young blacks to enter the University of Alabama. As he told our nation, "Every American ought to have the right to be treated as he would wish to be treated; as one would wish his children to be treated."

Later that same summer, on the steps of the Lincoln Memorial, Martin Luther King told Americans of his dream that one day the sons of former slaves and the sons of former slave owners would sit down together at the table of brotherhood; that one day his four little children would be judged not by the color of their skin, but by the content of their character. His words captured the hearts and steeled the wills of millions of Americans. Some of them sang with him in the hot sun that day. Millions more, like me, listened and wept in the privacy of their homes.

It's hard to believe where we were just three decades ago. When I came up here to Boys Nation and we had this mock congressional session, I was one of only three or four southerners who would even vote for the civil rights plank. That's largely because of my family. My grandfather had a grade school education and ran a grocery store across the street from the cemetery in Hope, Arkansas, where my parents and my grandparents are buried. Most of his customers were black, were poor, and were working people. As a child in that store I saw that people of different races could treat each other with respect and dignity.

But I also saw that the black neighborhood across the street was the only one in town where the streets weren't paved. And when I returned to that neighborhood in the late '60s to see a woman who had cared for me as a toddler, the streets still weren't paved. A lot of you know that I am an ardent moviegoer. As a child I never went to a movie where I could sit next to a black American. They were always sitting upstairs.

In the 1960s, believe it or not, there were still a few courthouse squares in my state where the rest rooms were marked "white" and "colored." I graduated from a segregated high school seven years after President Eisenhower integrated Little Rock Central High School. And when President Kennedy barely carried my home state in 1960, the poll tax system was still alive and well there.

Even though my grandparents were in a minority, being poor, southern whites who were pro–civil rights, I think most other people knew better than to think the way they did. And those who were smart enough to act differently, discovered a lesson that we ought to remember today: Discrimination is not just morally wrong, it hurts everybody.

In 1960, Atlanta, Georgia, in reaction to all the things that were going on all across the South, adopted the motto, "The city too busy to hate." And however imperfectly over the years, they tried to live by it. I am convinced that Atlanta's success—it now is home to more foreign corporations than any other American city, and one year from today it will begin to host the Olympics—that that success all began when people got too busy to hate.

The lesson we learned was a hard one. When we allow people to pit us against one another or spend energy denying opportunity based on our differences, everyone is held back. But when we give all Americans a chance to develop and use their talents, to be full partners in our common enterprise, then everybody is pushed forward.

My experiences with discrimination are rooted in the South and in the legacy slavery left. I also lived with a working mother and a working grandmother when women's work was far rarer and far more circumscribed than it is today. But we all know there are millions of other stories—those of Hispanics, Asian Americans, Native Americans, people with disabilities, others against whom fingers have been pointed. Many of you have your own stories, and that's why you're here today; people who were denied the right to develop and use their full human potential. And their progress, too, is a part of our journey to make the reality of America consistent with the principles just behind me here.

Thirty years ago in this city, you didn't see many people of color or women making their way to work in the morning in business clothes, or serving in substantial numbers in powerful positions in Congress or at the White House, or making executive decisions every day in businesses. In fact, even the employment want ads were divided, men on one side and women on the other.

It was extraordinary then to see women or people of color as television news anchors or, believe it or not, even in college sports. There were far fewer women or minorities as job supervisors, or firefighters, or police officers, or doctors, or lawyers, or college professors, or in many other jobs that offer stability and honor and integrity to family life.

A lot has changed, and it did not happen as some sort of random evolutionary drift. It took hard work and sacrifices and countless acts of courage and conscience by millions of Americans. It took the political courage and statesmanship of Democrats and Republicans alike, the vigilance and compassion of courts and advocates in and out of government committed to the Constitution and to equal protection and to equal opportunity. It took the leadership of people in business who knew that in the end we would all be better. It took the leadership of people in labor unions who knew that working people had to be reconciled.

Some people, like Congressman Lewis there, put their lives on the line. Other people lost their lives. And millions of Americans changed their own lives and put hate behind them. As a result, today all our lives are better. Women have become a major force in business and political life, and far more able to contribute to their families' incomes. A true and growing black middle class has emerged. Higher education has literally been revolutionized, with women and racial and ethnic minorities attending once overwhelmingly white and sometimes all-male schools.

In communities across our nation police departments now better reflect the makeup of those whom they protect. A generation of professionals now serve as role models for young women and minority youth. Hispanics and newer immigrant populations are succeeding in making America stronger.

For an example of where the best of our future lies just think about our space program and the stunning hookup with the Russian space station this month. Let's remember that that program, the world's finest, began with heroes like Alan Shepard and Senator John Glenn, but today it's had American heroes like Sally Ride, Ellen Ochoa, Leroy Child, Guy Bluford and other outstanding, completely qualified women and minorities.

How did this happen? Fundamentally, because we opened our hearts and minds and changed our ways. But not without pressure—the pressure of court decisions, legislation, executive action, and the power of examples in the public and private sector. Along the way we learned that laws alone do not change society; that old habits and thinking patterns are deeply ingrained and die hard; that more is required to really open the doors of opportunity. Our search to find ways to move more quickly to equal opportunity led to the development of what we now call affirmative action.

The purpose of affirmative action is to give our nation a way to finally address the systemic exclusion of individuals of talent on the basis of their gender or race from opportunities to develop, perform, achieve, and contribute. Affirmative action is an effort to develop a systematic approach to open the doors of education, employment, and business development opportunities to qualified individuals who happen to be members of groups that have experienced long-standing and persistent discrimination.

It is a policy that grew out of many years of trying to navigate between two unacceptable pasts. One was to say simply that we declared discrimination illegal and that's enough. We saw that that way still relegated blacks with college degrees to jobs as railroad porters, and kept women with degrees under a glass ceiling with a lower paycheck.

The other path was simply to try to impose change by leveling draconian penalties on employers who didn't meet certain imposed, ultimately arbitrary, and sometimes unachievable quotas. That, too, was rejected out of a sense of fairness.

So a middle ground was developed that would change an inequitable status quo gradually, but firmly, by building the pool of qualified applicants for college, for contracts, for jobs, and giving more people the chance to learn, work, and earn. When affirmative action is done right, it is flexible, it is fair, and it works.

I know some people are honestly concerned about the times affirmative action doesn't work, when it's done in the wrong way. And I know there are times when some employers don't use it in the right way. They may cut corners and treat a flexible goal as a quota. They may give opportunities to people who are unqualified instead of those who deserve it. They may, in so doing, allow a different kind of discrimination. When this happens, it is also wrong. But it isn't affirmative action, and it is not legal.

So when our administration finds cases of that sort, we will enforce the law aggressively. The Justice Department files hundreds of cases every year, attacking discrimination in employment, including suits on behalf of white males. Most of these suits, however, affect women and minorities for a simple reason—because the vast majority of discrimination in America is still discrimination against them. But the law does require fairness for everyone and we are determined to see that that is exactly what the law delivers.

Let me be clear about what affirmative action must not mean and what I won't allow it to be. It does not mean, and I don't favor, the unjustified preference of the unqualified over the qualified of any race or gender. It doesn't mean, and I don't favor, numerical quotas. It doesn't mean, and I don't favor, rejection or selection of any employee or student solely on the basis of race or gender without regard to merit.

Like many business executives and public servants, I owe it to you to say that my views on this subject are, more than anything else, the product of my personal experience. I have had experience with affirmative action, nearly twenty years of it now, and I know it works.

When I was attorney general of my home state, I hired a record number of women and African-American lawyers, every one clearly qualified and exceptionally hardworking. As governor, I appointed more women to my cabinet and state boards than any other governor in the state's history, and more African Americans than all the governors in the state's history combined. And no one ever questioned their qualifications or performance. And our state was better and stronger because of their service.

As president, I am proud to have the most diverse administration in history in my cabinet, my agencies, and my staff. And I must say, I have been surprised at the criticism I have received from some quarters in my determination to achieve this.

In the last two and a half years, the most outstanding example of affirmative action in the United States, the Pentagon, has opened 260,000 positions for women who serve in our Armed Forces. I have appointed more women and minorities to the federal bench than any other president, more than the last two combined. And yet, far more of our judicial appointments have received the highest rating from the American Bar Association than any other administration since those ratings have been given.

In our administration many government agencies are doing more business with qualified firms run by minorities and women. The Small Business Administration has reduced its budget by 40 percent, doubled its loan outputs, dramatically increased the number of loans to women and minority small-business people, without reducing the number of loans to white business owners who happen to be male, and without changing the loan standards for a single, solitary application. Quality and diversity can go hand in hand, and they must.

Let me say that affirmative action has also done more than just open the doors of opportunity to individual Americans. Most economists who study it agree that affirmative action has also been an important part of closing gaps in economic opportunity in our society, thereby strengthening the entire economy.

A group of distinguished business leaders told me just a couple of days ago that their companies are stronger and their profits are larger because of the diversity and the excellence of their workforces achieved through intelligent and fair affirmative action programs. And they said we have gone far beyond anything the government might require us to do because managing diversity and individual opportunity and being fair to everybody is the key to our future economic success in the global marketplace.

Now, there are those who say, my fellow Americans, that even good affirmative action programs are no longer needed; that it should be enough to resort to the courts or the Equal Employment Opportunity Commission in cases of actual, provable, individual discrimination because there is no longer any systematic discrimination in our society. In deciding how to answer that let us consider the facts.

The unemployment rate for African Americans remains about twice that of whites. The Hispanic rate is still much higher. Women have narrowed the earnings gap, but still make only 72 percent as much as men do for comparable jobs. The average income for an Hispanic woman with a college degree is still less than the average income of a white man with a high school diploma.

According to the recently completed Glass Ceiling Report, sponsored by Republican members of Congress, in the nation's largest companies only six-tenths of one percent of senior management positions are held by African Americans, four-tenths of a percent by Hispanic Americans, three-tenths of a percent by Asian Americans; women hold between 3 and 5 percent of these positions. White males make up 43 percent of our workforce but hold 95 percent of these jobs.

Just last week, the Chicago Federal Reserve Bank reported that black home loan applicants are more than twice as likely to be denied credit as whites with the same qualifications; and that Hispanic applicants are more than one and a half times as likely to be denied loans as whites with the same qualifications.

Last year alone the federal government received more than 90,000 complaints of employment discrimination based on race, ethnicity, or gender. Less than 3 percent were for reverse discrimination.

Evidence abounds in other ways of the persistence of the kind of bigotry that can affect the way we think even if we're not conscious of it, in hiring and promotion and business and educational decisions.

Crimes and violence based on hate against Asians, Hispanics, African Americans, and other minorities are still with us. And, I'm sorry to say, that the worst and most recent evidence of this involves a recent report of federal law enforcement officials in Tennessee attending an event literally overflowing with racism, a sickening reminder of just how pervasive these kinds of attitudes still are.

By the way, I want to tell you that I am committed to finding the truth about what happened there and to taking appropriate action. And I want to say that if anybody who works in federal law enforcement thinks that that kind of behavior is acceptable, they ought to think about working someplace else.

Now, let's get to the other side of the argument. If affirmative action has worked and if there is evidence that discrimination still exists on a wide scale in ways that are conscious and unconscious, then why should we get rid of it as many people are urging? Some question the effectiveness or the fairness of particular affirmative action programs. I say to all of you, those are fair questions, and they prompted the review of our affirmative action programs, about which I will talk in a few moments.

Some question the fundamental purpose of the effort. There are people who honestly believe that affirmative action always amounts to group preferences over individual merit; that affirmative action always leads to reverse discrimination; that ultimately, therefore, it demeans those who benefit from it and discriminates against those who are not helped by it.

I just have to tell you that all of you have to decide how you feel about that, and all of our fellow countrymen and women have to decide as well. But I believe if there are no quotas, if we give no opportunities to unqualified people, if we have no reverse discrimination, and if, when the problem ends, the program ends, that criticism is wrong. That's what I believe. But we should have this debate and everyone should ask the question.

Now let's deal with what I really think is behind so much of this debate today. There are a lot of people who oppose affirmative action today who supported it for a very long time. I believe they are responding to the sea change in the experiences that most Americans have in the world in which we live. If you say now you're against affirmative action because the government is using its power or the private sector is using its power to help minorities at the expense of the majority, that gives you a way of explaining away the economic distress that a majority of Americans honestly feel. It gives you a way of turning their resentment against the minorities or against a particular government program, instead of having an honest debate about how we all got into the fix we're in and what we're all going to do together to get out of it.

That explanation, the affirmative action explanation for the fix we're in, is just wrong. It is just wrong. Affirmative action did not cause the great economic problems of the American middle class. And because most minorities or women are either members of that middle class or people who are poor who are struggling to get into it, we must also admit that affirmative action alone won't solve the problems of minorities and women who seek to be a part of the American Dream. To do that, we have to have an economic strategy that reverses the decline in wages and the growth of poverty among working people. Without that, women, minorities, and white males will all be in trouble in the future.

But it is wrong to use the anxieties of the middle class to divert the American people from the real causes of their economic distress, the sweeping historic changes taking all the globe in its path, and the specific policies or lack of them in our own country which have aggravated those challenges. It is simply wrong to play politics with the issue of affirmative action and divide our country at a time when, if we're really going to change things, we have to be united.

I must say, I think it is ironic that some of those, not all, but some of those who call for an end to affirmative action also advocate policies which will make the real economic problems of the anxious middle class even worse. They talk about opportunity and being for equal opportunity for everyone; and then they reduce investment in equal opportunity on an evenhanded basis. For example, if the real goal is economic opportunity for all Americans, why in the world would we reduce our investment in education from Head Start to affordable college loans? Why don't we make college loans available to every American instead?

If the real goal is empowering all middle-class Americans and empowering poor people to work their way into the middle class without regard to race or gender, why in the world would the people who advocate that turn around and raise taxes on our poorest working families, or reduce the money available for education and training when they lose their jobs or they're living on poverty wages, or increase the cost of housing for lower-income working people with children?

Why would we do that? If we're going to empower America, we have to do more than talk about it; we have to do it. And we surely have learned that we cannot empower all Americans by a simple strategy of taking opportunity away from some Americans.

So to those who use this as a political strategy to divide us, we must say, no. We must say, no. But to those who raise legitimate questions about the way affirmative action works, or who raise the larger question about the genuine problems and anxieties of all the American people and their sense of being left behind and treated unfairly, we must say, yes, you are entitled to answers to your questions. We must say yes to that.

Now, that's why I ordered this review of all of our affirmative action programs—a review to look at the facts, not the politics of affirmative action. This review concluded that affirmative action remains a useful tool for widening economic and educational opportunity. The model used by the military, the Army in particular—and I'm delighted to have the Commanding General of the Army here today because he set such a fine example—has been especially successful because it emphasizes education and training, ensuring that it has a wide pool of qualified candidates for every level of promotion. That approach has given us the most racially diverse and best-qualified military in our history. There are more opportunities for women and minorities there than ever before. And now there are over fifty generals and admirals who are Hispanic, Asian, or African Americans.

We found that the Education Department had programs targeted on underrepresented minorities that do a great deal of good with the tiniest of investments. We found that these programs comprised forty cents of every $1,000 in the Education Department's budget.

Now, college presidents will tell you that the education their schools offer actually benefit from diversity—colleges where young people get the education and make the personal and professional contacts that will shape their lives. If their colleges look like the world they're going to live and work in, and they learn from all different kinds of people things that they can't learn in books, our systems of higher education are stronger.

Still, I believe every child needs the chance to go to college. Every child. That means every child has to have a chance to get affordable and repayable college loans, Pell Grants for poor kids and a chance to do things like join AmeriCorps and work their way through school. Every child is entitled to that. That is not an argument against affirmative action; it's an argument for more opportunity for more Americans until everyone is reached.

As I said a moment ago, the review found that the Small Business Administration last year increased loans to minorities by over two-thirds, loans to women by over 80 percent, did not decrease loans to white men, and not a single loan went to an unqualified person. People who never had a chance before to be part of the American system of free enterprise now have it. No one was hurt in the process. That made America stronger.

This review also found that the executive order on employment practices of large federal contractors also has helped to bring more fairness and inclusion into the workforce.

Since President Nixon was here in my job, America has used goals and timetables to preserve opportunity and to prevent discrimination, to urge businesses to set higher expectations for themselves, and to realize those expectations. But we did not and we will not use rigid quotas to mandate outcomes.

We also looked at the way we award procurement contracts under the programs known as "set-asides." There's no question that these programs have helped to build up firms owned by minorities and women, who historically had been excluded from the old boy networks in these areas. It has helped a new generation of entrepreneurs to flourish, opening new paths to self-reliance and an economic growth in which all of us ultimately share. Because of the set-asides, businesses ready to compete have had a chance to compete, a chance they would not have otherwise had.

But as with any government program, set-asides can be misapplied, misused, even intentionally abused. There are critics who exploit that fact as an excuse to abolish all these programs, regardless of their effects. I believe they are wrong, but I also believe, based on our factual review, we clearly need some reform. So first, we should crack down on those who take advantage of everyone else through fraud and abuse. We must crack down on fronts and pass-throughs, people who pretend to be eligible for these programs and aren't. That is wrong.

We also, in offering new businesses a leg up, must make sure that the set-asides go to businesses that need them most. We must really look and make sure that our standard for eligibility is fair and defensible. We have to tighten the requirement to move businesses out of programs once they've had a fair opportunity to compete. The graduation requirement must mean something; it must mean graduation. There should be no permanent set-aside for any company.

Second, we must, and we will, comply with the Supreme Court's Adarand decision of last month. Now, in particular, that means focusing set-aside programs on particular regions and business sectors where the problems of discrimination or exclusion are provable and are clearly requiring affirmative action. I have directed the attorney general and the agencies to move forward with compliance with Adarand expeditiously.

But I also want to emphasize that the Adarand decision did not dismantle affirmative action and did not dismantle set-asides. In fact, while setting stricter standards to mandate reform of affirmative action, it actually reaffirmed the need for affirmative action and reaffirmed the continuing existence of systematic discrimination in the United States.

What the Supreme Court ordered the federal government to do was to meet the same, more rigorous, standard for affirmative action programs that state and local governments were ordered to meet several years ago. And the best set-aside programs under that standard have been challenged and have survived.

Third, beyond discrimination we need to do more to help disadvantaged people and distressed communities, no matter what their race or gender. There are places in our country where the free enterprise system simply doesn't reach. It simply isn't working to provide jobs and opportunity. Disproportionately, these areas in urban and rural America are highly populated by racial minorities, but not entirely. To make this initiative work, I believe the government must become a better partner for people in places in urban and rural America that are caught in a cycle of poverty. And I believe we have to find ways to get the private sector to assume their rightful role as a driver of economic growth.

It has always amazed me that we have given incentives to our businesspeople to help to develop poor economies in other parts of the world, our neighbors in the Caribbean, our neighbors in other parts of the world. I have supported this, when not subject to their own abuses, but we ignore the biggest source of economic growth available to the American economy, the poor economies isolated within the United States of America.

There are those who say, well, even if we made the jobs available people wouldn't work. They haven't tried. Most of the people in disadvantaged communities work today, and most of them who don't work have a very strong desire to do so. In central Harlem, fourteen people apply for every single minimum-wage job opening. Think how many more would apply if there were good jobs with a good future.

Our job is to connect disadvantaged people and disadvantaged communities to economic opportunity so that everybody who wants to work can do so.

We've been working at this through our empowerment zones and community development banks, through the initiative of Secretary Cisneros of the Housing and Urban Development Department, and many other things that we have tried to do to put capital where it is needed. And now I have asked Vice President Gore to develop a proposal to use our contracting to support businesses that locate themselves in these distressed areas or hire a large percentage of their workers from these areas—not to substitute for what we're doing in affirmative action, but to supplement it, to go beyond it, to do something that will help to deal with the economic crisis of America. We want to make our procurement system more responsive to people in these areas who need help.

My fellow Americans, affirmative action has to be made consistent with our highest ideals of personal responsibility and merit, and our urgent need to find common ground and to prepare all Americans to compete in the global economy of the next century.

Today, I am directing all our agencies to comply with the Supreme Court's Adarand decision, and also to apply the four standards of fairness to all our affirmative action programs that I have already articulated: No quotas in theory or practice; no illegal discrimination of any kind, including reverse discrimination; no preference for people who are not qualified for any job or other opportunity; and as soon as a program has succeeded, it must be retired. Any program that doesn't meet these four principles must be eliminated or reformed to meet them.

But let me be clear: Affirmative action has been good for America.

Affirmative action has not always been perfect, and affirmative action should not go on forever. It should be changed now to take care of those things that are wrong, and it should be retired when its job is done. I am resolved that that day will come. But the evidence suggests, indeed, screams, that that day has not come.

The job of ending discrimination in this country is not over. That should not be surprising. We had slavery for centuries before the passage of the Thirteenth, Fourteenth, and Fifteenth Amendments. We waited another hundred years for the civil rights legislation. Women have had the vote less than a hundred years. We have always had difficulty with these things, as most societies do. But we are making more progress than many people.

Based on the evidence, the job is not done. So here is what I think we should do. We should reaffirm the principle of affirmative action and fix the practices. We should have a simple slogan: Mend it, but don't end it.

Let me ask all Americans, whether they agree or disagree with what I have said today, to see this issue in the larger context of our times. President Lincoln said, we cannot escape our history. We cannot escape our future, either. And that future must be one in which every American has the chance to live up to his or her God given capacities.

The new technology, the instant communications, the explosion of global commerce have created enormous opportunities and enormous anxieties for Americans. In the last two and a half years, we have seen seven million new jobs, more millionaires and new businesses than ever before, high corporate profits, and a booming stock market. Yet, most Americans are working harder for the same or lower pay. And they feel more insecurity about their jobs, their retirement, their health care, and their children's education. Too many of our children are clearly exposed to poverty and welfare, violence and drugs.

These are the great challenges for our whole country on the home front at the dawn of the twenty-first century. We've got to find the wisdom and the will to create family wage jobs for all the people who want to work; to open the door of college to all Americans; to strengthen families and reduce the awful problems to which our children are exposed; to move poor Americans from welfare to work.

This is the work of our administration, to give the people the tools they need to make the most of their own lives, to give families and communities the tools they need to solve their own problems. But let us not forget affirmative action didn't cause these problems. And getting rid of affirmative action certainly won't solve them.

If properly done, affirmative action can help us come together, go forward, and grow together. It is in our moral, legal, and practical interest to see that every person can make the most of his life. In the fight for the future, we need all hands on deck and some of those hands still need a helping hand.

In our national community we're all different, we're all the same. We want liberty and freedom. We want the embrace of family and community. We want to make the most of our own lives and we're determined to give our children a better one. Today there are voices of division who would say forget all that. Don't you dare. Remember we're still closing the gap between our founders' ideals and our reality. But every step along the way has made us richer, stronger, and better. And the best is yet to come.

Thank you very much, and God bless you.

In Apology for Tuskegee
Study on Black Men

THE WHITE HOUSE
MAY 16, 1997

Ladies and gentlemen, on Sunday Mr. Shaw will celebrate his ninety-fifth birthday. [Applause] I would like to recognize the other survivors who are here today and their families: Mr. Charlie Pollard is here. [Applause] Mr. Carter Howard. [Applause] Mr. Fred Simmons. [Applause] Mr. Simmons just took his first airplane ride, and he reckons he's about 110 years old, so I think it's time for him to take a chance or two. [Laughter] I'm glad he did. And Mr. Frederick Moss, thank you, sir. [Applause]

I would also like to ask three family representatives who are here—Sam Doner is represented by his daughter, Gwendolyn Cox. Thank you, Gwendolyn. [Applause] Ernest Hendon, who is watching in Tuskegee, is represented by his brother, North Hendon. Thank you, sir, for being here. [Applause] And George Key is represented by his grandson, Christopher Monroe. Thank you, Chris. [Applause]

I also acknowledge the families, community leaders, teachers, and students watching today by satellite from Tuskegee. The White House is the people's house; we are glad to have all of you here today. I thank Dr. David Satcher for his role in this. I thank Congresswoman Waters and Congressman Hilliard, Congressman Stokes, the entire Congressional Black Caucus, Dr. Satcher, members of the cabinet who are here, Secretary Herman, Secretary Slater. A great friend of freedom, Fred Gray, thank you for fighting this long battle all these long years.

The eight men who are survivors of the syphilis study at Tuskegee are a living link to a time not so very long ago that many Americans would prefer not to remember, but we dare not forget. It

261

was a time when our nation failed to live up to its ideals, when our nation broke the trust with our people that is the very foundation of our democracy. It is not only in remembering that shameful past that we can make amends and repair our nation, but it is in remembering that past that we can build a better present and a better future. And without remembering it, we cannot make amends and we cannot go forward.

So today America does remember the hundreds of men used in research without their knowledge and consent. We remember them and their family members. Men who were poor and African American, without resources and with few alternatives, they believed they had found hope when they were offered free medical care by the United States Public Health Service. They were betrayed.

Medical people are supposed to help when we need care, but even once a cure was discovered, they were denied help, and they were lied to by their government. Our government is supposed to protect the rights of its citizens; their rights were trampled upon. Forty years, hundreds of men betrayed, along with their wives and children, along with the community in Macon County, Alabama, the city of Tuskegee, the fine university there, and the larger African-American community.

The United States government did something that was wrong—deeply, profoundly, morally wrong. It was an outrage to our commitment to integrity and equality for all our citizens.

To the survivors, to the wives and family members, the children and the grandchildren, I say what you know: No power on Earth can give you back the lives lost, the pain suffered, the years of internal torment and anguish. What was done cannot be undone. But we can end the silence. We can stop turning our heads away. We can look at you in the eye and finally say on behalf of the American people, what the United States government did was shameful, and I am sorry. [Applause]

The American people are sorry—for the loss, for the years of hurt. You did nothing wrong, but you were grievously wronged. I apologize and I am sorry that this apology has been so long in coming. [Applause]

To Macon County, to Tuskegee, to the doctors who have been wrongly associated with the events there, you have our apology, as well. To our African-American citizens, I am sorry that your federal government orchestrated a study so clearly racist. That can never be allowed to happen again. It is against everything our country stands for and what we must stand against is what it was.

So let us resolve to hold forever in our hearts and minds the memory of a time not long ago in Macon County, Alabama, so that we can always see how adrift we can become when the rights of any citizens are neglected, ignored, and betrayed. And let us resolve here and now to move forward together.

The legacy of the study at Tuskegee has reached far and deep, in ways that hurt our progress and divide our nation. We cannot be one America when a whole segment of our nation has no trust in America. An apology is the first step, and we take it with a commitment to rebuild that broken trust. We can begin by making sure there is never again another episode like this one. We need to do more to ensure that medical research practices are sound and ethical, and that researchers work more closely with communities.

Today I would like to announce several steps to help us achieve these goals. First, we will help to build that lasting memorial at Tuskegee. [Applause] The school founded by Booker T. Washington, distinguished by the renowned scientist George Washington Carver and so many others who advanced the health and well-being of African Americans and all Americans, is a fitting site. The Department of Health and Human Services will award a planning grant so the school can pursue establishing a center for bioethics in research and health care. The center will serve as a museum of the study and support efforts to address its legacy and strengthen bioethics training.

Second, we commit to increase our community involvement so that we may begin restoring lost trust. The study at Tuskegee served to sow distrust of our medical institutions, especially where research is involved. Since the study was halted, abuses have been checked by making informed consent and local review mandatory in federally funded and mandated research.

Still, twenty-five years later, many medical studies have little African-American participation and African-American organ donors are few. This impedes efforts to conduct promising research and to provide the best health care to all our people, including African Americans. So today, I'm directing the secretary of Health and Human Services, Donna Shalala, to issue a report in 180 days about how we can best involve communities, especially minority communities, in research and health care. You must—every American group must be involved in medical research in ways that are positive. We have put the curse behind us; now we must bring the benefits to all Americans. [Applause]

Third, we commit to strengthen researchers' training in bioethics. We are constantly working on making breakthroughs in protecting the health of our people and in vanquishing diseases. But all our people must be assured that their rights and dignity will be respected as new drugs, treatments, and therapies are tested and used. So I am directing Secretary Shalala to work in partnership with higher education to prepare training materials for medical researchers. They will be available in a year. They will help researchers build on core ethical principles of respect for individuals, justice, and informed consent, and advise them on how to use these principles effectively in diverse populations.

Fourth, to increase and broaden our understanding of ethical issues and clinical research, we commit to providing postgraduate fellowships to train bioethicists especially among African Americans and other minority groups. HHS will offer these fellowships beginning in September of 1998 to promising students enrolled in bioethics graduate programs.

And, finally, by executive order I am also today extending the charter of the National Bioethics Advisory Commission to October of 1999. The need for this commission is clear. We must be able to call on the thoughtful, collective wisdom of experts and community representatives to find ways to further strengthen our protections for subjects in human research.

We face a challenge in our time. Science and technology are rapidly changing our lives with the promise of making us much healthier, much more productive, and more prosperous. But with these changes we must work harder to see that as we advance we don't leave behind our conscience. No ground is gained and, indeed, much is lost if we lose our moral bearings in the name of progress.

The people who ran the study at Tuskegee diminished the stature of man by abandoning the most basic ethical precepts. They forgot their pledge to heal and repair. They had the power to heal the survivors and all the others and they did not. Today, all we can do is apologize. But you have the power, for only you—Mr. Shaw, the others who are here, the family members who are with us in Tuskegee—only you have the power to forgive. Your presence here shows us that you have chosen a better path than your government did so long ago. You have not withheld the power to forgive. I hope today and tomorrow every American will remember your lesson and live by it.

Thank you, and God bless you. [Applause]

On the Fortieth Anniversary of the Desegregation of Central High School

LITTLE ROCK, AR
SEPTEMBER 25, 1997

Governor and Mrs. Huckabee; Mayor and Mrs. Dailey; my good friend, Daisy Bates, and the families of Wylie Branton and Justice Thurgood Marshall. To the cochairs of this event, Mr. Howard, and all the faculty and staff here at Central High; to Fatima and her fellow students [Applause] to all my fellow Americans: Hillary and I are glad to be home, especially on this day. And we thank you for your welcome. [Applause]

I would also be remiss if I did not say one other word, just as a citizen. You know, we just sent our daughter off to college, and for eight and a half years she got a very good education in the Little Rock school district. And I want to thank you all for that. [Applause]

On this beautiful, sunshiny day, so many wonderful words have already been spoken with so much conviction, I am reluctant to add to them. But I must ask you to remember once more and to ask yourselves, what does what happened here forty years ago mean today. What does it tell us, most importantly, about our children's tomorrows?

Forty years ago, a single image first seared the heart and stirred the conscience of our nation—so powerful most of us who saw it then recall it still: a fifteen-year-old girl wearing a crisp black-and-white dress, carrying only a notebook, surrounded by large crowds of boys and girls, men and women, soldiers and police officers, her head held high, her eyes fixed straight ahead. And she is utterly alone.

On September 4, 1957, Elizabeth Eckford walked to this door

for her first day of school, utterly alone. She was turned away by people who were afraid of change, instructed by ignorance, hating what they simply could not understand. And America saw her, haunted and taunted for the simple color of her skin, and in the image we caught a very disturbing glimpse of ourselves.

We saw not one nation under God, indivisible, with liberty and justice for all, but two Americas, divided and unequal. What happened here changed the course of our country here forever. Like Independence Hall where we first embraced the idea that God created us all equal. Like Gettysburg, where Americans fought and died over whether we would remain one nation, moving closer to the true meaning of equality. Like them, Little Rock is historic ground. For, surely it was here at Central High that we took another giant step close[r] to the idea of America.

Elizabeth Eckford, along with her eight schoolmates, were turned away on September 4, but the Little Rock Nine did not turn back. Forty years ago today, they climbed these steps, passed through this door, and moved our nation. And for that, we must all thank them. [Applause]

Today, we honor those who made it possible—their parents first. As Eleanor Roosevelt said of them, "To give your child for a cause is even harder than to give yourself." To honor my friend, Daisy Bates, and Wylie Branton and Thurgood Marshall, the NAACP, and all who guided these children; to honor President Eisenhower, Attorney General Brownell, and the men of the 101st Airborne who enforced the Constitution; to honor every student, every teacher, every minister, every Little Rock resident, black or white, who offered a word of kindness, a glance of respect, or a hand of friendship; to honor those who gave us the opportunity to be part of this day of celebration and rededication.

But most of all we come to honor the Little Rock Nine. Most of us who have just watched these events unfold can never understand fully the sacrifice they made. Imagine, all of you, what it would be like to come to school one day and be shoved against lockers, tripped down stairways, taunted day after day by your classmates, to go all through school with no hope of going to a school play or being on a basketball team or learning in simple peace.

Speaking of simple peace, I'd like a little of it today. [Applause] I want all these children here to look at these people. They persevered. They endured. And they prevailed. But it was at great cost to themselves. As Melba said years later in her wonderful memoir, *Warriors Don't Cry*, "My friends and I paid for the integration of Little Rock Central High with our innocence."

Folks, in 1957 I was eleven years old, living fifty miles away in Hot Springs, when the eyes of the world were fixed here. Like almost all southerners then, I never attended school with a person of another race until I went to college. But as a young boy in my grandfather's small grocery store, I learned lessons that nobody bothered to teach me in my segregated school. My grandfather had a sixth-grade education from a tiny rural school. He never made a bit of money. But in that store, in the way he treated his customers and encouraged me to play with their children, I learned America's most profound lessons: We really are all equal. We really do have the right to live in dignity. We really do have the right to be treated with respect. We do have the right to be heard.

I never knew how he and my grandmother came to those convictions, but I'll never forget how they lived them. Ironically, my grandfather died in 1957. He never lived to see America come around to his way of thinking. But I know he's smiling down today not on his grandson, but on the Little Rock Nine, who gave up their innocence so all good people could have a chance to live their dreams. [Applause]

But let me tell you something else that was true about that time. Before Little Rock, for me and other white children, the struggles of black people, whether we were sympathetic or hostile to them, were mostly background music in our normal, self-absorbed lives. We were all, like you, more concerned about our friends and our lives, day in and day out. But then we saw what was happening in our own backyard, and we all had to deal with it. Where did we stand? What did we believe? How did we want to live? It was Little Rock that made racial equality a driving obsession in my life.

Years later, time and chance made Ernie Green my friend. Good fortune brought me to the governor's office, where I did all I could to heal the wounds, solve the problems, open the doors so we could become the people we say we want to be.

Ten years ago, the Little Rock Nine came back to the governor's mansion when I was there. I wanted them to see that the power of the office that once had blocked their way now welcomed them. But like so many Americans, I can never fully repay my debt to these nine people. For, with their innocence, they purchased more freedom for me, too, and for all white people. People Like Hazel Brown Massery, the angry taunter of Elizabeth Eckford, who stood with her in front of this school this week as a reconciled friend. [Applause] And with the gift of their innocence, they taught us that all too often what ought to be can never be for free.

Forty years later, what do you young people in this audience believe we have learned? Well, forty years later, we know that we all benefit—all of us—when we learn together, work together, and come together. That is, after all, what it means to be an American. [Applause]

Forty years later, we know, not withstanding some cynics, that all our children can learn, and this school proves it. [Applause] Forty years later, we know when the constitutional rights of our citizens are threatened, the national government must guarantee them. Talk is fine, but when they are threatened, you need strong laws faithfully enforced and upheld by independent courts. [Applause]

Forty years later, we know there are still more doors to be opened, doors to be opened wider, doors we have to keep from being shut again now. Forty years later, we know freedom and equality cannot be realized without responsibility for self, family, and the duties of citizenship, or without a commitment to building a community of shared destiny and a genuine sense of belonging.

Forty years later, we know the question of race is more complex and more important than ever—embracing no longer just blacks and whites or blacks and whites and Hispanics and Native Americans, but now people from all parts of the Earth coming here to redeem the promise of America. Forty years later, frankly, we know we're bound to come back where we started. After all the weary years and silent tears, after all the stony roads and bitter rides, the question of race is in the end still an affair of the heart. [Applause]

But if these are our lessons, what do we have to do? First, we must all reconcile. Then we must all face the facts of today. And finally we must act. Reconciliation is important not only for those who practice bigotry, but for those whose resentment of it lingers, for both are prisons from which our spirits cannot break free. If Nelson Mandela, who paid for the freedom of his people with twenty-seven of the best years of his life, could invite his jailers to his inauguration and ask even the victims of violence to forgive their oppressors, then each of us can seek and give forgiveness. [Applause]

And what are the facts? It is a fact, my fellow Americans, that there are still too many places where opportunity for education and work are not equal, where disintegration of family and neighborhood make it more difficult. But it is also a fact that schools and neighborhoods and lives can be turned around if, but only if, we are prepared to do what it takes.

It is a fact that there are still too many places where our children die or give up before they bloom, where they are trapped in a web of crime and violence and drugs. But we know this, too, can be changed, but only if we are prepared to do what it takes.

Today children of every race walk through the same door, but then they often walk down different halls. Not only in this school but across America, they sit in different classrooms, they eat at different tables. They even sit in different parts of the bleachers at the football game. Far too many communities are all white, all black, all Latino, all Asian. Indeed, too many Americans of all races have actually begun to give up on the idea of integration and the search for common ground.

For the first time since the 1950s, our schools in America are re-segregating. The rollback of affirmative action is slamming shut the doors of higher education on a new generation, while those who oppose it have not yet put forward any other alternative. [Applause]

In so many ways, we still hold ourselves back. We retreat into the comfortable enclaves of ethnic isolation. We just don't deal with people who are different from us. Segregation is no longer the law, but too often, separation is still the rule. And we cannot forget one stubborn fact that has not yet been said as clearly as it should. There is still discrimination in America. [Applause]

There are still people who can't get over it, who can't let it go, who can't go through the day unless they have somebody else to look down on. And it manifests itself in our streets and in our neighborhoods and in the workplace and in the schools. And it is wrong. And we have to keep working on it—not just with our voices, but with our laws. And we have to engage each other in it.

Of course, we should celebrate our diversity. The marvelous blend of cultures and beliefs and races has always enriched America, and it is our meal ticket to the twenty-first century. But we also have to remember with the painful lessons of the civil wars and the ethnic cleansing around the world, that any nation that indulges itself in destructive separatism will not be able to meet and master these challenges of the twenty-first century. [Applause]

We have to decide—all you young people have to decide—will we stand as a shining example, or a stunning rebuke to the world of tomorrow? For the alternative to integration is not isolation or a new separate but equal, it is disintegration.

Only the American idea is strong enough to hold us together. We believe, whether our ancestors came here in slave ships or on the Mayflower, whether they came through the portals of Ellis Island or on a plane to San Francisco, whether they have been here for thousands of years, we believe that every individual possesses the spark of possibility; born with an equal right to strive and work and rise as far as they can go, and born with an equal responsibility to act in a way that obeys the law, reflects our values and passes them on to their children. We are white and black, Asian and Hispanic, Christian and Jew and Muslim, Italian and Vietnamese and Polish Americans and goodness knows how many more today. But above all, we are still Americans. Martin Luther King said, "We are woven into a seamless garment of destiny. We must be one America."

The Little Rock Nine taught us that. We cannot have one America for free. Not forty years ago, not today. We have to act. All of us have to act. Each of us has to do something. Especially our young people must seek out people who are different from themselves and speak freely and frankly to discover they share the same dreams. All of us should embrace the vision of a color-blind society, but recognize the fact that we are not there yet and we cannot slam shut the doors of educational and economic opportunity. [Applause]

All of us should embrace ethnic pride and we should revere religious conviction, but we must reject separation and isolation. All of us should value and practice personal responsibility for ourselves and our families. And all Americans, especially our young people, should give something back to their community through citizen service. [Applause] All Americans of all races must insist on both equal opportunity and excellence in education. That is even more important today than it was for these nine people; and look how far they took themselves with their education. [Applause]

The true battleground in education today is whether we honestly believe that every child can learn, and we have the courage to set high academic standards we expect all our children to meet. We must not replace the tyranny of segregation with the tragedy of low expectations. I will not rob a single American child of his or her future. It is wrong. [Applause]

My fellow Americans, we must be concerned not so much with the sins of our parents as with the success of our children, how they will live and live together in years to come. If those nine children could walk up those steps forty years ago, all alone, if their parents could send them into the storm armed only with school books and the righteousness of their cause, then surely together we can build one America—an America that makes sure no future generation of our children will have to pay for our mistakes with the loss of their innocence. [Applause]

At this schoolhouse door today, let us rejoice in the long way we have come these forty years. Let us resolve to stand on the shoulders of the Little Rock Nine and press on with confidence in the hard and noble work ahead. Let us lift every voice and sing, "till earth and heaven ring," one America today, one America tomorrow, one America forever.

God bless the Little Rock Nine, and God bless the United States of America. Thank you. [Applause]

First Black
President Speech

Ladies and gentlemen, the main thing I want to say tonight is thank you. Thank you to the Congressional Black Caucus for your leadership and your partnership, for your genuine friendship. Thank you to Jim Clyburn; to my friend of twenty-seven years, Eddie Bernice Johnson; to Eva Clayton; to the dean of the delegation, John Conyers; to your retiring member, and a great champion of education and human welfare, Bill Clay. [Applause] To Corrine Brown and Elijah Cummings, and Sheila Jackson Lee and all the other members of the CBC: I thank you for your kindness, your friendship, your support to me, to Hillary, to Al and Tipper Gore, to what we have done together.

I thank Senator Carol Moseley-Braun for her continuing willingness to serve. [Applause] I welcome and congratulate the award winners, my friends Julius Chambers and Alvin Brown and Tom Joyner. Can you imagine Tom Joyner and his son thanking Al and me for being on his radio program? [Laughter] You know, even the people that don't like us don't think we're stupid. [Laughter and applause]

And I want to thank and congratulate Rear Admiral Evelyn Fields, who has done such a great job. She started as a cartographer and went on to chart a new course of opportunity not only for African-American women, but for all women. And thank you for honoring them. I also would like to welcome the president of Haiti here, President Rene Preval. We're delighted to have him here and we thank him for his friendship. [Applause]

There are so many people here who have been associated with our administration, and they were all asked to stand. You know them well. I want to just mention two, if I might. One is my chief speech writer, Terry Edmonds—because he's the first African American to ever hold that job—and the reason I'm introducing him is, since Al and Eddie Bernice and Jim talked, I can't give half the speech that he wrote for me, so the least I can do is acknowledge that he did it. Thank you, my friend, you're doing great. [Applause]

The other person I want to thank for his extraordinary leadership as our special representative to the continent of Africa is Reverend Jesse Jackson, and I want to thank him very much for that. [Applause] And particularly his role in ending the disastrous conflict in Sierra Leone. [Applause]

I want to congratulate some of the current judicial nominees, more than half of whom are women and minorities, including Judge James Wynn, who will be the first African American to serve on the Fourth Circuit; Judge Ann Williams, the first African American on the Seventh Circuit. And this week I nominated Kathleen McCree Lewis to serve on the Sixth Circuit. I congratulate them. [Applause]

There are just two more people I want to thank. I want to thank my wife for her love, her friendship, and for her leadership for our children and our future; for the way she has represented us around the world and for having the courage to stay in public service.

After all we've been through she would be the best United States senator you could ever elect to anything. [Applause]

I also want to thank all the members of the administration here, the cabinet members—some are African American, some are not. But one of the most interesting things that anyone ever said to me is—the presidential scholar, that the vice president and I knew, came from Harvard one night to a dinner at the White House. And we were pretty low; it was after we had been waxed in the ninety-fourth congressional elections. And this man said, I have been studying administrations for a long time and you should know that I believe that yours will be reelected; and one reason is, you have the most loyal cabinet since Thomas Jefferson's second administration.

So to all who are here—Secretary Slater, Madame Attorney General, Secretary Herman, any other members of the cabinet who are here, our veterans affairs secretary, all the others, I want to thank them.

And, finally, and most of all, I'd like to thank the vice president, without whom none of the good things we have accomplished together would have been possible. He has been, by far, the most influential, active, passionate, intense, effective vice president of the United States in the history of our republic and I am very grateful to him. [Applause]

Now, you know, this has been an exciting year for African Americans, a lot of things have happened. I mean, Serena Williams became the first black woman since Althea Gibson to win the U.S. Open. [Applause] Ken Chenault was named the first black CEO of American Express. [Applause] And this is very important, I want you all to listen to this: the magnificent African-American writer Toni Morrison agreed with an extreme right-wing journalist that I am the first black president of the United States. [Laughter and applause]

Chris Tucker came to see me today. [Laughter] He's here somewhere tonight. Where are you? Stand up there. [Applause] So Chris Tucker is in there, he looks at me with a straight face and says he's come in to case the Oval Office because he's about to make a movie in which he will star as the first black president. I didn't have the heart to tell him I had already taken the position. [Laughter and applause]

I want to make a couple of points. Most of what needs to be said has been said. One of the most interesting books of the Bible is the Book of James. It challenges us to be "doers of the word and not hearers only." This, truly, is a caucus of doers. And I'm grateful for all the things that have happened that everyone else has mentioned. But none of it would have been possible without you.

Now we come again to what has become a fairly usual moment in the last two years—the end of another budget year in which we must all make an accounting of ourselves to the American people for what we have done and what we are about to do and what we are going to do with the money they give us from the sweat of their brow.

Now, our Republican friends have sent me a tax bill, and it is quite large. The middle-class and working-class and lower-income relief in it is, oh, about the size of our bill, but their bill is more than three times the size of ours. And people in upper-income groups who are doing pretty well in the stock market get all the rest of the relief.

But the main thing is that the bill makes choices. We all make choices in life, often when we pretend not to and often when we deny that we are, but we do. And so even when things don't seem to be happening, sometimes decisions of the most momentous consequences are being made. The vice president courageously presented himself for public office, for the highest office in the land. [Applause] Many of the rest of you will be running this year—perhaps the First Lady will be among you. [Applause]

But while we are doing these things which we know are big, decisions will be made in this Congress which will affect what they can do if the American people are good enough to send them into office.

Why do I want to veto this bill? Not because I enjoy these interminable partisan fights; I, frankly, find them revolting most of the time. It's not really what the framers had in mind. They wanted us to debate our differences in advance and then figure out what we could agree on and go on and do it. But there are choices here.

Do you know the number of people over sixty-five is going to double in the next thirty years? I hope to be one of them. When that happens there will be two people working for every one person drawing Social Security and Medicare. We ought to use this surplus to deal with the challenge of the aging of America, and take care of Social Security and Medicare and give a prescription drug benefit. [Applause]

Do you know we've got more kids in our schools than ever before? You heard the vice president talk about what our agenda is and what he wants to do. Well, you can't do it if you give away the store first. We ought to invest in our kids. We have the most diverse, largest group of children ever in our schools and they are carrying our future in their little minds every day when they show up. And we need to give them all a world-class education. [Applause]

And if we do this right, believe it or not, we'll be paying down the debt. We could actually make America debt free for the first time since Andrew Jackson was president in 1835. Now, here's why progressives ought to be for this, because if we do that we'll drive down interest rates and we'll be able to get more people to go invest money in places that haven't yet felt our prosperity. We'll keep interest rates down for homes, for college loans, for car loans, for credit cards. We'll guarantee that we'll have a generation of prosperity. We will pass something on to our children. This is a choice.

What I want to say to you is, I want us to get as much of this done as we can, so that we leave for our successors in office the chance to do something meaningful. Nothing, in some ways, is more important than trying to make sure every American has a chance to participate in our prosperity. I was so proud of Alvin Brown tonight when I was listening to his speech on the film—getting ready to give him his award; so grateful that the vice president gave him a chance to lead our empowerment zone and enterprise community programs; so glad that we are continuing to try to involve businesses—the vice president is determined to bridge the so-called digital divide and put computers in every classroom in America, not just those who can afford it on their own, and make sure they can afford to use them. Thank you, Chairman Kenard, for what you've done on that. [Applause]

It's very important that we fund the next round of empowerment zones, that we fund the new markets initiative, that we give Americans the same incentives to invest in poor neighborhoods here as we give them to invest in poor places overseas. I want to continue with all these incentives. I wish we did more for the Caribbean, for Central America, for South America, and for Africa. I just want to do the same thing for the poor neighborhoods of Appalachia, of the Mississippi Delta, of the Indian reservations, of the cities that have been left behind. [Applause]

All the things that have been mentioned, I just want to say, me, too. To the fair and accurate census: me, too; to making sure that our children have safe and good places to learn. Me, too, to meeting the challenge of quality health care and passing an enforceable patients' bill of rights, and doing more in the battle against AIDS, here at home and around the world; and restoring trust between the community and police, passing the hate crimes legislation; and passing the other things that we talked about.

I want to say a few words, seriously, about a topic that the vice president touched on, and I really appreciated it. And I don't want to trivialize this. I think the killing of innocent people en masse in America has been the most painful thing that he and I and our families have had to endure in discharging our responsibilities to the American people: the bombing at Oklahoma City; the terrible school violence at Littleton, Colorado, and, before that, across the country, Arkansas and Mississippi, all the way to Oregon, and all the other places that were affected; this awful spate of race-related killings, and then, apparently, people just with their anger out of control, from Illinois and Indiana out to Los Angeles, over to Georgia and back to Fort Worth, Texas.

None of us should seek to make any capital out of this, but all of us should seek to make sense out of it. That's why we started this big grassroots campaign against youth violence, that I hope all of you will be involved in. Two or three people came up to me tonight and said you were doing things back in your home communities, and I'm grateful.

But the vice president brought up this subject about whether it was evil rather than guns, since that is the debate as it has been posed in the paper and by some others, to explain the terrible things that happened in the church in Texas, and many of these other things.

And he said, essentially, both. I just want to ask you to think about this, because—you think about how many times in your life you're in a bind and would like to avoid taking responsibility for something that you could actually do something about in your personal life, in your work life, as citizens. You can always find some other cause for the problem that you can still do something about.

You know our country has the highest murder rate in the world. And here, I'll tell you another thing you probably didn't know: the number of children who die accidentally from gun deaths in the United States is nine times higher than the number who die in the next twenty biggest economies combined. Now, if you believe this is about the human heart, you must believe two things. If the murder rate is higher here, and the accidental death rate is exponentially higher, you must believe that we are both more evil and more stupid than other countries—don't laugh. I know it's kind of funny, but don't laugh.

The point I'm trying to make is, the NRA and that crowd have got to stop using arguments like this as an excuse to avoid our shared responsibilities. [Applause] It may be true that if we had passed every bill that I have advocated, and every bill that the vice president says he'd pass if he were president, that some of these killings would have occurred. But it is undoubtedly true that many would not. And that is what we have to think about.

And when we go into this political season, where everybody will turn up the rhetoric, you ought to have your antennae working real good, and ask yourself: are these people looking for a way to assume responsibility, or to duck it? [Applause]

And when I say that, I mean no disrespect to anyone. Of course, it is because something horrible had happened to that man's heart that he walked into that church in Texas and killed those people—of course it is. And the same things that happened to the children in Los Angeles and the Filipino postal worker, and the same thing that happened to all those people in Illinois and Indiana. Of course it is.

But we cannot use that as an excuse not to ask ourselves, what's the difference between our setup here and everybody else's setup? And is it worth the price we're paying, or is there something we can do collectively to make America a safer place, and make it clear that more of our children are going to grow up safe and sound and healthy?

That's what we ought to be doing. Make this election year about assuming responsibility, not ducking it, for America's future. You can do it, and we need you to do it. [Applause] Finally, let me just say— for the record and for the press here—most of the things the Congressional Black Caucus has really worked for in the nearly seven years I've been privileged to be president, have not benefited African Americans exclusively—sometimes not even primarily. Most of the things that you have fought for were designed to give all Americans a chance to live up to the fullest of their God-given capacity; designed to give all Americans a chance to live on safe streets; designed to give all Americans a chance to come together.

And in that sense, it may be that in the end, the efforts we have made—now manifested in our office for One America in the White House that Ben Johnson leads—to bring this country together as we move forward, may be the most important of all. You know, no one can foresee the future. I have loved doing this job, and I'm going to do it to the best of my ability every day that I have left on my term. I am going to do it to the best of my ability. I am going to be a good citizen for the rest of my life, and tell people exactly what I think. [Applause]

But no one can see the future, and no one has all the answers.

But I know this, and you do, too: if every American really believed that we were one nation under God; if every person really believed that we are all created equal; if every person really believed that we have an obligation to try to draw closer together and to be better neighbors with others throughout the world, then all the rest of our problems would more easily melt away.

And so I ask you, as we go through the last difficult and exhilarating challenges of this year, as you head into the political season next year, keep in your mind—especially those of you in this Congressional Black Caucus—the enormous potential you have to reach the heart and soul of America, to remind them that we must be one.

Thank you, and God bless you. [Applause]

Martin Luther King Jr.
Holiday Speech

UNIVERSITY OF THE DISTRICT
OF COLUMBIA, WASHINGTON, D.C.
JANUARY 15, 2001

Thank you very much. Normally, I don't think presidents should get awards. But I believe I'll accept these, if it's all the same to you.

I want to begin by saying that I am delighted to be here at this university, in this great hall, with all the people who are here on the stage. I brought something to Mayor Williams and to Representative Eleanor Holmes Norton. He mentioned that we signed the—that we passed the Southeast Federal Center Bill to spur community development with a public/private partnership on federal property. At the time it passed, we weren't able to do a formal signing ceremony, so I brought Mayor Williams and Eleanor Holmes Norton a copy of the bill and the pens I used to sign it, and I'd like to give it to them now.

I want to thank the D.C. City Council chair Linda Cropp, Kathy Patterson, and the other council members who are here who helped to make my stay in Washington, along with my family's, so wonderful. I want to thank Robie Beatty and Shirley Rivens Smith from the King Holiday Commission.

I'd like to thank the people who are here from my administration, present and former. I want to thank Frank Raines, former director of OMB [Office of Management and Budget], and Jack Lew, our present director, for all the work they did, along with the indomitable Alice Rivlin, to make sure that the federal government became a better partner for the District of Columbia in the allocation of our money.

On this Martin Luther King Holiday, I want to thank my friend of almost twenty years, the secretary of transportation, Rodney Slater, who is always serving. And I want to thank the present head of the Corporation of National Service and the person who started our national service program, first Senator Harris Wofford, then Eli Segal. Thank you for bringing AmeriCorps to life.

And I know we have AmeriCorps award winners and their families here and members and alumni. Thank you for your service. And thank you, Nancy Rubin, for your support. I also am proud to announce on Eli Segal's birthday that under the leadership of Nancy Rubin, a group of people are creating a new Eli Segal AmeriCorps Award for Entrepreneurial Leadership, and I thank you for that.

And I want to thank the members of the new D.C. Commission on National and Community Service. I just came from the kickoff, and I swore in the first community service volunteers—swore in, not swore at—[Laughter]—the first community service volunteers. And we did some painting, and I can prove it because I've got paint on my pants and shoes to show it—[Laughter]—not the ones I'm wearing now.

I want to thank Mayor Williams for this award and for what he said about our common efforts to make this great city even greater. It has been a real honor for me to live and work in Washington these last eight years. I went to college here, and I worked here when I was a young man.

And I love this city. I loved all of its neighborhoods. Even when I was in college, I spent a lot of time in all the neighborhoods. I was a community service volunteer in Northeast Washington when I was a student at Georgetown. And one of the first things I did after I got elected was to take a walk down Georgia Avenue. It looks better today than it did eight years ago, I might add.

And I'm very proud of the work that we have done. I'm also— you might be interested to know that when Hillary was elected to the Senate and we had to find a place for her to live, she absolutely insisted on living in the District of Columbia. She wanted to be here. So I'll be back from time to time. [Laughter]

[Audience member:] Don't go! [Laughter]

[The President:] Don't say that. [Laughter] I want you to know that while I think we have done a reasonably good job these last few years of relocating government functions and getting more funds to the District of Columbia and getting some of the burdens off your back that should be lifted, I believe that you should still have your votes in Congress and the Senate. I think that, maybe even more important, you should have the rights and powers and responsibilities that statehood carries.

[At this point, reveille was played on a bugle.]

[The President:] We practiced that for an hour yesterday. How did we do? [Laughter] We did great. It's okay. It's all right. It was good. I mean, it—[Laughter]—you know, look, I've only got five days left; it's hard to hold your interest. So we did the best we could. [Laughter]

And I want you to know that the Secret Service delivered to me this morning, so I get to ride around in it for five days, the newest presidential limousine, which, I might add, is an enormous improvement in terms of the workability of the inner space. But we still have the license plates on it that calls for D.C. statehood. So I hope you'll keep working on that and keep making the case.

Meanwhile, we have worked together to use federal resources to help spark economic growth, housing development, and job creation: over a billion dollars in new tax incentives for businesses and homeowners; $25 million to build the New York Avenue Metro station; $110 million for new and better public housing in Anacostia; $17 million for the D.C. College Access Act—three thousand young people now taking advantage of that in its very first year. Congratulations. I want to thank all of you who worked in the vineyards to make all these things happen.

This is a day we celebrate not only the life but the service of Martin Luther King, and not only the service of the famous but the service of those who are not known, embodied in the famous statement of Dr. King that everybody can be great because everybody can serve. You forget the rest of it—"you only need a heart full of grace and a soul generated by love."

In 1992 when I ran for president, and Eleanor and I actually jogged up Pennsylvania Avenue in the rain together, some people thought that America had become so divided and cynical that somehow the spirit of service was gone, especially among our young people. I never believed that. Then I read all these articles about young people, this so-called Generation X group, and how self-absorbed and selfish they were. I never believed that. I saw people serving together everywhere and yearning to be part of a higher calling.

In 1993 in my Inaugural Address, I challenged the American people to a new season of service. And I proposed national service legislation to give young people in America the chance to serve in their own communities or other communities across the country and earn some money for college while doing it. Well, I think that what these young people have done in the last seven years, since we had the first AmeriCorps class of 1994, has proved that what I saw eight years ago was right. I'll say more about that in a moment.

In 1994 I signed the King Holiday and Service Act, sponsored by then Senator Harris Wofford and Congressman John Lewis of Atlanta, who worked with Dr. King. They wanted to make this holiday a day on, not a day off. Today, as a result of what they did, hundreds of thousands of our fellow citizens are serving in their communities today, including over a thousand here in Washington.

I've just come from the Greenleaf Senior Center with some very dedicated young people from four AmeriCorps projects, including City Year, a program that I found in Boston in 1991 that helped to inspire the creation of the national service program we have today. Today I swore in the first new members of City Year here in Washington, D.C. When I became president, there were a hundred of them around the country—a hundred members; today there are over a thousand in thirteen cities.

But listen to this. When we created the AmeriCorps program in 1994, we wanted to give young people the chance to serve. Obviously, we didn't know how many people would do it. The pay is modest. The scholarship benefits are not inconsiderable, but they're not enormous. But listen to this. Since the first class of volunteers in 1994, almost 200,000 men and women have participated, more than have served in the Peace Corps in the forty years since it was created.

I say that not to diminish the Peace Corps; I'm a huge supporter of the Peace Corps. We've dramatically increased enrollment there, and I'd like to see the Congress continue to do so. But I just want to make the point that people do want to serve in our communities; they do want to make a difference.

And today, the young people that I painted the columns with over at the Greenleaf Community Center, three of them were from the D.C. area, but one was a young woman from Seattle. And the other young AmeriCorps volunteers I swore in, they were from all over America. And that's the great thing about it. You get all kinds of people, all different races and ethnic groups and backgrounds and income groups, coming together in all kinds of communities, dealing with all kinds of other people. And pretty soon, before you know it, you've got America at its best just happening there at the grassroots level. This is a big deal. And these 200,000 people have not only changed their own lives but the lives of millions and millions of other Americans. We must continue to do this.

So far there have been 677 D.C. residents in AmeriCorps. They've earned a total—listen to this—of two and a half million dollars for college education. And I want to thank, by the way, since we're here, the University of the District of Columbia, along with seven other of Washington's colleges and universities, for their participation in the AmeriCorps Heads Up program. AmeriCorps volunteers who are students here work as reading and math tutors at Davis Elementary School in Benning Heights, gaining valuable teaching experience. And the young people they are tutoring are gaining a head start on learning that will last a lifetime.

Citizen service changes people for the better. I don't know how many times I've heard volunteers in the classroom say they have learned more than their students have. And that makes every one of our young volunteers a winner. But today I want to congratulate some very special ones, those who won this year's All-AmeriCorps Award, ten men and women selected for outstanding service to AmeriCorps.

And I want to talk about it a little bit to try to illustrate that this is not just about numbers. Yes, we've got 200,000 people in Ameri-

Corps in seven years of classes, more than forty years in the Peace Corps.

Yes, they've gone all across this country and had a transforming effect. But that's the key. It's not the numbers, it's the impact. The adult literacy programs, the community learning centers, the volunteer programs—that these award winners are getting today—are still going strong, in some cases, years after their service has ended.

One young woman is a former migrant worker who used the skills she learned in AmeriCorps to teach 2,400 farm workers about pesticide safety. One man has been elected mayor of the community in which he served. Shoot, I wish we would have had this around when I was a kid. [Laughter]

Right here in Washington, Carey Hartin started a diversity club to help the many cultures at Roosevelt High School understand one another better. The kids in that club were so inspired, they went out and got a grant to expand Carey's program to other D.C. schools. Carey is now studying for her master's in education and student teaching at Cardozo High School. Where are you, Carey? Stand up there. Give her a hand. [Applause] Good for you.

She also has with her today another success story, the young woman who was the first president of Roosevelt High's diversity club, and is now in college studying music education. Stand up—where are you? [Applause] Give her a hand.

Now I want all the award winners to stand up. Let's give them all a big hand. [Applause] Thank you all, and bless you.

Let me say, when you see their numbers, you should multiply in your head times twelve, because studies show that every full-time AmeriCorps volunteer generates on average a dozen more volunteers.

Now, all across America, you should also know that one million students are doing public service as a part of their school curriculum. And I might say, I would like to see every state in America follow the lead of the state of Maryland, under Lieutenant Governor Kathleen Kennedy Townsend, and require, as a course, community service as a condition of graduation from high school. I think it would be a very good thing.

The United Nations has named 2001 the International Year of Volunteers. Americans have a lot to be proud of on that score. Our citizens are volunteering more and giving more to charitable causes than ever before. And the most generous donors by percentage are families with incomes of less than $10,000 a year.

I came here today, on Martin Luther King's holiday, to talk about citizen service and AmeriCorps because it is the embodiment of my dreams of one America, an America in which we not only tolerate but respect and even celebrate our differences, but in which we work together and live together knowing that our common humanity is even more important. Part of Martin Luther King's dream was somehow we would learn to "work together, pray together, struggle together, go to jail together, stand up for freedom together." If I could leave America with one wish as I depart office, it would be that we become more the one America that we know we ought to be.

Today I'm sending a message to Congress—you can read about it in the papers; I won't go through it all—but it follows up on the work I have done on this One America initiative over the last several years.

And I wanted to basically inform the Congress and the incoming administration about where we are in dealing with our racial issues, our opportunities, and our continuing difficulties, about what progress we have made in the last eight years and what still needs to be done to build one America.

I advocated some things that will doubtless be somewhat controversial, but I have been working on them: improvements in the criminal justice system; restoring voting rights to people when they complete their sentences, so they don't have to get a presidential pardon; a national election commission headed by Presidents Ford and Carter to look into why some Americans have so much difficulty voting and how we can ever avoid—always avoid having another election like the last one, with all the controversies that we had there; and new steps forward in closing the disparities in health and education and economic development.

But what I want to say to you is that building one America is like life. It's a journey, not a destination. And the main thing will always be whether we're still making the trip. Did any of you see the jazz series on TV this week? It was fabulous, wasn't it? My favorite line in the whole thing—my favorite line was uttered by that great Washington, D.C., native Duke Ellington. When he was asked, "What's your favorite jazz tune," he said, "The one coming up." [Laughter] Well, believe me, that's what I believe about our country. I see these young people, I see these volunteers, and it's been an honor for me to serve. It's been an honor for me to help make Washington stronger and better. But when somebody asks you what the best day is, think about these young folks and say, "The one coming up."

Thank you very much, and God bless you.

Clinton Administration
Black Appointees

CABINET OFFICERS

Jesse Brown	Secretary of Veterans Affairs
Ronald H. Brown	Secretary of Commerce
Mike Espy	Secretary of Agriculture
Hazel O'Leary	Secretary of Energy
Togo West	Secretary of Army and Secretary of Veterans Affairs
Alexis Herman	Secretary of Labor
Rodney Slater	Secretary of Transportation
Lee P. Brown	Director, Office of National Drug Control Policy (Drug Czar)

SUBCABINET APPOINTEES

David Satcher *Surgeon General*	Department of Health and Human Services
Eric Holder *Deputy Attorney General*	Department of Justice
Robert Mallet *Deputy Secretary*	Department of Commerce
Clifford Wharton Jr. *Deputy Secretary*	Department of State
Walter Broadnax *Deputy Secretary*	Health and Human Services
James Johnson *Undersecretary for Enforcement*	Department of Treasury
Shirley Watkins *Undersecretary of Agriculture for Food*	Nutrition and Consumer Affairs
Cheryl Shavers *Undersecretary for Technology*	Department of Commerce
Carla Faison *Undersecretary*	Department of the Treasury
Ronald Noble *Undersecretary for Enforcement*	Department of the Treasury

Edwin Dorn *Undersecretary*, Office of Personnel & Readiness	Department of Defense
James Klugh *Deputy Undersecretary*, Logistics	Department of Defense
Charles Baquet *Deputy Director*	Peace Corps
Emmett Paige *Assistant Secretary*, Command, Control, Communication & Intelligence	Department of Defense
Rodney McCowan *Assistant Secretary*, Human Resources & Administration	Department of Education
Sharon Robinson *Assistant Secretary*, Ed., Res., & Improvement	Department of Education
Archer L. Durham *Assistant Secretary*, Human Resources	Department of Education
Avis LaVelle *Assistant Secretary*, Public Affairs	Health and Human Services
Wardell Townsend *Assistant Secretary*, Administration	USDA
Shirley Watkins *Assistant Secretary*, Food & Commercial Service	USDA
Helen T. McCoy *Assistant Secretary*, Financial Management	Department of Defense Army
Cyril Kent McGuire *Assistant Secretary*	Department of Education
Leslie Turner *Assistant Secretary*, Territorial & International Affairs	Department of the Interior
Clarence Irving Jr. *Assistant Secretary*, Communications & Information	U.S. Department of Commerce
Joan Logue-Kinder *Assistant Secretary for Public Affairs*	Department of the Treasury
Marilyn Davis *Assistant Secretary*, Administration	Housing & Urban Development

Bernard Anderson *Assistant Secretary,* Employment & Training Administration	U.S. Department of Labor
Deval Patrick *Assistant Attorney General,* Office of Civil Rights	Department of Justice
Reginald Robinson *Deputy Assistant Attorney General,* Justice Programs	Department of Justice
James Lewis *Director,* Office of Minority Economic Impact	Department of Energy
Robert Stanton *Director,* National Park Service	Department of Interior
Clyde Hart Jr. *Administrator,* Maritime Administration	Department of Transportation
David Andrews *Legal Adviser*	Department of State
Vivian Derrych *Assistant Administrator*	Agency for International Development
Cassandra Wilkins *Commissioner,* SSA	Health & Human Services
Jeffrey Rush Jr. *Inspector General*	USAID

WHITE HOUSE SENIOR STAFF

Terry Edmonds	Assistant to the President and Director of Presidential Speechwriting
Alexis Herman	Assistant to the President and Director, Office of External Liaisons
Franklin Raines	Director, Office of Management and Budget
Robert Benjamin Johnson	Assistant to the President and Director of the White House Office on the President's Initiative for One America
Mark F. Lindsay	Assistant to the President and Director of Political Affairs
Thurgood Marshall Jr.	Assistant to the President and Cabinet Secretary
Bob Nash	Assistant to the President and Director of Presidential Personnel

Veronica Biggins	Assistant to the President and Director of Presidential Personnel
Minyon Moore	Assistant to the President and Director of Political Affairs
Joseph "Jake" Simmons	Deputy Assistant to the President and Director of the Military Office
Michelle Balantyne	Special Assistant to the President and Special Counsel to the Chief of Staff
Betty Currie	Special Assistant to the President and Personal Secretary to the President
Parnice Green	Special Assistant to the President and Associate Director of Presidential Personnel
Janis Kearney	Special Assistant to the President and Special Adviser, Presidential Historian
Tonya Lombard	Special Assistant to the President and Southern Political Director
Zina Pierre	Special Assistant to the President for Intergovernmental Affairs
Dawn Marie Chirwa	Associate Counsel Office of Counsel to the President
Jean V. Roscoe	Associate Director Office of Public Liaison
Maggie Williams	Chief of Staff to the First Lady

WHITE HOUSE STAFF

Tonia Butler-Bush	Speech Writer, Correspondence
Florence Champagne	Staff Assistant, Office of General Counsel
Sheryll Cashin	Assistant to the Director, Office of Policy Development
Betty W. Currie	Secretary/Reception to the President
Paul Deegan	Deputy Administration Officer, Office of Policy Development
Ruth Eaglin	Secretary to the Director, Presidential Personnel
Kumild Gibson	Counsel to the Vice President
Charlotte Hayes	Domestic Policy Assistant, National Drug Control Policy
Alexis Herman	Assistant to the President, Office of Public Liaison
Steven Hilton	Deputy Assistant to President, Office of Public Liaison

Ben Johnson	Associate Director, Office of Public Liaison
Joycelyn Jolley	Executive Assistant to Deputy Director, Office of Legal Affairs
Arthur Jones	Deputy Press Secretary, Office of Communications
Reta Lewis	Special Assistant to President, Office of Political Affairs
Alphonso Maldon	Deputy Assistant to President, WH Military Office
Sonyia Matthews	Staff Assistant, NEC
Floydetta McAfee	Assistant Director, Office of Public Liaison
Lorraine Miller	Deputy Assistant to the President, Legal Affairs
Rosalyn Miller	Executive Assistant, Office of Domestic Policy
Cheryl Mills	Associate Counsel, Office of WH Counsel
Bob Nash	Director, Presidential Personnel
Andre Oliver	Special Assistant to Chief of Staff
Ada Posey	Director, General Services Division
R. Paul Richard	Deputy Staff Secretary, Office of Staff Secretary
Ronald K. Saleh	Staff Assistant
Margaret P. Smith	Executive Assistant to the Deputy Assistant to the President, Economic Policy
Alan P. Sullivan	Deputy Assistant to the President, Director, Military Office
Tracey Thornton	Special Assistant, Office of Legal Affairs
Ann Walker	Special Assistant to the President & Director, Communications Research
Angelina Walker	Executive Assistant to the Counsel for the Vice President
Margaret A. Williams	Assistant to the President, Chief of Staff, Office of the First Lady
Gwendolyn Weaver	Deputy Assistant Director, Office of Administration

SENIOR EXECUTIVE BRANCH APPOINTEES

William Kennard *Chair*	Federal Communications Commission
Cheryl Thomas *Chair*	Railroad Retirement Board
Roger Walton Ferguson *Member*, Board of Governors	Federal Reserve System

AMBASSADORS

Carol Moseley Braun	New Zealand
James Joseph	South Africa
Delano Lewis	South Africa
Charles Stith	Tanzania
George Haley	Gambia[1]
Diane Watson	Micronesia
Leslie Alexander	Mauritius
Aurelia Brazeal	Kenya
Walter Carrington	Nigeria
Johnnie Carson	Zimbabwe
Jerome Cooper	Jamaica
Irvin Hicks	Ethiopia
Howard Jeter	Botswana
Bismarck Myrick	Lesotho
Carl Stokes	Seychelles
Sidney Williams	Bahamas
Johnny Young	Togo

JUDICIAL APPOINTEES[2]

Court of Appeals

Theodore McKee	3rd Circuit
Carl Stewart	5th Circuit

[1] Haley, the brother of author Alex Haley and a descendant of Kunta Kinte who was bought to the United States from Gambia in a slave ship. As U.S. ambassador he arrived in Gambia aboard a 747.

[2] Appointments made between January 20, 1992, and May 30, 2002. Source: Bob J. Nash, Clinton administration director of presidential personnel.

Eric Clay	6th Circuit
R. Guy Cole	6th Circuit
Ann Claire William	7th Circuit
Judith Rogers	12th Circuit

District Court

Reginald Lindsay	1st Massachusetts
Alvin Thompson	2nd Connecticut
Deborah Batts	2nd New York, Southern
Barrington Parker	2nd New York, Southern
George B. Daniels	2nd New York, Southern
Gregory M. Sleet	3rd Delaware
Joseph Greenaway	3rd New Jersey
William Walls	3rd New Jersey
Gary Lancaster	3rd Pennsylvania, Western
Raymond Finch	3rd Virgin Island
Andre Davis	4th Maryland
Alexander Williams	4th Maryland
James Beaty	4th North Carolina, Middle
Margaret B. Seymour	4th South Carolina
Raymond Jackson	4th Virginia, Eastern
Gerald Bruce Lee	4th Virginia, Eastern
Ivan L. R. Lemelle	5th Louisiana, Eastern
Ralph E. Tyson	5th Louisiana, Middle
Sam A. Lindsay	5th Texas, Northern
Vanessa Gilmore	5th Texas, Southern
Denise Hood	6th Michigan, Eastern
Victoria A. Roberts	6th Michigan, Eastern
Solomon Oliver Jr.	6th Ohio, Northern
Algenon L. Marbley	6th Ohio, Southern
Curtis Collier	6th Tennessee, Eastern
William Joseph Haynes Jr.	6th Tennessee, Middle
Bernice Donald	6th Tennessee, Western
David Coar	7th Illinois, Northern
Charles Clevert	7th Wisconsin, Eastern

Michael Davis	8th Minnesota
Charles Shaw	8th Missouri, Eastern
Raner Christercunean Collins	9th Arizona
Audrey Collins	9th California, Central
Martin J. Jenkins	9th California, Northern
Napoleon Jones	9th California, Southern
Ancer Haggerty	9th Oregon
Franklin Burgess	9th Washington, Western
Wiley Daniel	10th Colorado
Vicki Miles-LaGrange	10th Oklahoma, Western
Henry Adams	11th Florida, Middle
Stephan P. Mickle	11th Florida, Northern
Wilkie Ferguson Jr.	11th Florida, Southern
W. Louis Sands	11th Georgia, Middle
Clarence Cooper	11th Georgia, Northern
Henry Harold Kennedy Jr.	12th DC District of Columbia
Richard W. Roberts	12th DC District of Columbia
Emmet Sullivan	12th DC District of Columbia

U.S. ATTORNEYS

Eric T. Washington, Associate Judge	D.C. Superior Court
Rhonda R. Winston, Associate Judge	D.C. Superior Court
Brice H. Holder Jr. U.S. Attorney, DC	U.S. Attorney's Office
Charles R. Wilson U.S. Attorney, FL, Middle	U.S. Attorney's Office
Don C. Nickerson U.S. Attorney, IA, Southern	U.S. Attorney's Office
Eddie J. Jordan Jr. U.S. Attorney, LA, Eastern	U.S. Attorney's Office
Saul A. Green U.S. Attorney, MI, Eastern	U.S. Attorney's Office
Zachary W. Carter U.S. Attorney, NY, Eastern	U.S. Attorney's Office
Janice M. Cole U.S. Attorney, NC, Eastern	U.S. Attorney's Office
Veronica F. Coleman U.S. Attorney, TN, Western	U.S. Attorney's Office

Gaynelle G. Jones *U.S. Attorney, TX, Southern*	U.S. Attorney's Office
Audrey Thomas Francis *U.S. Attorney, VI*	U.S. Attorney's Office
Theodore A. McKee *Judge, 03 Circuit*	U.S. Circuit Court
Carl E. Stewart *Judge, 05 Circuit*	U.S. Circuit Court
Judith W. Rogers *Judge, 12 D.C. Circuit*	U.S. Circuit Court
Reginald C. Lindsay *Judge, 01 MA*	U.S. Circuit Court
Alvin W. Thompson *Judge, 02 CT*	U.S. Circuit Court
Debora A. Batts *Judge, 02 NY, Southern*	U.S. Circuit Court

EXECUTIVE BRANCH POLITICAL APPOINTEES

Lauri Fitz-Pegado *Assistant Secretary,* USFCS	U.S. Department of Commerce
Beverley Gallimore *Special Assistant,* Office of Executive Secretary	U.S. Department of Commerce
Lawrence Goffney *Assistant Commissioner,* Patents	U.S. Department of Commerce
John Scott Gray, III *Special Assistant*	U.S. Department of Commerce
Parnice Green *Congressional Affairs Specialist,* NOAA	U.S. Department of Commerce
Wilma Greenfield *Chief of Protocol,* OS	U.S. Department of Commerce
James Hackney *Counselor to the Secretary*	U.S. Department of Commerce
Carol Hamilton *Special Assistant,* Commerce	U.S. Department of Commerce
Phillip Hampton *Assistant Commissioner,* Trademarks	U.S. Department of Commerce
Gwen Harmon *Director, Public Affairs,* EDA	U.S. Department of Commerce
Wilbur Hawkins *Deputy Assistant Secretary,* EDA	U.S. Department of Commerce

C. Howie Hodges *Assistant Director,* *Program Development & Policy*, MBDA	U.S. Department of Commerce
Kathryn Hoffman *Special Assistant*, OS	U.S. Department of Commerce
Emma Horton *Confidential Assistant,* *Executive Secretary*	U.S. Department of Commerce
LaJuan Johnson *Director*, Office of Consumer Affairs	U.S. Department of Commerce
Theresa Youngblood *Confidential Assistant*	U.S. Department of Commerce
Renata L. Anderson *Special Assistant* *to Commander Pletcher*	U.S. Commission on Civil Rights
Rosalind Gray *Executive Assistant to Staff Director*	U.S. Commission on Civil Rights
Stella G. Youngblood *Special Assistant to the Commissioner*	U.S. Commission on Civil Rights
Bettie A. Davis *Administrative Assistant* *to the Chairman*	Commodity Futures Trading Commission
Patricia H. Adkins *Chief of Staff*	U.S. Consumer Product Safety Commission
Clarence T. Bishop *Executive Assistant* *to Commissioner Smith*	U.S. Consumer Product Safety Commission
Thomas H. Moore *Commissioner*	U.S. Consumer Product Safety Commission
William Coleman, *General Counsel*	Department of Defense Army
Dennis Collins *Deputy for Equal Opportunity,* Reserve Affairs	Department of Defense Air Force
Ruby DeMesme *DAS*, Force Management & Personnel	Department of Defense Air Force
Alicia Edmonds *Staff Assistant*, OAS for Reserve Affairs	Department of Defense
Elbert Hampton *Staff Assistant*, Office of Legal Affairs	Department of Defense

Shelia Helm *Special Assistant*	Department of Defense
Lori Hendricks *Defense Fellow*	Department of Defense
Patricia Irvin *DAS,* Humanitarian, Refugee & Peacekeeping	Department of Defense
Rhonda F. King *Confidential Assistant,* OAS for Economic Security	Department of Defense
Bill Leftwich EEO	Department of Defense
Robert Mills *Special Assistant,* Policy	Department of Defense
Otis Pearson *Chauffeur,* ODS	Department of Defense ODS
Raymond Pierce *DAS,* Office of Civil Rights	Department of Education
Bryant Robinson *Special Assistant,* OSEC	Department of Education
Henry Sterling *Special Assistant,* Office of White House Initiative on HBCUs	Department of Education
Leslie Thornton *Deputy Chief of Staff*	Department of Education
Sandra Walker *Secretary's Regional Representative*	Department of Education
(Sandra) Eulada Watt *Special Assistant*	Department of Education
Patricia DeVeaux *Senior Adviser, Diversity,* Office of Science, Education, and Technology	Department of Energy
Joan Duncan *Confidential Assistant,* OS	Department of Education
Elaine B. Heath *Confidential Assistant,* OS	Department of Education
Loveless Johnson *Staff Assistant,* Office of Public Accountability	Department of Education
Almira D. Kennedy *Special Assistant*	Department of Education

Marcus King *Staff Assistant,* Office of the Undersecretary	Department of Education
William Donald Magwood, IV *Special Assistant*	Department of Education
Kneeland Youngblood *Member,* Board of Directors	Enrichment Corporation
George Wesley Allen *Executive Assistant to* *Assistant Administrator,* PP&TS	Environmental Protection Agency
Shantrel Atris Brown *Legal Adviser,* OPPTS	Environmental Protection Agency
Michelle D. Jordan *Deputy Regional Administrator,* *Region V*	Environmental Protection Agency
Elliot Laws *Assistant Administrator,* SW&ER	Environmental Protection Agency
Gretchen Graves *Program Adviser,* OA&R	Environmental Protection Agency
Arnita Hannon *Congressional Liaison Specialist,* OCLA	Environmental Protection Agency
Clifford G. Stewart *General Counsel*	Equal Employment Opportunity Commission
Cheryl Tates Macias *Director.* Office of Congressional & Public Affairs	Farm Credit Administration
Meredith J. Jones *Chief*	Federal Communications Commission
William E. Kennard *General Counsel*	Federal Communications Commission
Karen E. Watson *Director*	Federal Communications Commission
Carrie Brown *Administrator,* US Fire Administrator	Federal Emergency Management Agency
Louis Elisa *Regional Director*	Federal Emergency Management Agency
Anna Towns *Special Projects Officer,* Office of Special Actions	Housing & Urban Development
Bessie Williams *Special Assistant,* Office of Assistant Secretary for Administration	Housing & Urban Development

Patricia Hill Williams *Member*, Board of Directors	Inter-American Foundation
Karrye Braxton *Special Assistant*, Water & Science	Department of the Interior
Rhea Lydia Graham *Director*, US Bureau of Mines	Department of the Interior
Barry Hill *Director*, Office of Hearings & Appeals	Department of the Interior
James Oliver Horton *Special Assistant Interpretation*	Department of the Interior
Glynn Key *Special Assistant*, OS	Department of the Interior
Wilma Lewis *Associate Solicitor*	Department of the Interior
Richard Pecante *Public Affairs Specialist*, Bureau of Reclamation	Department of the Interior
Cynthia Quarterman *Deputy Director*, Minerals Management Service	Department of the Interior
Mary Thompson *Press Secretary*, MIB	Department of the Interior
Juliette W. Pryor *Staff Assistant*	Interstate Trade Commission
Sharon Rankins *Special Assistant*	ICC
Kim S. Humphries *Special Assistant to* *Assistant Attorney General*	Department of Justice
Renee Lenders *Senior Counsel*, Office of Policy Development	Department of Justice
Kirsten Irvingston *Special Assistant*, Civil Division	Department of Justice
Pamela Neal *Assistant to Director for Scheduling*, Office of Attorney General	Department of Justice
Jennifer Rose *Staff Assistant*	Department of Justice

Elaine McReynolds *Administration,* Federal Insurance Administrator	Federal Emergency Management Agency
Vicky A. Bailey *Commissioner*	Federal Energy Regulatory Commission
Mary Helen Mathis *Special Assistant DAS for Legal* (Health Service)	Health & Human Services
Portia Mittelman *Principal DAS for Aging,* Administration on Aging	Health & Human Services
Kimberly Parker *DAS for Legislation* (Congressional Affairs)	Health & Human Services
David Satcher *Director,* Center for Disease Control & Prevention, Region IV	Health & Human Services
Donald Sykes *Director,* Community Services Admin. for Children & Families	Health & Human Services
Helen Taylor *Associate Commissioner,* Head Start	Health & Human Services
Melvin Whitfield *Director,* Correspondence Controller	Health & Human Services
Mitch Dasher *Director,* Office of Distressed & HUD Troubled Housing	Housing & Urban Development
Otha Dillihay *Director,* Hospital Mortgage Ins. Staff, Office of Housing	Housing & Urban Development
Abram Emerson *Special Assistant,* D.C. Field Office	Housing & Urban Development
Davey Gibson *Secretary's Representative*	Housing & Urban Development
Arlee W. Gist *Intergovernmental Relations Specialist*	Housing & Urban Development
Greg Hyson *Special Assistant,* Office of Housing	Housing & Urban Development
Zenobia Johnson Black *Special Assistant*	Housing & Urban Development

Dwight Robinson *President*, Government National Mortgage Association	Housing & Urban Development
Nancy Smith *Special Assistant to the Secretary*, OS	Housing & Urban Development
Joseph A. Stripling *Special Projects Officer*	Housing & Urban Development
Teresa Roseborough *Deputy Assistant Attorney General*, Office of Legal Counsel	Department of Justice
Carol Waller Pope *Executive Assistant General Counsel*	Federal Labor Relations Authority
Jeanette L. Cole *Special Assistant*	Federal Maritime Commission
Joe Scroggins Jr. *Commissioner*	Federal Maritime Commission
Vella M. Traynham *Staff Assistant*	Federal Mediation & Conciliation Service
Monica U. Gainey *Confidential Assistant*	Federal Mine Safety & Health Review Commission
Robin A. Newman *Confidential Assistant to* *Commander Jordan*	Federal Mine Safety & Health Review Commission
Richard Thomas White *Member*	Foreign Claims Settlement Commission
William Burke *Regional Administrator*	General Service Administration
Gloria Steele Branker *Special Assistant to Solicitor General*	Department of Justice
Geovette Washington *Special Assistant*	Department of Justice
Tracy Shawn Washington *Special Assistant*, Criminal Division	Department of Justice
Anthony D. West *Special Assistant to* *Deputy Attorney General*, DAG	Department of Justice
Robyn A. White *Confidential Assistant*, Tax Division	Department of Justice
Lisa Marie Winston *Special Assistant*, Civil Rights	Department of Justice

Gail Black *Executive Special Assistant,* ESA	U.S. Department of Labor
Delia Bostic *Special Assistant,* OS	U.S. Department of Labor
Alexis R. Yeoman *Public Affairs Specialist*	Office of Nat'l Drug Control Policy
Charlotte Hayes *Director*	Office of Nat'l Drug Control Policy
Cynthia Brock-Smith *Deputy Director,* Congressional Relations	Office of Personnel Management
Lorraine Green *Deputy Director*	Office of Personnel Management
Gerri Hall *Counselor to the Deputy Director*	Office of Personnel Management
Thomas Hicks *Staff Assistant,* Office of Congressional Relations	Office of Personnel Management
Michele Hunt *Director,* Federal Quality Institute	Office of Personnel Management
Courtenay L. Miller *Special Assistant*	Office of Personnel Management
Gordon J. Linton *Administrator,* Federal Transit	Department of Transportation
Rodney E. Slater *Administrator,* Federal Highway Administration	Department of Transportation
Devonalu Robinson *Special Assistant,* FHA	Department of Transportation
Christopher Brown *Special Policy Analyst*	Department of the Treasury
Walter Corley *Ombudsman,* U.S. Customs	Department of the Treasury
Jamir Couch *Deputy to Assistant for Legal Affairs*	Department of the Treasury
Dennis DaCosta *Staff Assistant,* Office of Assistant Secretary	Department of the Treasury
Davis Douglass *Senior Trial Attorney,* Litigation Division, Office of Comptroller of Currency	Department of the Treasury

Maurice Foley *Deputy Tax Legal Counsel*	Department of the Treasury
Douglass Harris *Senior Deputy Comptroller*	Department of the Treasury
Rebecca Hedlund *Director*	Department of the Treasury
Erika Irish *Senior Policy Analyst,* Office of DAS, Government Finance	Department of the Treasury
Rebecca Lowenthal *Special Assistant to Assistant Secretary* *for Public Affairs*	Department of the Treasury
Brian Mathis *Senior Adviser,* Office of Assistant Secretary for Financial Institutions	Department of the Treasury
Jonathon Murchinson *Public Affairs Specialist*	Department of the Treasurey
Zina Pierre *Special Assistant,* Electronic Media	Office of Personnel Management
Evelyn Turner *Executive to Assistant Deputy Director*	Office of Personnel Management
Douglas Walker *Director,* Program Management	Office of Personnel Management
Karen Johnson Pittman *Executive Director*	Ounce of Prevention
Walter Jones *Africa/Middle East Manager*	Overseas Private Investment Corp.
Louie L. Shackelford *Member*	Overseas Private Investment Corp. Board of Directors
Sandra Robinson *Regional Director,* Africa	Peace Corps
George W. Haley *Commissioner*	Postal Rate Commission
Marianne C. Spraggins *Member*	Securities Investor Protection Corp.
Wayne A. Budd *Member*	U.S. Sentencing Commission
James W. Breedlove *Regional Administrator*	Small Business Administration
Ed Cleveland *Special Assistant,* Investment	Small Business Administration

Janice Kearney *Assistant Administrator,* Public Commission	Small Business Administration
Rebecca McKenzie *Public Affairs Specialist*	Small Business Administration
Robert Neal *Associate Deputy Administrator*	Small Business Administration
Cassandra Pulley *Deputy Administrator*	Small Business Administration
Shirley Wilcher *Deputy Assistant Secretary,* Office of Federal Contracts	Department of Labor
Michael Wilson *Special Assistant, ESA*	Department of Labor
Thomas Williamson *Solicitor*	Department of Labor
Sherri Wood *Special Assistant*	Department of Labor
La Veeda M. Battle *Member,* Board of Directors	Legal Services Corp.
Ernestine P. Watlington *Member,* Board of Directors	Legal Services Corp.
Dennis L. Miller *Legal Specialist to the Chairman*	Merit Systems Protection Board
Greg Gibbs *Public Affairs Specialist*	NASA
Bruce Henderson *Special Assistant to the* *Associate Administrator, OEO*	NASA
Charles P. Henry *Member*	National Council on the Humanities
Tom Holt *Member*	National Credit Union Administration
Joyce N. Jackson *Deputy Director of Community Development*	National Credit Union Administration
Olive Mosier *Director,* Policy, Planning & Research	National Endowment for the Arts
LaVerne Walker *Executive Secretary*	National Endowment for the Arts
Richard Woodruff *Congressional Liaison*	National Endowment for the Arts

Miguel A. Gonzalez *Executive Assistant to the Chair*	National Labor Relations Board
William B. Gould, IV *Chair and Member*	National Labor Relations Board
William R. Stewart *Chief Counsel to the Chair*	National Labor Relations Board
Kinshasha Holman Conwill *Chair*	National Museum Services Board
Ruth Y. Tamura *Member*	National Museum Services Board
Shirley M. Malcom *Member*	National Science Board
Claudia Mitchell Keman *Member*	National Science Board
Warren M. Washington *Member*	National Science Board
Herschelle S. Challenor *Member*	National Security Education Board
Shirley Ann Jackson *Member*	Nuclear Regulatory Commission
Linda Bowen *Special Assistant to the Commissioner,* Administration for Children, Youth, & Families	Health and Human Services
Lavarne Burton *Senior Adviser to the Assistant Secretary* *for Management & Budget*	Health and Human Services
Carolyn Colvin Watts *Deputy Commissioner,* Policy & External Affairs, SSA	Health and Human Services
Martis Davis *DAS,* Health (Communications)	Health and Human Services
Patricia Fleming *Special Assistant to the Secretary*	Health and Human Services
Pamela J. Gentry *Deputy Director, Public Liaison,* Health Care Financing Administration	Health and Human Services
Lisa A. Gilmore *Special Assistant to the Assistant,* Secretary for Planning & Evaluation	Health and Human Services

Geralyn Goins *Confidential Assistant to the Assistant* *Secretary*, Planning & Evaluation	Health and Human Services
Grantland Johnson *Regional Director*, Region IX	Health and Human Services
Susan Johnson *Special Assistant Deputy Secretary*	Health and Human Services
Monica Lewis *Special Assistant to DAS*, Public Affairs (Policy & Strategy)	Health and Human Services
Lisa M. Mallory *Special Assistant to the Deputy Secretary*	Health and Human Services
Mozelle Thompson *Deputy Assistant to Secretary,* Government Financial Policy	Department of the Treasury
R. Keith Walton *Senior Policy Analyst*, Enforcement	Department of the Treasury
Bruce Bennett	USAID
Jennifer Douglas	USAID
Nathaniel Fields *Deputy Assistant Administrator,* Bureau for Africa	USAID
Patrick Fn'Piere	USAID
John F. Hicks Sr. *Assistant Administrator*, Africa	USAID
Nyka Jasper	USAID
Alison King *Public Liaison Officer*	USAID
Alan Lang	USAID
Sheree McManus *Special Assistant*	USAID
Wandra Gail Mitchell *General Counsel*	USAID
Valerie Newsom	USAID
Sheila Price *Assistant Chief of Staff*	USAI
Jeffrey Rush Jr. *Inspector General*	USAID
Samuel Phipps *Confidential Assistant*, FCIC	USDA

Vivian Portis *Confidential Assistant*, FCIC	USDA
Dallas Smith	USDA
Earl Taylor *Confidential Assistant*, RE&CD	USDA
Betty Thomas *AIDS Specialist*	USDA
Eloise Thomas	USDA
Samuel Thornton *Deputy Director,* Office of Communications	USDA
Anthony Williams *Chief Financial Officer*, Administration	USDA
Joyce Willis *Confidential Assistant*	USDA
Brenda Young *Private Secretary*, Administration	USDA
Theodore A. McKee	USDA